The
AUCTIONEER

The
AUCTIONEER

ADVENTURES IN
THE ART TRADE

SIMON DE PURY

and William Stadiem

ST. MARTIN'S PRESS ❧ NEW YORK

www.stmartins.com

Designed by Steven Seighman

Library of Congress Cataloging-in-Publication Data

Names: De Pury, Simon, author. | Stadiem, William, author.
Title: The auctioneer : adventures in the art trade / Simon de Pury ; and William Stadiem.
Description: First Edition. | New York : St. Martin's Press, 2016.
Identifiers: LCCN 2015048746| ISBN 9781250059789 (hardcover) | ISBN 9781250094094 (e-book)
Subjects: LCSH: De Pury, Simon. | Auctioneers—Switzerland—Biography. | Art—Economic aspects—History—20th century. | Art—Economic aspects—History—21st century. | BISAC: BIOGRAPHY & AUTOBIOGRAPHY / Artists, Architects, Photographers. | ART / Art & Politics. | ART / Business Aspects.
Classification: LCC N8605.S92 D43 2016 | DDC 381/.17092—dc23
LC record available at http://lccn.loc.gov/2015048746

Our books may be purchased in bulk for promotional, educational, or business use. Please contact your local bookseller or the Macmillan Corporate and Premium Sales Department at 1-800-221-7945, extension 5442, or by e-mail at MacmillanSpecialMarkets@macmillan.com.

First Edition: May 2016

10 9 8 7 6 5 4 3 2 1

To my children: Alban, Charles, Loyse, Balthasar, and Diane Delphine

Contents

Acknowledgments   ix

1.   My Nude Portrait   1
2.   Going Contempo   9
3.   Artopolis   19
4.   L'Artiste   25
5.   The Apprentice   33
6.   London Calling   45
7.   My Role Model   52
8.   The Auction House Wars   66
9.   Simon de Monaco   75
10.   Our Man in Geneva   84
11.   A Royal Courtship   95
12.   Me and the Baron   104
13.   The Merry Wives of Heini; or, The Making of a Collector   116
14.   Foreign Intrigues   131
15.   If I Had a Hammer   147
16.   Teams of Rivals   162
17.   The Women   172
18.   My Oligarchs   194
19.   Courting Medicis   206
20.   The Cutting Edge   216

ACKNOWLEDGMENTS

G iven my extremely short attention span, I have read only a very few books in my life. One of the few that I have read is *Haute Curiosité*, written by Maurice Rheims in 1975. The memoirs of this art-obsessed French auctioneer had a great impact on the young man I was when I read it. "This is the kind of life I want to live!" was my instant conclusion. I feel blessed for, so far, not having discovered what routine is and not having encountered any boredom in my life; at times, things have even become a little too exciting for my own taste. As one of the works by artist Jenny Holzer so aptly says: "Protect me from what I want"! This is the impact that the Rheims memoirs, way back, had on my own life that always made me wish to one day write my own book.

It is my old friend Stanley Buchthal who kept encouraging me to do it. It was equally he who suggested the title *The Auctioneer* for it. I am most grateful to him for having given me the key push to do it.

Having the patience to read a book is one thing, but having the discipline to put pen to paper is quite another. I was introduced to a lovely "ghostwriter." After two sessions together she sent to me a sample chapter; reading it, I was bored by my own story. Shortly after that, by pure coincidence, Jeffrey Deitch (at the time director of the MoCA in Los Angeles) introduced me to Bill Stadiem. Bill, a successful writer of books and screenplays, had approached Jeffrey to write his memoirs, but Jeffrey then had other fish to fry and was unable to embark on such a vanity project. I am grateful to Jeffrey for the introduction.

Thus began lengthy Skype sessions between London and L.A. It felt like having a shrink, with me doing a lot of talking and Bill every now and then asking me pointed questions. Being Swiss and discrete by nature doesn't go well with writing a book. Bill kept asking me, "Give me names, give me names!"

When I eventually saw what all this talking had morphed into I recognized some of my stories, but certainly didn't recognize my "voice." I rapidly realized that this was in fact an advantage and was impressed by how Bill had transformed some of my very approximate "impressionistic brush strokes" into very detailed and precise descriptions. Reading him I was definitely no longer bored by my own story! I am most grateful to him and thank him for his collaboration and for his patience.

The real engine behind everything I do is my love, curiosity, and passion for art. I feel privileged to be able to indulge in it professionally. If you love candies there is no better place to work than in a candy store!

At the end of the day everything we do in our lives is meaningless compared to the unconditional love our families represent for us. I am infinitely grateful to my wife, business partner, and mother of my youngest daughter, Michaela, for all of her totally amazing support. I am also immensely grateful to Isabel, the mother of my four adult children, for her really incredible support and for having been the only person besides Stanley to have read the manuscript for this book.

Only a fraction of the extraordinary stories I have lived on a near daily basis are in this book, and many key players in the art world and close collector friends could not be mentioned, maybe to their relief.

I want to thank my two invaluable colleagues, Harmony Hambly-Smith and Mark Ferkul, who have provided help at every stage.

My thanks go to our book agent, Dan Strone, who found in St. Martin's the best house to publish this book.

Finally, my thanks to Jennifer Weis, my wonderful editor, and Sylvan Creekmore, Sally Richardson, and the whole team at St. Martin's Press.

The AUCTIONEER

My Nude Portrait

I f anybody needed a rebound, it was I. Professionally, my plans to turn the auction-house duopoly that was Sotheby's and Christie's into a triumvirate that included myself had gone up in the terrible smoke and ash of 9/11. I couldn't have had a greater financial partner than the French luxury-goods tycoon Bernard Arnault, or a greater business partner than my former Sotheby's colleague turned co-gallerist Daniella Luxembourg. Alas, both the real world and the often unreal art world had been upended in the fall of 2001 by al-Qaida and by the resultant financial terror that shook the confidence of even the most deep-pocketed and geopolitically indifferent collectors. Arnault had gone, and Daniella was going. An incurable optimist, I refused to believe that the ship everyone else said was sinking faster than the *Titanic* could not be righted and sailed gloriously into the sunset. O Captain! The art world groaned and collectively crossed the street to avoid me, to them a dead man walking, whether the thoroughfare was Madison Avenue, Bond Street, or the Ginza.

Romantically, things were just as disastrous. My wife, Isabel, and I had parted ways. For our decades of marriage I had viewed Isabel as the most intellectually brilliant of women. I next was involved with Louise Blouin MacBain, a female tycoon by whose entrepreneurial gifts I had been smitten. Her power and success, not to mention the Marie Antoinette splendor of her lifestyle, were aphrodisiacal. Her gilded aura surely played into the ambitions I had in wanting to challenge the giants Sotheby's and Christie's. But that love affair had gone the fiery way of the Twin Towers, and now I was adrift. I had always found solace, as well as inspiration, in art. Now, at low tide, I found it in an artist.

Anh Duong could surely be said to be the distaff trophy of the art world, and in falling for her, I may have been a victim of the same megalomania that had drawn me to the likes of Bernard Arnault and Louise MacBain. A similar siren call had lured Odysseus to near-disaster. The Greeks, as ever, had a word for it. Unfortunately, I didn't have anyone left on my putatively sinking ship, now christened Phillips de Pury, to tie me to the mast to prevent me from succumbing to whatever fatal attractions the world had in store. Please forgive my delusions of grandeur, which actually did have some foundation in reality. I had been blessed with a fabulous wife, four fabulous children, and a fabulous career, having held two of the plum jobs in art, first as the curator of the Thyssen-Bornemisza Collection, the greatest private assemblage in the world, only rivaled by that of the Queen of England, and then as chairman of the colossus that was Sotheby's Europe. I couldn't help but think big; it was an occupational hazard. And now all the hazards were coming home to roost.

Luckily for me, Anh Duong's remarkable beauty and talent didn't add up to her being a *femme fatale*. Anh was a true exotic, half Spanish, half Vietnamese, born in Bordeaux, educated to become an architect in Paris at the École des Beaux-Arts. Instead, she became a ballerina and then a top model, gracing *Vogue* covers and Yves Saint Laurent and Christian Lacroix runways. She eventually stole the heart of Julian Schnabel, away from his fashion-designer wife, Jacqueline. And now she was about to steal mine, away from nothing at this point but shell shock, loneliness, and the battle fatigue of the challenge of saving Phillips de Pury from its predicted oblivion.

What surely excited me the most about Anh Duong wasn't that she was a top model, but rather that she was an intriguing artist. She had been encouraged by Schnabel, who became famous for his huge paintings set on broken fragments of ceramic plates. Many consider that Schnabel has one of the biggest egos of any living artist. He boasted about being the next Picasso the way Cassius Clay used to boast that he was the greatest thing since Joe Louis. So the fact that this ego allowed Anh to develop as an artist meant that there was something special there. Schnabel bought her an easel, brushes, and paint, and she began to play around. Eventually she developed a style evocative of Frida Kahlo. Her trademark was her self-portraits, often nude or in transparent lingerie.

Anh and Schnabel had broken up when he went on to marry his second wife, Olatz, a Spanish actress. Ahn lived in her studio on West 12th Street, near my new Phillips de Pury offices on 15th Street, where I had beaten a hasty retreat when our disastrous auction efforts had necessitated fleeing from the skyscraper rents on 57th Street. This was well before Manhattan's Meatpacking District had become the new SoHo, and I like to think I helped plant the seed of cultural gentrification here. I had met Anh at a dinner at Pastis, then the neighborhood canteen, and suggested quite flippantly across the table that I would like to commission her to do my portrait. Equally flippantly, she agreed. Was this a modern version of the old seduction ploy of inviting the object of your affections to come up and see your etchings? I don't think so. I wasn't even thinking romance, at least not consciously.

Anh had been developing quite a reputation as a portraitist. She had recently painted the major contemporary collector Aby Rosen, a global realty mogul who had moved to New York from Frankfurt and would eventually buy both Lever House and the Seagram Building, two of New York's greatest architectural trophy properties. Ahn had painted Aby in his boxer shorts. She was currently painting the model Karen Elson, legendary for her pale skin and flaming hair, wearing nothing at all. I wondered what she had in store for me.

These portrait sessions tend to be very long and very intimate. I remember that when Heini Thyssen commissioned Lucian Freud to do his portrait, it took over 150 hours of sittings, over the course of fifteen months in 1981 and 1982.

I wasn't sure what I wanted in Anh's portrait, other than that it not take as long as Freud's of Heini and that it not be in the nude. I requested that I wear my uniform of a double-breasted Caraceni suit, a tailoring obsession I had contracted from my former boss, Baron Hans Heinrich Thyssen-Bornemisza, who was a devoted Caraceni man and had sent me to Milan for my first fittings, after which I was totally hooked. The tailor of kings and the king of tailors, Caraceni had dressed the crowned heads of Italy and Greece, when they still wore crowns, as well as Gianni Agnelli, Cary Grant, Gary Cooper, and even couturiers like Yves Saint Laurent and Valentino. I liked being in such heady company, and really didn't want to be captured for posterity any other way. Matching the suit's navy color, I wore my habitual navy tie and white shirt and carried my other trademark, my red leather diary from Smythson of Bond Street. Auctioneers are notorious for their superstitions. One of mine was to eat an apple before every sale. Another was always to be bearing something red. Anh was very tolerant of these fetishes.

As we began our sessions, what drew me most to Anh was her striking, observant eyes. They put me on the spot and created a particular tension, which is essential to making art. The other thing that lured me in was that her taste in music mirrored my own. There had to be music in these sessions, and Anh's mix was an eclectic mélange of opera, classical, rock, pop, French chansons, and movie soundtracks. Every tune touched a chord in me. Ever since childhood my three obsessions have been art, music, and soccer. With Anh two out of three was as good as it would get. Over the course of our sittings something just happened. Anh gave me a sculpture of herself. I ended up buying her Karen Elson portrait for myself. Despite its full frontal nudity, Anh wasn't the slightest bit jealous. This was art, not sex. Such was Anh's immersion in *la vie bohème*, Chelsea version. But art is sexy, as sexy as anything, and eventually something started between us.

Enter Eric Fischl, an artist I have always greatly admired. I saw him as the continuation of the great American realist tradition, the spiritual descendant of Winslow Homer and Edward Hopper. In the eighties, no one was much bigger than Eric. He was up in the stratosphere with Schnabel and Ross Bleckner. The three of them were a juggernaut, the "Boone Boys," all discovered and represented by the queen of that decade's SoHo art firmament, Mary Boone, a modern-day commercial Cleopatra, who, most fittingly, was of Egyptian descent. When I was running Sotheby's in Geneva, I had invited Eric, at the height of hot, to come to Switzerland to be part of my monthly lecture series. Jeff Koons, Karl Lagerfeld, and Philippe Starck were fellow invitees, proof that I was not behind the curve in the emergence of contemporary art and style as the next big thing.

Given the vagaries of the market, Eric has never gotten any bigger than he was in the eighties, nor has Mary Boone. Eric had become famous as the Degas of American suburbia, painting transgressive images of his alter ego staring at his naked sleeping mother in bed while picking her purse (*Bad Boy*) or that same alter ego masturbating into a backyard swimming pool (*Sleepwalker*). Eric was anything but bitter, but to pretend that schadenfreude did not exist in art the way it does in Hollywood would be a very Pollyanna-ish perspective. That his works sold in the high six figures rather than the seven he used to sell for or the eight of some of his fellow boy wonders was no one's tragedy. In fact, to me it was nothing but sheer opportunity. A dealer loves nothing more than an undervalued artist. The fact that I couldn't afford Eric in the eighties stoked my desire to buy him at bargain prices in the new millennium.

In 2002 I saw a Fischl at a Mary Boone show that I just had to have, in the same way I just had to have Anh's Karen Elson, and ultimately just had to have Anh herself. The piece was called *Living Room, Scene 2,* painted in a Mies van der Rohe house-turned-museum in Krefeld, Germany; Eric turned it back into a house and hired actors to do for German suburbia what he had done to that of his childhood in Arizona. *Living Room* depicted a wealthy couple in their sleek abode with their proudest possessions: a Gerhard Richter, a Warhol, and a Bruce Nauman. That painting spoke to me as a collector and, especially, as a dealer. I went to Mary and bought it on a handshake.

Alas, that handshake quickly went the way of all flesh. Mary called me to tell me that she wanted to bail and void the sale. She had gotten another offer from the hot and rising Seattle Art Museum and wanted to take it. Microsoft's Paul Allen, Mr. Seattle, was a huge benefactor of the emerging art scene in that Nirvana of tech. Mary liked the idea of bringing the mountain to Mohammed. Of the many superstars Mary had represented in her eighties glory days, only Eric and Ross Bleckner had stayed true blue. Schnabel had moved on, as had David Salle, Georg Baselitz, Barbara Kruger, and Brice Marden. Jean-Michel Basquiat was, sadly, dead.

My first reaction was to be incensed and refuse to succumb to Mary's perfidy. No way, I insisted angrily. A deal is a deal. But no one on earth is as persistent as Mary Boone. She wanted her deal as much as I wanted that Fischl. She came up with a compromise: Back off on *Living Room*, and I will personally get Eric to do your portrait. They're very rare, Mary said, selling hard. He only does them for his closest friends, like Steve Martin.

Forget it, I told her. I already had one portrait in the works by Anh. How many portraits did I need? Who was I, Louis XIV? Certainly not after my recent debacles. Instead, Mary was making me feel like Rodney Dangerfield, the great comedian whose trademark was "no respect." Besides, who wanted a one-man picture of me from Eric Fischl? That would be so boring compared to a real Eric Fischl, whose hallmark is the intense tension between two individuals on the same canvas. To me, Eric was right up there with Lucian Freud in creating that tension. Give me my *Living Room* or give me death, I declared to Mary and hung up.

Then I began having second thoughts, but not noble thoughts, like *Let Mary have what she wants. We've both been up and down, and she deserves a break.* No, I wasn't that altruistic or noble. Instead I saw a great opportunity to do Mary a big favor and do myself one as well, by turning this portrait into a real Eric Fischl and not some tribute to myself. My brainstorm was to get that trademark tension by having not only me in the portrait but another person as well. And that other person would be Anh Duong. And Anh Duong would be *in the nude*. As I previously noted, Anh is one of the only true bohemians I know. She has no false modesty, no prudery. There's nothing *Swiss* about her, like the high-propriety people I grew up around.

Anh had done so many nude self-portraits that I didn't even bother to ask her first. Instead, I pitched the concept to Mary, who loved it. Then I called Eric and pitched it to him, and he loved it, too. Only then did I pitch it to Anh, who said all systems go. Anh had done nudes for other artists, such as Peter McGough, a close friend of Schnabel's from the eighties, who created the daguerreotype-style *Anh Duong, 1917*, painting her like a pinup of the Jazz Age. Besides, Eric Fischl and Anh were good friends, and she loved his work.

So out to Montauk we went one summer weekend for our rendezvous with naked destiny. Eric lived in Sag Harbor with his wife, April Gornik, an acclaimed landscape painter. He had fled SoHo and the druggy excesses of being a millionaire artist of the eighties for the relative rusticity of the east end of Long Island, before the hedge-funders moved in. Eric was anything but an effete artist. He was a sporty guy, having traded art for tennis lessons with his pal John McEnroe. He had been a security guard in a Chicago museum in his early years.

Unlike Anh, who worked from life, Eric worked solely from photographs and memory. Eric's hardcore policy was that I would have no say whatever in the portrait and that I could not even see it until it was done. I had expected that Eric would give very specific instructions for what he wanted from us. Instead, he didn't tell us anything. "So what do you guys want?" he asked. Anh and I were both clueless. She had undressed and was standing around aimlessly in the nude, while I was standing around aimlessly in my Caraceni suit. Finally, Eric broke the ice by starting to snap an endless series of photos, sort of like the David Hemmings character in *Blow-Up*, but minus any stage directions, like Hemmings gave to Veruschka. Somehow I noticed a rocking chair on the wooden floor of the studio. I went and sat in the chair. Then Anh, by instinct, came over and sat on my knee. Eric climbed up a ladder and began shooting from above. "My God, I feel like Helmut Newton," Eric exclaimed. At that moment, I had a flash that this particular angle, this overhead shot, was what would end up as the portrait.

The whole session lasted an hour and a half. Anh redressed. Then we had tea, very demurely, with Eric and April and drove back to Montauk, where we were staying with friends. My relationship with Anh lasted ten months. Our romance ended before the painting was delivered. I had warned Anh that we might not last forever, but Anh had no regrets. What she did, she did for art. That was her philosophy. When I did see the painting I was pleased. It was no portrait. It was a *real* Eric Fischl. The psychological tension fairly screamed from the canvas, so much so that I wondered if I had ever understood how tenuous my relationship with Anh must have been. I look completely alone, notwithstanding Anh's sultry naked presence on my knee. There was a total disconnect between us. The work was proof of how artists like Eric can see beyond the medium.

I own the painting, but I never show it to anyone. I feared my friends might have written it off to a midlife crisis, or worse. In 2012, Mary Boone had an Eric Fischl portrait exhibition at her new gallery in Chelsea and asked to borrow it. I said yes, with some trepidation. She hung me, or rather the Fischl, on the first wall, all by itself. It was the first thing anyone saw on entering the gallery. Anh came to see it. She burst out laughing. Mary's exhibit got a scathing review in *The New York Times*. The critic savaged the exhibition for painting the 1-percenters. I got defensive for Mary. Didn't every artist throughout history paint the princes of his time? What were the Medicis if not 1-percenters?

I felt bad for Mary, and I felt bad for Eric. He remains on my list of the ten to fifteen major artists who are underappreciated. The critic had singled out my portrait for special flaying, describing it as "a blasphemous Pietà." This was my brilliant idea, and poor Eric was getting all the blame. As for the other portrait, the one that started this whole thing off, Anh did finish that one, too, just before we broke up. It was not her best work. Our initial split was anything but cordial, and I wondered if bad art was imitating bad life. Eventually, we both were able to look back in laughter at how art illuminated the naked truth about a relationship that might have been better left unpainted.

2

GOING CONTEMPO

C ontemporary art is the New Old Masters. That's because there aren't any more Old Masters for dealers and auction houses to sell. They're all in museums. The same is becoming the case for Impressionists and Post-Impressionists, which are increasingly rarely found in private collections. And as time goes by, even twentieth-century modern art gets a bit long in the tooth. The Abstract Expressionists, Jackson Pollock et al., seem Old Masterly. In 1998 Christie's changed the art game altogether by changing the rules, or at least the terms, redefining contemporary as work created, not after World War II ended in 1945, but after the1960s revolution ended in 1970. Even though rival Sotheby's tried to hold the line at 1945, 1970 became the new "sell after" date.

And sell we have. Thanks to longevity and procreativity, the supply of contemporary artists is infinitely elastic and, notwithstanding occasional episodes of market remorse, has been matched by demand. That demand is best symbolized by the Michael Douglas "Greed is good" speech in the 1987 film *Wall Street,* inspired by the convicted arbitrageur Ivan Boesky. As Wall Street has gone, so has the contemporary art market. Who, some old-time purists may ask, other than barbarians at the gate would be attracted to such creations as Damien Hirst's ashtray of cigarette butts, which I had sold at Phillips in 2001 for what was then a world record price of $600,000, a record that has been broken since then by 137—and counting—other works of his.

Or the Jeff Koons *Woman in Tub,* depicting a headless woman in a bubble bath clutching her breasts as she is attacked from below by a snorkel-wearing intruder. Christie's sold that for $1.7 million in 2000, after which they dressed half of New York's unemployed actors in Pink Panther costumes to hype the upcoming sale of the Koons sculpture of the same name. The hype paid. *Pink Panther* sold for $1.8 million, surprising even Christie's, whose high estimate was only half that amount. I was the underbidder, for a private collector, on the *PP,* as well as for the $420,000 *Fool,* by Christopher Wool. Soon after those underbids, a journalist approached me and asked, flat out, "Aren't you crazy?" I laughed and told him that *I* was the fool not to get *Fool.* The ever-soaring prices have proved me right—and not foolish.

Greed was good, indeed. And so it has remained. Here's a case in point, one of many greedy nights to remember in the world of top-dollar art. It was spring 2013. Christie's didn't feel like an auction house. It felt like a gambling house. The electricity in the muggy May air in Rockefeller Center was akin to that of a big night at the Casino in Monte Carlo. The players, or collectors, if you must, were there from all over the world, high rollers from Russia, Asia, and the Persian Gulf, as well as the home-team Americans. By evening's end, I realized that my instinct that this would be a huge night had not been exaggerated. A staggering total of $495 million in contemporary art had been sold. Fifteen world records for artists had been broken. It was the biggest art auction in history—to that point.

The largest sale of this enormous evening was the $48 million for Jean-Michel Basquiat's *Dustheads.* The times were changing, and fast. Just a year and a half earlier, as chairman of Phillips de Pury, the only rival to the Christie's-Sotheby's duopoly, I had stood on the podium and auctioned another Basquiat for a then-record $16.3 million. And now I had not just been doubled, but trebled. I had thought that I was pretty hot stuff. I loved setting records. Records are a dealer's, an auctioneer's, lifeblood. I was hot, all right. But, as it turned out, things were just warming up. The world that seemed to be crashing in 2008 was having a dramatic V-shaped recovery, if not renaissance. The stock market seemed to be invincible, on rocket fuel, and as stocks went, so did art, and at far greater multiples of propulsion.

In today's pecuniary scorecard of greatness, the price of an artist's work is often taken to be the measure of the man. What else could serve as a common denominator for the diverse tastes of Wall Street, Russia, China, and Arabia? By that quantifiable standard Jean-Michel Basquiat is the Van Gogh of contemporary art. These two tortured geniuses have been posthumously elevated into the pantheon of cultural capitalism. I do hope Jean-Michel is smiling down on me from that pantheon, for I am proud to have played a role in making the market for him as adulatory as it has become. It all started just a few years ago, when Phillips de Pury set three world records.

The first, in 2007, was the $8.8 million for Basquiat's *Grillo* ("cricket," the insect, not the game, in Spanish), a monumental-sized (over thirty feet wide) tribute to his Puerto Rican maternal roots. I had been mesmerized by this painting nearly a decade before when I was chairman of Sotheby's Europe. An Israeli dealer, Micky Tiroche, owned it, and promised to let me sell it one day. I had assumed it was all promises, promises—art hype. Amazingly, Micky came through, and I stepped up my own auction game to do him proud, making the huge sale to a phone buyer at our New York auction. So many of these monster sales are over the phone, with the buyers, famous though many be, insisting on anonymity in their extravagances.

In 2008, I set another record of $11 million, in the New York auction of Basquiat's own Winged Victory, *Fallen Angel*. This one was from his *annus mirabilis*, 1981. This was before he met Warhol and their deep friendship began, at the dawn of his discovery and embrace by the illuminati, yet the works from this year were the cream of his crop. My auction of this piece, sold by an Italian and bought, again, by a mystery phone bidder, was immortalized by the director Tamra Davis, wife of Beastie Boy Mike D, in her documentary *Jean-Michel Basquiat: The Radiant Child*. Alas, my stellar performance on the podium would end up on the cutting room floor.

But the only way for Basquiat was up. When in 2009 Sotheby's beat my last record, the competitive adrenaline pushed me to try even harder. This led to the 2012 sale of *Untitled*, a portrait of a haloed black man with a flaming red skeleton. This, too, was from that vintage year 1981. Its owner, Robert Lehrman, was a low-key collector in Washington, D.C., a town not known for its embrace of the avant-garde. A lawyer and heir to the Giant Foods supermarket fortune, Lehrman had bought two Basquiats back then for $5,000 apiece.

He had sold one for a normal profit before art became like big game hunting; now was the time for an abnormal profit. The market was euphoric. Was the exuberance irrational? Time will tell, but the exuberance continues to snowball. Having sold in 2008 an interest in Phillips de Pury to the Mercury Group, the leading Russian luxury-goods conglomerate, I was flush enough with oligarch wealth to compete with Christie's and Sotheby's and give Mr. Lehrman the guarantee he required. That was the amount he would get even if *Untitled* sold for below its estimated sales price of between $9 million and $12 million. It was a high-risk strategy, but this was a game of no pain, no gain. I was used to rolling the dice.

Contrary to popular belief that an auction is a roomful of waving paddles and multiple bidders, for *Untitled* there were only three bidders, and none of them were in our packed auction room in Chelsea. Some auctions are filled with battling bidders, but not this one. This was quality over quantity. Still, there was immense excitement. If the Romans came to the Coliseum to see blood, the New Yorkers came to Phillips to see money. The anonymous collectors were all represented telephonically by Phillips experts, but they were all watching the auction online, and it was my job as auctioneer to make them as desperate to bid, and bid high, as if they were right there below my podium.

Although it may have seemed that in selling to my employees, I was preaching to the choir, in truth I was working as hard as a missionary trying to convert a tribe of headhunters. My gospel was one of transcendent inspiration mixed with eternal value. I knew precisely who the bidders were. I knew who was on those phones. I'd get one bid, and I would look at my experts, beseeching them and their clients to step up, and step high, or else they might lose the treasure. The signs were simple, an arched eyebrow, an extended stare, a change of tone; whatever, the challenge was to deliver the message of a great headmaster with Oscar-worthy finesse: You must do better. It was essential to convey my bullishness. I was high on Basquiat.

Also contrary to popular belief, most of these eight-figure auctions are not drawn-out affairs. Short and sweet, they can last anywhere from one minute to a dozen. This one lasted six minutes. When I banged the gavel and smiled at the phone bank, the price was $16.3 million. The high estimate had been shattered. The record was mine. The crowd breathed a collective "wow." Loud applause filled the room. It felt great. But I knew it wouldn't, couldn't last. And I was glad. That was what made the business so exciting. You could never rest on your laurels. You could never get bored.

The new-record $48 million *Dustheads* had been sold—over the phone—to a thirtyish Malaysian bon vivant named Taek Jho Low. Nobody knew what he did for a living. Some said oil, some construction, others arms. He was a Wharton grad, and he must have learned something, and learned it well. We were in the Wharton age, when MBA was more likely to be the title of the super-collector than OBE, "von," or "de." Inherited wealth was being dwarfed by tech wealth, by oil, by hedge funds. These were where the new players at the auction houses—and at the casinos of the world—were coming from.

The talented Mr. Low was one of the few major collectors I didn't know. Where had he been keeping himself, I wondered, as I put him on my "to meet" list. I looked around Christie's auction room. The paneling gave it a much warmer, library-like feel than Sotheby's clinical white chamber, which was more like an operating room. But wasn't that what was going on, operating, at the highest level? I knew just about every face in the room, certainly every face connected with a hand that might raise and bid. I had to. In art, knowledge—of the art, and of the buyers— was power, and knowledge meant business. Ignorance could only be measured in misery and failure, never bliss.

Five rows in front of me, right in front below the podium, was Laurence Graff, the poor Stepney-born London diamond merchant who had become the new Harry Winston. Graff had proven to be as astute in art as he had been in jewelry. The two were very closely related, objects of beauty. Tonight his quarry was Roy Lichtenstein's 1963 Pop riff on Picasso, *Woman with Flowered Hat*. It was being sold by Revlon's Ron Perelman, with an estimate of $28 million. I had just had tea with Graff, resplendent in Savile Row bespoke, looking like the king of diamonds that he was. Graff was in New York for the sale with his stunning half-Brazilian, half-English fellow jeweler girlfriend, Josephine Daniel, thirty-plus years his junior and mother of two of his children.

At tea Graff had told me he was fond of Lichtenstein. How fond I would now see, as he went mano a mano with Brett Gorvy, Christie's young (fiftyish) chairman, who was representing an anonymous phone buyer on the hotline bank beside the podium. Notwithstanding his high office, Gorvy, in contrast to Graff, was soberly and unobtrusively dressed—like a banker, a lawyer, some sort of fiduciary. The idea was that in this service business you should never steal the thunder of your clients. Where Gorvy did dazzle was in his seriousness and dedication. The Graff-Gorvy competition was like a tennis match, round by round, with Graff bidding less with his nearly imperceptible hand gestures than with his eyelids. Up and up it all went, until Graff broke Gorvy with a bid of $55 million, nearly double the estimate.

The gallery swooned. All the top dealers in the world were there, following the action. First and foremost was Larry Gagosian, the unflappable Beverly Hills–Armenian silver fox who had become the Duveen of his generation. If Gagosian was the new Duveen, the Nahmads, Syrian Jews who had empires in both London and New York, were the new Wildensteins. Several Nahmads were in attendance. Conspicuously absent was Hillel "Helly" Nahmad, the thirty-something owner of a distinguished Madison Avenue gallery, envied playboy/serial dater of supermodels, and an art Pied Piper who had turned his Hollywood friends, like Leonardo DiCaprio, on to the joys of contemporary art. Alas, Helly had just been arrested in Los Angeles on charges of involvement in an international high-stakes gambling ring, for which he would ultimately serve several months in jail, after which he returned to art, where he remains at the top of the game. On this night, the family showed up, and Helly was not discussed. The art show must go on.

Then there were the Mugrabis, also Syrian Jews, who had emigrated to Bogotá, where they became fabric merchants and had built their collection by buying up huge lots of paintings whenever the art market crashed. They had the world's largest trove of Warhols, over eight hundred strong, not to mention more than a hundred Basquiats, plus many important pieces by Damien Hirst, Jeff Koons, and Richard Prince. They owned giant warehouses in Geneva and in Newark. Saying hello to father Jose, and sons David and Alberto, I mused at how the art market seemed to be dominated by these men with Levantine roots. I guess they shared some kind of genius trading gene. The only one of these gilded Middle Easterners missing tonight was London's Charles Saatchi, the advertising mogul who became the Iraqi Cosimo Medici of the Young British Artists, as responsible as any collector for the contemporary fiscal fireworks I was witnessing tonight.

Observing the scene from one of Christie's skyboxes, which are often obscured with semitransparent curtains that protect the identities of Garbo types and Arab princes, was Christie's big boss, François Pinault, the French tycoon who also controls Gucci, Bottega Veneta, and Stella McCartney, but is most famous to Americans for being the father-in-law of movie star Salma Hayek. Pinault is totally hands-on. At Art Basel, he once disguised himself as a porter wearing workman's overalls just to get an early look at what would be for sale. Such is Monsieur Pinault's competitive drive, his passion to win. That I had dared to challenge this giant, backed by his archrival Bernard Arnault (LVMH, plus Dior, DKNY, Marc Jacobs, you name it), in the auction wars of the new century had seemed to many like suicidal madness. Whatever, François waved down a warm hello.

We had seen each other a few nights before at the "kids' auction," a charity sale to benefit the Leonardo DiCaprio Foundation, dedicated to bird and wild-animal sanctuaries around the globe. Save that tiger! While only $31 million was raised, compared to the $500 million tonight would bring, the publicity value was worth the difference if it got young people to follow their beloved stars' burgeoning interest in art. In addition to Leonardo and Salma, Tobey Maguire, Bradley Cooper, Mark Ruffalo, and Owen Wilson were all in avid, camera-ready attendance. Larry Gagosian showed his appreciation by paying over $7 million for a Mark Grotjahn, winning even more of Young Hollywood's hearts and minds, as if he needed any, by proving he was "with the program." Larry *is* the program.

An auction is only as big as its buyers, and tonight boasted what on the old New York Yankees was known as "Murderers' Row." In addition to Graff, there was the Emperor of Los Angeles, Eli Broad, who nearly singlehandedly transformed the movie capital into an art capital, godfathering the city's main museums and building a classic one (and more) of his own. Eli, now in his eighties, has the energy of a teenager. His fountain of youth is art, which sends him and his wife, Edythe (they're known as E&E), Gulfstreaming around the world on what has become an infinite loop of glamorous yet serious art events, all of which started with Art Basel, in the city of my birth and own conversion to the religion of art.

I was highly flattered that I had made Eli Broad's impressive short list of candidates to become the director of LA's MOCA (Museum of Contemporary Art). When he had interviewed me in 2009 in his South Beach hotel suite at Art Basel Miami, I was preoccupied with my own business of Phillips and passed with regret. I recommended my friend and fellow candidate, the brilliant art dealer and SoHo gallerist Jeffrey Deitch, as the ideal man for the job, and was thrilled that Eli eventually chose him. Jeffrey's appointment, his turbulent three-year reign at MOCA notwithstanding, was testament to how far outside the box Eli Broad is willing to think, hiring someone far off the conventional curatorial/art-history-academic/nonprofit career track. Jeffrey's shows at MOCA, such as his "Art in the Streets" graffiti exhibition, were beyond original and reflected the innate originality of his staid-seeming patrons the Broads.

For all their billions, the Broads are as plain as their collection is grand. It's all on their walls, not on their backs. Talk about insurance salesmen. Trained as an accountant, Eli made one fortune in tract homes, another in insurance, before he got hooked on paintings. It all started with a Toulouse-Lautrec poster and a Braque print that Edythe brought home. She passed on a Warhol soup can, because she thought Eli would shoot her for its $100 price tag. The Broads are living proof that you don't have to be fancy to be a collector.

The Broads' opposite number was there as well. Peter Brant, the polo-playing playboy billionaire, published *Art in America* and *Interview*. He produced the films *Basquiat* and *Pollock*. He had a great new foundation/museum in Connecticut. He genuinely loved art. Befriended by Warhol as a young heir and converted into a patron at an early age, he turned his Bulgarian-born father's paper company into a vast empire that enabled Brant to pursue his multiple passions of art, horses, and distaff pulchritude. Tonight his oft-embattled wife, Stephanie Seymour, supermodel and Axl Rose ex, who greatly disappointed the tabloids by reuniting with Brant, was not in attendance. But Peter Brant never needed a prop.

Even with the tens of millions changing hands tonight, Peter was setting the stage for a still bigger auction coming up in November by consigning to Christie's his massive orange Jeff Koons balloon dog sculpture. The estimate was from $35 million to $55 million, which would belittle even tonight's record Basquiat sale and set a new high for Koons. There were four other Koons balloon dogs, each in a different color, and the owners constituted an oligarchy of their own: Brant, Broad, Pinault, Greek tycoon Dakis Joannou, and hedge-fund overlord Stevie Cohen, whose troubles with the SEC had kept him, just as legal woes had kept Helly Nahmad, off the floor tonight.

Speaking of exclusion, I was still sorting out my emotions regarding my major life change in leaving Phillips de Pury that past December. The Russians at Mercury had bought out all my shares in the company in 2012. Now I was gone. I had changed the once-stuffy auction house into the cutting-edge beacon of contemporary art, and, as was my historical wont, decided to move on to new challenges. But I was gone, and so was my name. When Joseph Stalin eliminated his rivals, they ceased to exist, and were known as "non-people." So it seemed to go with the new de-Pury-less Phillips. I had given it my best shot, taking on the two giants, and while my David had not slain the double Goliaths, I had certainly shaken their firmament. A non-person I could never be.

Sure, whenever I saw a podium, I wanted to be on it. I witnessed the joy of my friend Tiqui Atencio, who had put the Basquiat *Dustheads* on the block. Tiqui, an elegant Venezuelan who has the greatest home and gives the wildest parties on the French Riviera (and that's saying something), is no stranger to exuberance. When the $48 million hammer dropped, she leapt out of her chair and threw both arms high in the air, as if her team had just won the World Cup. I missed sharing that moment of triumph. The call of the gavel was the call of the wild. That's why I kept my hat in the ring, even minus the auction house, by doing charity auctions around the world, often once a week.

I watched Christie's Finnish auctioneer, Jussi Pylkkanen (a spelling-bee showstopper), run up the millions. It wasn't that hard. For someone worth billions, as were so many of these auction-house habitués, raising a bid by a million was play money. Meaningless. There was no pain involved, only the pleasure of high rolling. Again, this was the casino effect. Was the casino rigged? That's been the cry of reforming legislators in New York for years, trying vainly to outlaw the so-called chandelier bids, in which the auctioneer raises the ante by pointing to a vague rich someone in the back of the room. That someone could be a chandelier. That someone doesn't exist. It's within the auctioneer's discretion to make up bids throughout a sale, just to keep a slow auction rolling, up to whatever confidential minimum reserve price has been agreed upon by the seller and the auction house. By the way, it's all completely legal and is likely to remain so.

Remembering the eighties, when a million dollars would create a huge sensation, I watched these big bidders spread around the room. Christie's knew better than to seat two rivals anywhere near each other. The seating chart at these auctions was just as fraught as those at the "power" art-crowd restaurants, from La Grenouille in New York to Harry's Bar in London to the Kronenhalle in Zurich to the China Club in Hong Kong. I figured that there were 25 to 35 people in the world capable of spending, and prepared to spend, over $100 million on a single piece of art. Another 100 to 125 could, and might, spend $50 million. The pyramid got increasingly wide from there. Works selling for $1 million, once front-page news, are never even mentioned now. At the base of the pyramid is eBay, with, at last count, 85 million collectors bidding and buying in what is the world's largest flea market. Of those 150 or so highest rollers, all of them seemed to be here, in body or spirit, tonight.

I thought how I'd do this auction, how I might get even bigger numbers—you know, the nobody-does-it-better syndrome that is an occupational hazard of the auctioneer. Big art demands big egos. But as much as I hate to confess it, I had to admit to myself that Jussi was doing an amazing job. In all honesty, what I wasn't feeling was seller's remorse, or auction envy. My biggest emotion was extreme exhilaration, the thrill of an exploding market that I was figuring out how to reposition myself in. Contemporary art had become the Gold Rush of the millennium, and I was one prospector who could never be deterred from the thrill of the chase and the endless eureka moments that came with it.

3

ARTOPOLIS

As an art dealer, an art collector, an art obsessive, I would like to think, without being overly chauvinistic, that someone as mad for art as I am could have only come from one place. That place is Basel. A lot of cities in the world have great art—Florence, Paris, St. Petersburg come quickly to mind—but in no other city does art flow in the veins of its citizens as it does in my Swiss home. Today, you say the word "art," and the first urban free association is Art Basel, whether it's taking place in Basel itself or in Miami, Hong Kong, or wherever else the world's preeminent art fair may be cloned in the future. Say "Basel," and you think Art Basel; say "art," and you think Art Basel. But Art Basel is a very new phenomenon, dating back only to 1970, while art *in* Basel has been going on for centuries in this little, perfect city on the Rhine, where France, Germany, and Switzerland all meet. Basel is the perfect intersection of culture and wealth, a fertile crescent of art collectors.

Basel is home to Switzerland's oldest and finest university, the Harvard of the Rhine, where Erasmus and Nietzsche both taught. The University of Basel goes back to 1460. Deeply connected to it is the Kunstmuseum, which goes back to 1661 and is the world's oldest public-access art museum. And then there are the pharmaceutical companies; that's where the big money is, and that's where collections get started. Novartis, Hoffmann–La Roche, Syngenta, and many others are all right here.

Put simply, the chemistry here is literally perfect for great art collections to form. There's a basic art instinct in that Rhine water, and the Swiss business gene has created the ways and means to harness money to culture and build something beautiful. Those are my roots.

I was born in Basel in 1951. My father was a lawyer there for Hoffmann–La Roche. His family was from Neuchâtel, that picturesque castle town a hundred kilometers from Basel. My father was a baron, though that was a title he kept in the closet. (Just for the record, I'm one, too, and I keep my title in the closet as well. Self-effacement runs in the family.) Our ancestors had been governors of Neuchâtel for centuries and had been ennobled by Frederick the Great of Prussia, in effect for their role in keeping Frederick's Protestant faith vis-à-vis the Catholic one of France. Because of its proximity to these frequently warring powers, Neuchâtel was something of a political football. Having enough of this game of nations, my ancestor David de Pury left the scene altogether and moved to Lisbon, where he became banker to the King of Portugal. However, when he died, he left his Portuguese fortune to Neuchâtel; hence his statue in Neuchâtel's main square, Place de Pury, and hence my royal welcome when I wed my first wife in the castle that is the emblem of the city.

I do have ties to America. In 1731 David de Pury's son Jean-Pierre petitioned the English king to establish a settlement of six hundred Neuchâtel peasants, in search of a better life, on the swampy banks of the Savannah River south of Charleston, South Carolina, then the Paris of the New World. The de Pury colonists sailed from Genoa. Adding an extra "r" for good measure, they called the town they founded Purrysburg. Alas, despite the Protestant work ethic of the settlers, malaria and other diseases of the Low Country, as that area is known, rendered Purrysburg a ghost town not long after the American Revolution, though not before George Washington put the town on the map by having breakfast there. They couldn't brag that "George Washington slept here," which is the ultimate American validation, like "By Appointment to Her Majesty." But it was close.

The lost colony provided ever-historic-minded South Carolina with a host of Swiss names that became entrenched in that state's founding Huguenot (French Protestant) aristocracy. In the 1980s, a Neuchâtel-

Purrysburg exchange was initiated by descendants of these South Carolina grandees, and I was invited to help commemorate Purrysburg's 250th anniversary. The celebration of this gone-with-the-wind settlement was so romantically nostalgic that I couldn't help feel a little like a Swiss Rhett Butler.

As a boy in Basel, however, I felt more like a Swiss Oliver Twist. When I was ten, I became a drug orphan. That wasn't as grave as it sounds. But I was indeed cut adrift when my father was given the career opportunity of his lifetime, to transfer to Tokyo and run the Hoffman–La Roche business there. What was a small ten-man operation when my father arrived in 1961 grew under his leadership to a giant corporation employing over ten thousand people. My three siblings, two brothers and a sister, were all older than I, and on their own. I had to be sacrificed on the altar of my father's brilliant career and was placed with family friends.

I had been a terrible student in the famous Humanistisches Gymnasium that had been founded by Erasmus. Despite being tall, I was awkward and awful at sports, always the last to be chosen. I still loved soccer, if only vicariously. I loved art even more, which amazed my parents, and doubly amazed my "stepfamily," the Bonhotes, headed by an executive from Father's pharmaceutical rival Ciba-Geigy. The Bonhotes were as acultural as my parents had been culture vultures. Once when Mrs. Bonhote asked me where I had been that afternoon and I told her I had gone to a Klee exhibition, she thought I had gone to look at a show of keys. Key in French is *clef,* pronounced Klee. Maybe Mrs. Bonhote thought I had a future as a locksmith. She was living proof that while Basel was a great art town, not everyone there was bitten by the art bug.

My personal infection had started on childhood trips with my mother to Florence, where I had been transfixed by the Uffizi and the Bargello even more than by the *gelati* that had been the reward for most normal kids for putting up with the art. Adding fuel to the fire was my first trip to Paris, staying with an uncle on Île Saint-Louis and being unleashed at the Louvre. Maybe if Euro Disney had been around, I might have been distracted into a totally different life path, but it wasn't, nor were Disney's *Davy Crockett* episodes available on European television.

We were stuck with Old World culture, and insulated from the small-screen pop-culture seductions of the New.

So art was my "thing." I adored school excursions to the Basel Kunst-museum the way others would adore going to movies. The father of one of my friends had inherited part of the art collection of Basel's first great collector, Raoul La Roche. My friend's house was completely banal, but the art was heavenly. I would be transfixed by the Picassos, the Legers, the Braques, the Grises, the way my friend, who was indifferent to his father's art, would devour comic books.

Eventually, I went with this friend to Paris, a four-hour train ride from Basel, to visit the amazing modern house designed for La Roche, who was not one of the drug La Roches but a banking La Roche, by his best friend, Le Corbusier, which housed most of his collection after he died in 1965. La Roche, who began collecting the modern art of his Parisian friends in 1918, when he was only twenty-nine, became a role model for my young self, something unusual to aspire to. My older brothers, both brilliant students, were stars at a young age. One was a theologian, the other a lawyer. I had no hope of competing with them. So I looked for another path, a road not taken.

During my lonely adolescence, an event occurred in Basel that illuminated why, when it came to art, this town was different from all other towns. The year was 1967. I was sixteen, deep into my obsession with Anglo-American pop music. I liked American Pop Art as well. One of my art buddies had an American mother. She introduced me to Rauschenberg and Warhol, who I thought were cool and captured the essence of an America that existed in my dreams and in my ears. Andy Warhol created one image, Jimi Hendrix another. Marilyn, Elvis, Campbell's Soup, "Purple Haze." I later learned that American boys of my generation escaped the confines of their lives by reading *National Geographic*. I escaped mine with art and music. While the idea of becoming the next Raoul La Roche was beyond adolescent fantasy, I collected my Beatles, Stones, Beach Boys, and Bob Dylan albums the way my friends' families would collect their art.

No family in Zurich had better art than that of my school friend Ruedi Staechelin. Rudi's grandfather, Rudolf, had one of the world's preeminent collections of French Impressionists (Monet, Renoir, Sisley) and

Post-Impressionists (Van Gogh, Gauguin). Ruedi himself would also go on to work at Sotheby's. In April 1967, a disaster befell the Staechelin family. They were the owners of Switzerland's biggest charter airline, Globe Air. One of their planes, a Bristol Britannia en route from Bangkok to Basel, crashed in a thunderstorm near Nicosia, Cyprus, killing 126 mostly Swiss vacationers. Both pilots had violated the limits on hours, and one of them had insufficient training on the aircraft. The Staechelin family was being sued to death. They didn't have enough insurance to pay the victims. The only way they could survive their financial crisis was to start selling their art. This was my first exposure to fiscal dire straits. Money troubles for rich Swiss were a rarity in a country as famous for its banks as for its cheese and watches.

First the Staechelins sold a Van Gogh to Walter Annenberg, just before he became Nixon's ambassador to the Court of St. James's. But one Van Gogh would not a legal firestorm quell. They had to sell more, and Annenberg was the Qatari of his day, an insatiable collector with pockets as deep as the Mindanao Trench. Next on the block were two of the world's most valuable Picassos, then on permanent loan to the Basel Kunstmuseum. Both were masterpieces: 1906's Pink Period *Two Brothers* and 1923's *The Seated Harlequin*. When word got out about the Annenberg acquisition, the people of Basel went up in arms—and not only because Annenberg was an American, and a *nouveau riche* American whose own father had gone to prison and made his fortune not printing Gutenberg Bibles but peddling *The Racing Form*, the bible of horse racing and betting.

Even if the buyer were the Queen of England, the Baselers would have gotten deeply proprietary. Picasso had only spent one night of his life in Basel, staring at the Rhine from his room in the city's grand hotel Les Trois Rois, having been stood up by the Swiss artist Paul Klee, whom he had come to visit. Nevertheless, Basel had adopted Picasso as a native son. His biggest collectors were Baselers: La Roche, Staechelin, and the city's premier art dealer, Ernst Beyeler, who had sold over four hundred of the Spaniard's works, albeit around the world. The Basel city fathers and the museum heads went to the Staechelins and asked what it would take to keep those two Picassos here. It turned out the Staechelins wanted close to $1.5 million, which would have made these paintings among the world's most valuable. Basel was rich, but not Annenberg rich. So the city decided to put it to the people, letting the voters choose— or not—to assume what many thought was a scandalous expense, artistic greenmail.

What followed was one of the most colorful election campaigns in history. Politicians dressed as harlequins to get out the vote. There were huge street fairs. Local artists sold their own imitation Picassos at booths throughout the city, hard by bratwurst stands and beer gardens. Bands played "All You Need Is Picasso," to the Beatles' "All You Need Is Love." People wore "I Like Pablo" badges, evoking the "I Like Ike" buttons of the Eisenhower presidential campaigns in America. The opposition, those thrifty, conservative Swiss, as tight as the Scots, attacked the municipal purchase as a huge waste of money.

It also became a showdown between young and old, with the youth vote heavily leaning toward Pablo. However, some of the poorer kids thought this was effete snobbery at its worst. Rudi Staechelin became a marked man on the city's playgrounds and soccer fields. His parents sent him out of town to another school so he wouldn't get beaten up. In the end Picasso won—by a landslide. It was the first time in democratic history that a city had voted for art in this way. This was Basel's finest hour. Picasso himself was so moved by the results of the referendum that he made a gift of four more paintings to the Kunstmuseum, plus a priceless 1907 study drawing of *Les Demoiselles d'Avignon*. His generosity inspired that of others, including Mrs. Maja Sacher, one of the Hoffman–La Roche heiresses, whose husband, the best friend of Igor Stravinsky, was another avid patron of the arts. Mrs. Sacher donated her own Picasso Cubist masterpiece to the Kunstmuseum, completing the transformation of the Globe Air tragedy into a triumph for our city.

4

L'Artiste

———————

Growing up in Basel, I had three adolescent pipe dreams: to become a soccer star or a rock star or a great artist. Pele, Paul (McCartney), and Picasso were my Holy Trinity, though there were plenty of possible substitutions. However, because I couldn't play, and I couldn't sing, I had no choice but to take the one road to my dreams that wasn't already closed. I Like Pablo. That became my mantra, and long before my parents decamped for Japan, I was sketching, then taking art classes and starting to paint. And much to my parents' surprise, my teachers didn't think I was half bad, although I was largely an autodidact. I was such a dud in academics that my parents' wishful thinking may have made them see art when someone else would see folly. Nonetheless, they encouraged me to continue, and to try to be good at *something*.

The most exciting part of my childhood was my summers, when I got to travel. Going to Japan to visit my parents, who were living in splendor in the Okura Hotel, was a real adventure. The Okura was the pinnacle of sixties modernity, as cool architecturally as Raoul La Roche's Le Corbusier house. I loved the neon fantasyland that was the Ginza by night, so much the opposite of traditional Basel, yet I also loved the ancient traditions and inscrutable serenity that counterpointed the frenzy of the new. To wit, I ate sushi in Tokyo for the first time; I also had my first Big Mac, at the booming McDonald's on the Ginza.

While my father was becoming a captain of industry, building his company's Japan base, Nippon Roche, my mother was becoming a serious artist in her own right. She had studied and become an expert in ikebana, the Japanese fine art of flower arranging. She became the first non-Japanese to receive the highest-level diploma of Sogetsu, the most avant-garde of Japan's ikebana schools. When my parents retired back to Basel, Mother opened a branch of Sogetsu there. While I totally lacked a green thumb, I was enormously proud and personally encouraged to have an artist in the immediate family. In time my father got into the art act as well, taking lessons in sculpture in Tokyo from the master Yukio Inoue.

When I was just seventeen, I made my first trip to New York City, en route to my brother's wedding in Washington, D.C. At first my parents had disinvited me because of my bad marks in school. I was never so disappointed. Finally, they relented and took pity on me. My father told me to enjoy myself, for, given my perceived lack of promise, he was certain that I would never have the chance to travel again. Of course, now I live most of my life on airplanes. I laugh at this, thinking perhaps I travel so much simply to redeem myself to my father and rebut his vote of no confidence.

Whatever, my father was right about enjoying this first opportunity to see the world. The most exhilarating moment of my young life was seeing the majestic Manhattan skyline on the drive in from Kennedy Airport. I stayed in Greenwich Village with my cousin Marianne de Pury, who was living *la vie bohème américaine*, acting in very-off-Broadway underground theaters, hanging out with long-haired artists and musicians. I was so impressed when she dropped the name Charlie Mingus. My highest moment of Manhattan ecstasy was the entire day I spent in the Museum of Modern Art. To see Picasso's *Guernica* in the flesh galvanized me in my commitment to become an artist. I Like Pablo!

Then I took the Metroliner to Washington for the wedding and got my first taste of American power politics. My future sister-in-law was the daughter of Ernest Cuneo, one of the most influential Democratic lawyers in the nation's capital. Cuneo had been a football star at Columbia and in the pros, and then the right hand of New York mayor Fiorello La Guardia, as well as a top adviser to Franklin Roosevelt. Cuneo then became one of the top media attorneys in the world, as the counsel to fifties über-gossip-columnist Walter Winchell. Lots of senators, former cabinet officers, and press lords were at the wedding. Again, however, art conquered all.

My biggest thrill in Washington was not meeting the future secretary of state Cyrus Vance but spending another glorious museum day, this time at the National Gallery. The Gallery's rising-star director, Carter Brown, whose roots went back before the *Mayflower* and who had been mentored, after Harvard, by Bernard Berenson, would, in the years ahead, actually become a colleague of mine. That was science fiction at the time. Right then, I was delighted just to be there. Visiting the National Gallery was a state of grace.

The next year I finished high school, without honors. What faced me now was six months of compulsory military service (no jokes about the Swiss navy, please) and then the even harsher reality of law school, where I was expected to follow in my brother David's footsteps, without any hope of filling his shoes. Becoming a major theologian like my other brother, Albert, was even further out of the question. He was already a professor of Old Testament studies, the youngest tenured professor at the University of Geneva, where he held a special chair. He was fluent in Hebrew and Arabic. My sister Marie-Isabelle suffered no such career imperatives, although today she might be railing at the sexism of such reduced expectations. She became a nurse, went to live and work in a village in Dahomey, then came home to marry a prominent lawyer and has lived happily ever after.

Before I would surrender my youth and face the music of someone else's idea of a brilliant career, I wanted to take one last shot at sowing my artistic oats. Accordingly, I moved to Tokyo for a few months to enroll at the Todai-Tokyo Academy of Fine Arts in Ueno Park, where so many of the city's major museums are located, analogous to Berlin's Museum Island. I studied *sumi-e,* or ink wash painting. This is brush painting that uses black ink, the same as in Eastern calligraphy, in various concentrations. Fifty shades of gray is the idea.

I was entranced with the whole process: the bamboo brushes, which were *objets d'art* themselves; the plant-based *washi* paper, which was the most beautiful in the world; the intricacy of the technique. It looks simple, but so does Fred Astaire's dancing. Each stroke must be mastered, repeated thousands of times. The process was anything but tedious. I felt born again. I also studied *nihonga,* classic Japanese painting, using watercolor on silk, and accompanied my father to his sculpture lessons and borrowed some of Inoue's beautiful models to use for my academic drawings. I never dreamed that my father and I would bond over art this way.

The entire mythology of Japanese art appealed to me, such as the story of a seventeenth-century priest who needed a huge brush for a large-scale opus grew his hair to create a human brush that was dipped in Chinese ink. It struck me that Japanese ancient art was in many ways much more contemporary than the classical European art of the same period. I also found that postwar Abstract Expressionism, the nonrepresentational, emotional, nontraditional "new school" of Pollock, Rothko, Newman, and de Kooning, which was the rage in New York before Pop emerged, had a lot in common with Japanese painting. I shared Van Gogh's fascination with and inspiration by Japanese woodprints. That love would be returned in the late 1980s, when I was at Sotheby,'s by the rich Japanese who created the greatest bull market in the history of art by paying unbelievable prices for the works of Van Gogh and Renoir.

The biggest of the big was in 1990, when paper-products tycoon Ryoei Saito paid $82.5 million at a Christie's auction in New York for Van Gogh's 1890 *Portrait of Dr. Gachet.* The next night I had the chance to enter the record books and to top this. I was working for Sotheby's and was on the phone with a very serious bidder at our auction of Renoir's 1876 *Bal du Moulin de la Galette.* I was thus getting into the ring with Ryoei Saito in the art equivalent of a sumo wrestling match. Mr. Saito had made his fortune in the paper that had obsessed me so, a fitting career for an art collector. He was the Japanese counterpart of the great American collector and paper tycoon, Peter Brant.

The prize Renoir here had been owned by an American imperial dynasty, the Whitneys. I had a rather dynastic client who wanted the Renoir badly—but in the end, not as much as Mr. Saito, who outbid us with the staggering sum of $78 million. I turned out to be the underbidder, one bid away from the record books. Close but no cigar. These were two nights, back to back, that shook the art world, the greatest concentrated shopping spree in the history of luxury, as dramatic a display of the power of the Japanese as their recent purchase of Rockefeller Center, Pebble Beach, and Columbia Pictures.

Mr. Saito's moment of glory turned out to be short-lived. First he shocked the art world by announcing that he planned to have both the Van Gogh and the Renoir cremated with him when he died. Later he said he was joking, but his humor was lost on the art press. Then he got ensnared in a corruption scandal, having turned to bribery to expedite the rezoning of forest land where he wanted to create a golf club named after none other than Vincent van Gogh. After Mr. Saito, that most passionate of collectors, died in 1996, of a stroke, possibly precipitated by his fall from the grace he sought art to give him, the Van Gogh was not seen publicly again. Sadly, this was a case of *après moi, le deluge*. The market soon crashed, and for a while everyone was looking for scapegoats for the bulling—and killing—of the art market. That was the one compensation for not having made the record books.

But 1990 was a long way, a whole career away, from 1969. Right now I was about as out of the art market as a novice painter could be. I found out how out I was on my way home to face the military. I decided to stop in New York City en route from Tokyo and try to sell the paintings I had done in Japan. I took an airport bus from JFK into the city, awed as ever by that mighty skyline. Despite my shock and awe at the view, I was too green and naïve to be intimidated by the prospects of rejection faced by any new artist, if it wasn't hubristic to call myself that.

Crashing again with my artsy cousin in Greenwich Village, I made a battle plan. I decided to present myself to the galleries with the largest ads in *The New York Times*. This was the Big Apple, home of the big everything. Bigger was better here, or so it seemed. My first stop was at Manhattan's oldest and most prestigious gallery, Knoedler, in grand town-house quarters on 57th Street off Fifth Avenue, across the street from Tiffany's, Bonwit Teller, and Harry Winston. You could feel the money, the luxury, the splendor, in the air, even if there were anti–Vietnam War protesters marching with placards, a jarring counterpoint to the crowds of chic female conspicuous consumers.

"I'd like to speak to Mr. Knoedler," I said, as charmingly as I could muster, to the stern receptionist.

"There *is* no Mr. Knoedler," she shot back at me, glaring at my large cardboard portfolio as if I were a homeless person carrying all my belongings in one box.

I had done some homework, but not enough. Because Knoedler had European roots, having opened in 1846 as a branch of a Paris gallery, and its first manager was German, I was assuming that my European-ness would get me in the door. Ha! Knoedler had made its name and fortune in America's Gilded Age, selling Old Masters to the *nouveau* robber barons, like Astor, Frick, Vanderbilt, Mellon, and Rockefeller. The last generation of the Knoedler family, whose name was Roland Balay, would soon be selling the gallery to industrialist Armand Hammer, whom I would later get to know through Heini Thyssen. The receptionist did not have a crystal ball. She could have introduced me to Mr. Balay, who was technically a Knoedler, but she saw no need. What she saw was what she got, and what I got was the door.

In 2011 this colossus of art closed suddenly and ignominiously when it was caught in a scandal selling—for millions—Pollocks, Diebenkorns, and Rothkos that had been forged by a Chinese craftsman in Queens who started out selling fakes on a street corner. He was only discovered when it turned out some of the paint used didn't even exist when the artists were alive. One of my good friends, Domenico De Sole, the resurrector of Gucci and currently chairman of the board of Sotheby's, was caught by this ruse, having bought a fake Rothko from Knoedler, proof that even the most sophisticated collectors, with the resources for investigating provenance, could get fooled.

In any event, Knoedler couldn't get fooled by me. So I took a long walk up Madison Avenue to 77th Street and my next stop, the Leo Castelli Gallery. In two years Castelli would move to West Broadway and shift the axis of the New York art world downtown. But for the moment, Artland was the Upper East Side, anchored by the squat fortress of the Sotheby Parke Bernet auction house. Castelli's was right around the corner, between Madison and Fifth, like Knoedler in a fancy town house. Castelli was the first art dealer since Jospeh Duveen to become a household name, assuming your household was on Park Avenue or in Greenwich.

The tiny, elegant, courtly Castelli, born Krausz, had grown up in Trieste and been trained as a lawyer before going to work for an insurance company in Bucharest. The unartisticness of this background was always an inspiration to me when I suffered through law school. It was at the Romanian insurance office where artistic lightning—and romance—struck. There he met his wife, a garment-maufacturing heiress named Ileana Schapira, whose father bought the couple a Matisse for a wedding gift and would soon finance Leo's first gallery, in Paris at the Place Vendôme, across from the Ritz. Leo was off to a grand start, which only got grander when Ileana's family connections enabled them to escape the Nazis via Tangier and Havana to New York.

In postwar New York, the worldly Castellis joined an artistic circle that included many of the emerging Abstract Expressionists, like Pollock and de Kooning, as well as the cutting-edge gallerist of the time, Sidney Janis, who took Castelli in as his protégé. By 1957 Castelli had his own gallery, the one I was eagerly approaching, and was representing the stars of AE, like Pollock, de Kooning, and Twombly, as well as the future princes of Pop, Johns, Rauschenberg, Lichtenstein, and, after an initial rejection, Warhol. How insane was I to even think of approaching this closed circle? I didn't know any better. They had a big ad. There was business to do.

"Can I speak to Mr. Castelli?" I inquired.

"He's traveling," the stylish, impenetrable receptionist said.

"I wanted to show him my work—"

She cut me off. "Mr. Castelli is only interested in *American* art," she announced. She was judging me—and finding me guilty—solely by my accent. She had no idea what kind of art I was lugging in that clumsy cardboard portfolio.

"Actually it's Japanese art." I tried to stay alive.

"Mr. Castelli only represents *American* artists," she snarled.

In all my travels, some before and many since, I had never felt like such a stranger in a strange land. And Americans complained about the haughty *French* maître d's at temples of gastronomy like Le Pavillon. This imperious woman could have given Gianni Agnelli an inferiority complex. I apologized for intruding and slunk out the door.

My third stop was Staempfli. It was conveniently located also on 77th Street, just east of Madison. George Staempfli was well known as the dealer of Salvador Dali. More important for me was that he was Swiss, from Bern. We had a national tie. No way could I get the Castelli "no Europeans wanted" treatment from him. Staempfli had made his career at Knoedler and then gone out on his own, opening this gallery in 1959. He proudly represented European artists. I thought I was one.

"I'd like to see Mr. Staempfli," I said as my opening.

"I'm sorry, he's not here," the receptionist said. She was the classic all-American blonde, someone you would see more as a sunny football cheerleader, not a black-clad, austere gatekeeper. True to her friendly looks, she didn't cut me dead. "He'll be back. Why don't you leave your portfolio. Come back in three hours."

I was elated. Where there was art, there was hope. For the next three hours I wandered the canyons of upper Madison. I strolled through Central Park. I went to the Met and the Guggenheim. I thought about how glorious life would be as an artist in New York. Then from those heights, I dove into the depths of speculation about how horrible life would be as a lawyer in Switzerland. I thought of the Charles Dickens book about lawyers, *Bleak House.* The choice was clear, but it wasn't mine to make. It was all up to my compatriot, George Staempfli. My future, my career as an artist, was in his hands.

"Mr. Staempfli loved your stuff," the cheerleader gushed as I came in the door. For one split second, all my artistic dreams had come true. Staempfli, Dali, and de Pury. What a trio. I Like Pablo. "But . . ."

I don't remember what the excuse was. The "but" was all I heard. The beautiful receptionist had delivered a bleak messahge in the brightest possible way. It hurt the same. I gathered up my portfolio and departed. I knew my New York idyll was over. It was back home to the Swiss army, or navy for all it mattered to me. At least I had tried. As I trudged, eyes downcast, past the temple of art that was Sotheby Parke Bernet, the idea that I would one day return to these rarefied precincts as a player in a game where the captains, as in all the games of my youth, wouldn't choose me for the team was as far from my realm of possibility as playing guitar onstage with the Rolling Stones.

5

THE APPRENTICE

My endless weeks of military training and service were a mortification of the flesh, an atonement for the delicacy and refinement of life that I had enjoyed in Japan. The only saving grace of the military experience was that I had fallen in love with the daughter of a Japanese general while studying art in Tokyo, and that romance sustained me through the rigors of basic training. The general had become military attaché in Paris, where the daughter was modeling for the couture house Céline. Desperate to visit her, I needed a three-day pass. I approached my commander with great trepidation, thinking of various excuses such as deaths in the family or some exotic disease that only a Paris specialist could cure. The commander saw right through me. He knew my disease was love. "I'm a man as well," he told me. "Go and enjoy."

Knowing my passion for art, some family friends had given me a birthday gift of an envelope of money to purchase my first work of art. Instead, I took the money and ran with my girlfriend to the Côte d'Azur, where I blew every cent of it on extravagant hotels and restaurants on what I saw as a pre-honeymoon. So much for my art collecting, at least then. Art might have been a jealous mistress, but art was no match for a real mistress. In the end, my girlfriend went back to Japan; our relationship was done in by the then-prohibitive cost of long-distance calls. I kept art out of my mind and prepared to face that other famously jealous mistress, the law.

If I thought the military was bad, law school was even worse. Not that the school was bad. The University of Geneva, where my theologian brother held a chair, was founded in 1559 by John Calvin, and its modern law school had a special exchange program with Harvard Law School, so the two were considered sister schools, at least by the Swiss. If the University of Basel was the Harvard of the Rhine, Geneva's law school was the Harvard of the lakes. Whatever it was, it was way too good—and too hard—for me.

Basel was a city of culture. Zurich was a city of money. And Geneva was a city of jewelry. Art was an afterthought. There were only five decent galleries in the whole city. The rich people there, and there were many, preferred tangible assets; hence the lavish outposts of glittering enterprises like Harry Winston, Cartier, Van Cleef, Bulgari, and all the rest. If it was breakfast at Tiffany's in New York, it was fondue at Winston's in Geneva. I had little interest in jewels, nor in money. I missed Basel and its art. I rented a tiny *chambre de bonne,* or maid's room, on the picturesque Rue des Granges in the Old Town and tried to study law. On my first set of exams, I froze. I couldn't answer a single question. So I became a dropout. I left Geneva as ignominiously as I had left the Castelli Gallery.

When I arrived home in Basel and the news reached my mother in Japan, she was briefly beside herself. But my mother didn't dwell on failure. She was a woman of action. Instead, she called her old friend Ernst Beyeler and told him she was in despair, maybe exaggerating her plight for dramatic effect—and results. *I don't know what on earth to do with this boy. I'm at a total loss. Can you help me?* Send him around, Beyeler said.

Ernst Beyeler, who was around fifty when he received this hopeless case at his gallery, or should I say temple of art, at 9 Bäumleingasse near that other temple the Kunstmuseum, was a big man in a small town. Because it was small, everyone knew each other; hence my mother's easy access. This was decades before Beyeler created his Renzo Piano–designed museum outside of town, probably the greatest private museum in the world, and slightly before he helped create Art Basel in 1971. Then he was just Monsieur Beyeler, a great man and a family friend—and a total genius.

Without the Basel homeboy connection, going to see him would have been far more intimidating than trying to see Leo Castelli. Ernst Beyeler wasn't intimidating personally, unless you knew his achievements. He was considered the world's ultimate connoisseur of, and dealer in, twentieth-century art. That was quite an accomplishment for the son of a Swiss railway worker, from a family with no interest in art whatsoever. Tall and athletically thin and aquiline, Beyeler looked more like a ruggedly handsome skiing teacher than an art expert. His kindness in seeing me made a huge impression. Because of that I have made it a point to advise any young people who are considering careers in art; hence my role as mentor on the reality series *Work of Art*. I needed all the help I could get, and now I will give all the help that I can. The notion that one day I would be dispensing it to millions on television would have blown my mind at the time.

During World War II, Beyeler, like myself a university dropout, went to work in Basel for Oskar Schloss, a rare-book and print dealer and a German-Jewish refugee who put himself forth as a German Buddhist. I guess the world was safer for Buddhists in those days, even in neutral Switzerland. Like myself again, Beyeler developed a passion for Japanese art. When Schloss died in 1945, Beyeler bought the business. His first exhibit was Japanese woodcuts. We thus had something to talk about, other than my anomie. One of the first things Beyler said to me has always stuck in my mind: "The pretty is the enemy of the beautiful." He was quoting Fernand Léger, whose Cubist paintings nonchalantly lined a wall, but the riddle-of-the-Sphinx quote woke me up and made me think, and my first thought was that I'd better be on my toes with Ernst Beyeler.

When I was sitting with this great art dealer, I still saw myself as an artist, an aspiring artist, to be sure, a failed artist thus far as well, but nonetheless an artist, a creative person, not a businessman. However, Beyeler had a way of making what he did, that is, buying and selling art, as magical and intriguing as making art. Obviously nobody did it better, and when you're great at something, your greatness makes what you do fascinating. I was therefore enthralled when I told him about my recent visit to America and the cold, rather frozen, shoulder I had gotten in New York, and he responded by telling me how that same American cold shoulder had made his career.

The cornerstone of what would become the Beyeler colossus was a self-made steel tycoon from Peru, Indiana, whose other famous success story was Cole Porter. The nonmusical Peruvian was named G. David Thompson. Thompson, yet one more dropout, was a casualty of the Carnegie Institute of Technology in Pittsburgh, Andy Warhol's alma mater, where Thompson flunked out of his engineering degree. Undaunted, he went to Wall Street and made his fortune in finance, then returned to Pittsburgh, where by 1945, and barely into his forties, he headed four steel companies. That steel supported Thompson's real passion, which was art, a passion inspired by his Peru childhood when the local department store put an "artist" in the window and offered a free painting with every purchase over ten dollars. Thompson then offered all the store's shoppers he could hustle a pittance for their free art. A collector was born. In 1928 Thompson bought his first "real" painting, a Klee. He never stopped.

Pittsburgh must have had something in the waters of the Allegheny and Monongahela Rivers that intersect there. That city of industry gave America some of its greatest art collectors, most notably Henry Clay Frick (of the Frick), Paul Mellon (of the National Gallery), and Duncan Phillips (of Washington's Phillips Collection), not to mention Gertrude Stein, a Pittsburgher before finding her name and fame in Paris. Unfortunately, all of these patrons built and housed their collections elsewhere. When Thompson was nearing sixty, in 1959, he offered his vast collection, one of America's finest, to Pittsburgh, plus his super-modern futuristic mansion to house it. Pittsburgh turned him down flat.

Thompson was no refined Paul Mellon. He was rough and aggressive, less a brainy collector than a self-described "country horse trader." He also made his philosophy plain and simple. "During the early years, I classified art as abstract or realistic, and by schools such as Dada and Surrealist, " he wrote. But Thompson dropped out of those schools the same way he dropped out of Carnegie Tech. "Today I recognize but two kinds . . . Good Art and Bad Art." Stung by the rejection of Pittsburgh's old guard, he began focusing solely on modern art, which the old guard knew or cared little about, regarding it as *nouveau*, like Thompson himself. In the end Thompson had the last laugh, but Ernst Beyeler laughed even louder, all the way to the bank and to the Kunstmuseum.

If Thompson couldn't show his art, he decided, to hell with it, he would sell it. Like the Syrian-Colombian-American Mugrabi family today, who made their fortune stockpiling artists (nearly a thousand Warhols), and might also be viewed as "country horse traders," Thompson was one of the first collectors to buy in bulk. If he thought Klee was undervalued, he bought every Klee he could find. Just as he bought Klee, he sold Klee, and to whom better than his fellow Swiss Ernst Beyeler, who purchased nearly a hundred Klees from Thompson in 1961. He also bought ninety Giacomettis and hundreds more by Matisse, Miró, and Cézanne. His failure to be a prophet in his own country of Pittsburgh may have broken Thompson's heart. He died of heart failure in 1965. A few years later his wife continued his great deacquistion, selling a hundred Kandinskys to Beyeler.

By Thompson's death Ernst Beyeler had become the biggest horse trader in the art world. But there was nothing crass or commercial about him. He had the right stuff, and he merchandised it in the right way, the master of the soft, smart sell. Beyeler showed me some of his catalogues, which were artworks in themselves. The craftsmanship of those catalogues won the heart of Picasso, who invited Beyeler to visit him in his villa in Mougins, France, in 1966. Beyeler came away with twenty-six works to sell and to show. Beyeler described himself to me and to others as a "hunter." No one ever bagged more big game than he.

I met Beyeler's wife, Hildy, who ran the business with him, with an iron fist. They had no children. Their paintings were their family, and besides, they knew everyone in the world. They were never lonely. I wondered why Beyeler didn't become an international concern the way that Frank Lloyd, the head of the Marlborough Gallery, had recently done, opening outposts in London, New York, Monaco, Madrid, Buenos Aires, Tokyo, and beyond, a playbook that Larry Gagosian has taken and run with around the world today. I think the answer was that Beyeler loved Basel and loved the art vibe there. The world would come to him; he didn't need to expand. In a twist on his Léger quote, he might have said the big is the enemy of the important.

I was so entranced at our meeting that I decided then and there to forget becoming an artist. No, what I wanted to be now was an art dealer. I obviously was totally impressionable, but who in art, short of Picasso

himself, could have made a bigger impression than Ernst Beyeler? He
tried to focus my ambitions. Aside from being an artist, there were two
ways to make a future out of a love of art, he told me. The first was
to study and maybe teach or write about art. The second was to go
into the art market. Beyeler asked me about my preferences. "Is your
attraction to art physical or intellectual?" he pointedly asked me. "Purely
physical," I shot back without a second's hesitation. I admitted, if my
mother hadn't already told him, that I was a dreadful student, and that
my interest in art was anything but bookish. "Then you must never
study art history, for all you will see are books and slides," Beyeler said.
"You must become a dealer!"

How, I wondered out loud. Beyeler had a plan all worked out. "I will
send you to Kornfeld in Bern for three months. Then you will go to Sotheby's in London, for a year. Then to New York, for another year at
Sotheby's, and then one more at Marlborough. And then back to me."
It was a four-year plan, like a college education, albeit in a global university, one without walls, and with the pot of gold in working for the
King of Art at the end of a rainbow of Picassos.

Off to Bern I went. As the capital of Switzerland, Bern shared a
certain dullness with other capitals from Brasilia to Canberra to Ottawa
to Washington that were not a country's commercial and cultural hub.
That the liveliest spot in this ancient and elegant city was the *Bären-
graben,* or bear pit, that housed Bern's mascot, namesake, and symbol
was some commentary on the stolidity of life in the capital. If only there
had been a Goldilocks or two to cavort with the bears in the pit . . . Oh,
well. I was in Bern to work, and not to frolic. Abstinence was a small
price to pay for the opportunity to follow in the footsteps of Ernst Beyeler.

Galerie Kornfeld might be described as the Sotheby's of Switzerland.
It was an auction house, but what it was really known for was being
one of the world's preeminent dealers of prints and drawings. The gallery
had a long and proud history, having been founded in Stuttgart, Germany, in 1864 by H. G. Gutekunst, whose name felicitously translated
into "Good Art." In 1919 the gallery moved to Bern, and in 1951 Eberhard Kornfeld took over and gave it his name. In contrast to Beyeler,
who was austere and quiet, Ebi Kornfeld was a playful laugh riot, and
still remains so today, going strong in his nineties. He had the most

beautiful handwriting I'd ever seen, and would personally write out the provenance of all the art he sold. Kornfeld was of medium height, with long red hair and bushy eyebrows, something of a more theatrical version of Albert Einstein, who, along with Lenin, was Bern's most famous temporary resident. Einstein had worked as a clerk in the Swiss Patent Office in the early 1900s, before becoming "Einstein." If he could take a boring apprenticeship, so could I.

Luckily, mine was anything but boring. Kornfeld referred to me as *ein Schnupperlehring,* which roughly translates as an intern who is always sniffing around. My brief was to sniff around, truffle-pig-like, for hidden treasures. From Kornfeld, I quickly learned precision. The Swiss don't make the best watches for nothing. Kornfeld made the best catalogues, as good as if not better than Beyeler's. He was a leading seller of Picasso's prints and had become close friends with Pablo, as well as with Giacometti, Tinguely, de Saint Phalle, and Chagall. He had a rich, refined wife, Marlies, whose father, Jacques Koerfer, was a major art collector who lived in a Marcel Breuer home in Ascona, Switzerland, that was in all the architecture books. The Kornfelds had their own famous house, in Davos, that had belonged to the German Expressionist Ernst Ludwig Kirchner, who was driven to suicide by the Nazis after being branded as a "degenerate" artist. My first job at Kornfeld was to decipher and transcribe the huge cache of Kirchner's letters in Kornfeld's possession.

I lived atop the gallery, which was in the compound of the Kornfelds' Bern villa, and totally enjoyed this first real job. I was, unfortunately, less of a sniffer than a gofer. Still, I got to meet fabulous people, none more fabulous than Kornfeld's best friend, Heinz Berggruen, to whom I was assigned as chauffeur when he visited from Paris. Berggruen was another remarkable character I would eventually get to know on a more equal footing. Right now I was in awe of this swashbuckling, dapper man in his late fifties who was known to everyone as "Picasso's dealer," even more than Ernst Beyeler.

Berggruen was German, but beyond international. Educated in Berlin and Grenoble, he had become a journalist in Frankfurt in the thirties, but when the Nazis replaced his byline with his initials, Berggruen, who was from a wealthy Jewish family, saw in his denial of credit the handwriting on the wall. In 1936 he fled to California and enrolled in art history classes at Berkeley. Before long he had become the art critic of the *San Francisco Chronicle*. There wasn't much competition, as very few Americans, practical as they are, saw art as a "real" career, like banking or law or medicine or engineering. Berggruen married very well, wedding Lillian Zellerbach, the "pulp heiress" of the Crown Zellerbach paper colossus. He was then able to start collecting. His first acquisition, like G. David Thompson's, was a Klee. Klee is something of a starter kit for modernist collectors. Berggruen paid $100 for it.

Because Berggruen was one of the few "art men" in the Bay Area, he also became a curator at the San Francisco Museum of Modern Art, the repository of the millionaire collectors, most of whose fortunes were made in the Gold Rush but who now styled themselves not as 49er miners who had struck a big vein but as refined *culturati* whose art gave them an instant patina. One of his first shows at the museum was of Diego Rivera, with whom Berggruen struck up a fast friendship. Berggruen was ahead of the curve in his fascination with modern art—and modern artists. He had no idea how modern that world could be when Rivera took his new pal to a local hospital where his wife, Frida Kahlo, was undergoing therapy for the chronic pain from the bus accident she had suffered years before. "You will fall in love with my wife," Rivera trilled on their way to the hospital. How prophetic those words were.

Berggruen was twenty-five, Kahlo thirty-two. Her previous lover Leon Trotsky had just been assassinated in Mexico. She and Rivera were on the rocks. Despite her pain and her loss, she was triumphant, coming off a major success in a Paris Surrealist show. Despite his indulgent millionaire wife, Berggruen fell hard for the artist and followed her to New York, where they had a torrid romance that lasted six weeks, during which Kahlo divorced Rivera. Then she dumped Berggruen as fast and hard as he had fallen and went back to Rivera, remarrying him. Later in life, when Madonna was trying to get the film rights to play Frida Kahlo, she discovered Heinz and developed a dialogue that Heinz loved to boast about to all his friends. Too bad for him that the part eventually went to Salma Hayek (aka Madame Pinault).

Berggruen dealt with his heartbreak over Frida by joining the American army. His language skill and knowledge of Germany made him a valuable asset to the Allied forces. After the war he divorced Zellerbach and moved to Paris, opening a bookshop on the Île Saint-Louis specializing in illustrated tomes. Through the shop he met Picasso; the rest is history, art history.

Fortunately, in serving the likes of Heinz Berggruen, I didn't have to wear a uniform, and I didn't have to keep the car warm when Berggruen went to the fancy restaurants and hotels he loved. The most memorable of these was the Kronenhalle in Zurich, the most famous "art restaurant" in the world. The Kronenhalle is to Zurich what the Four Seasons is to New York, what Harry's Bar is to Venice, what Brasserie Lipp is to Paris: a power venue, where you can see everyone you need to see. In the past you could have seen the two Alberts, Einstein and Schweitzer, Thomas Mann, James Joyce, and every captain of finance who ever visited Zurich, the city of gnomes. But the main thing to see is the art, art everywhere, looming over the hearaldic shields and red leather banquettes. There's a self-portrait of Picasso, Mirós, Bonnards, Kandinskys, Chagalls, Varlins, all the friends of Kornfeld and Beyeler and Berggruen, and of Gustav Zumsteg, who made his fortune in silks in Paris but kept the Zurich restaurant as a hobby and a very lively museum.

When dealers and their top clients congregated here, as they always did, it was both an elite convention and a gemütlich homecoming. Plus the women were as beautiful and soigné as the *grandes horizontales* at Maxim's in Paris, except here they were devouring hearty platters of bratwurst and *rösti* potatoes, as opposed to *lièvre à la royale*. Among the other big names in art I met at Kornfeld was Theo van Gogh, the elderly nephew of the artist, who had the exact eyes of his uncle. Shaking his hand was like touching art. I was moved by this, and by meeting Aljoscha Klee, Paul's grandson, who had Paul's haunting dark eyes. Again, it was meeting history. Aljoscha was the author of a long and fascinating monograph on scleroderma, the atrophic skin disease from which Paul Klee suffered, and how illness affected his art. Meeting these legends, I felt I was in a club, an art club, and one I wanted to join. For the moment, I was delighted to be their mascot, their sniffer, their driver, whatever. I was extremely lucky to have a foot, or even a toe, in the door.

Notwithstanding my exposure to these super-dealers, I still hadn't fully let go of my initial dream of being an artist. At that point, however, aside from my Japanese art instructors, I hadn't met any real artists, Western style. Eberhard Kornfeld filled that void by adding to my list of duties that of "genius babysitter," the genius in this case being the legendary American abstract painter Sam Francis, the leader of the postwar expat school in Paris. Francis was coming to Bern for a high-profile exhibition of his recent works at Kornfeld. The problem was that Francis, forever high on pot, hadn't painted *any* recent works. So Kornfeld locked Francis up in his luxurious atelier behind the gallery and installed me as the go-between who would stir this genius to new heights (and not cannabis highs). That was a tall order.

Francis, then in his late forties, was a fascinating character. He had grown up outside San Francisco, his mother a pianist, his father a math professor. He had studied medicine at Berkeley before serving as a test pilot during World War II. A near-deadly plane crash, and two years in the hospital, turned the would-be doctor into an artist. After his release from the hospital, he returned to Berkeley and studied art. He was highly influenced by Jackson Pollock and Mark Rothko. After he got his master's degree, he moved to Paris, where he was lionized as a genius, the Jerry Lewis of art, and recognized as the leader of what became known as the "Second Generation" of Abstract Expressionists. I remember being transfixed by his painting *Big Red* at the Museum of Modern Art on my first visit to New York.

Francis and I also had other reasons to bond. He was fascinated and influenced by Japanese art, was considered a hero there, and had married a Japanese painter, Teruko Yokoi. So we had Japan to talk about, as well as Basel, where he was also a local hero and had done a large painting at our Kunsthalle, down the road from the Kunstmuseum, where many of Basel's large temporary exhibitions were held. The reason Sam smoked so much pot, he explained, was not because he was a Berkeley hippie (which would have been cool with me) but because he had developed renal tuberculosis as a sequel to his war injuries and was in the same kind of intractable pain that had sent Frida Kahlo to hospitals around the world. That made me think of Klee, of Kahlo, of Van Gogh, and wonder if great pain was a prerequisite to great art. We talked about it a lot.

Sam Francis once gave me, indirectly, one of the great compliments of my young life. Sam had a special technique of doing drip painting that involved putting a sponge into clear water, making lines on a canvas, then dipping his brushes into paint and letting them drip on the lines. One day, when he was in the bathroom, I couldn't resist trying to do an imitation of his work. When Sam emerged from the loo and began assembling his canvases for the show, he packed up my work among his, thinking the Simon de Pury was a Sam Francis. My Swiss honesty got in my way, and I had to confess to him my little experiment. He was incredibly polite and encouraging, but I insisted on throwing it into the trash. Sam was a hard act to follow, but I was pleased and proud that I was helpful at least in getting his Kornfeld show up and completely sold out.

Another of my Kornfeld assignments turned out far less well and could have ended my career in art even before it began. Mr. Kornfeld had assigned me to create a *passe-partout,* a kind of cardboard framing mat to place under the glass in a frame, for a priceless Max Ernst Surrealist drawing. Using a very sharp cutting knife, I created the *passe-partout* without realizing the Ernst was right beneath the cardboard. In the process I had cut the Ernst itself into four huge pieces. It was worse than when in 2006 Vegas casino mogul/collector Steve Wynn, whose vision suffered from retinitis pigmentosa, accidentally put his elbow through Picasso's *Le Rêve,* which he had just sold to hedge-fund mogul/collector Steven A. Cohen for $139 million. The painting cost nearly $100,000 to restore, and the elbow killed the sale and cut the value in half. Wynn sued his insurers, Lloyd's of London, for the difference. Lloyd's balked at paying the claim. An art donnybrook was averted when Cohen decided in 2013 he had to have the Picasso after all, now for $155 million.

In my case I had no Lloyd's insurance, no assets, and, I assumed, no future. I was terrified to tell Mr. Kornfeld the awful truth. Finally, I mustered my courage and revealed all. Kornfeld kept his ineffable cool. I have the world's best restorer, he assured me. The Ernst was imperceptibly restored. There was no way to see the traces of my cuts with the naked eye. The accident was never revealed in the Kornfeld catalogue. When the Ernst was offered at auction, I was still trembling that the damage I had done would somehow be exposed. But the shoe never dropped, the Ernst sold for a high price, and the buyer of the perfect restoration (and to guilty me, the perfect crime) was as happy with his restored Ernst as Stevie Cohen would be with his restored Picasso. And I was so happy with Eberhard Kornfeld that I stayed there eighteen months, far longer than the three that had been prescribed for me on the Beyeler Plan. But now it was time for my sophomore year at Sotheby's. In 1974, off to London I went.

6

LONDON CALLING

I was in love at first sight with London. My first sight was in London's prime time, the summer of 1967, the height of Beatlemania, Carnaby Street, *Blow-Up*, miniskirts, everything that made London in the late sixties the coolest city on the globe. I had been sent to a place called Basingstoke, an old market town in Hampshire, to live with a family and polish my English. The next summer I went to Cambridge and took a formal course, which enabled me to escape into London by train every chance I had. Punting on the River Cam seemed romantic, but I was hooked on the cutting-edge music and culture that only a city, and that city at that moment, could provide. I'm not sure how many kids who made their pilgrimages to Carnaby Street and Abbey Road also made pilgrimages to the Tate Gallery, but that was what made me the odd duck that I was.

When I returned in 1974, London was having an entirely different moment. The Beatles had broken up. Carnaby Street was a grotesque tourist trap. Did I have to come to London to hear ABBA, Yes, and Barry White? Most startlingly, London had gone from one of the biggest bargains in the world to one of the most expensive of cities. The reason was the Arab Oil embargo/crisis following the 1973 Yom Kippur War in Israel that had made the Gulf oil-producing nations rich beyond Croesus. London suddenly became Mecca-on-Thames, as the richest of the rich sought to live in cool Albionic splendor. But just as the price of oil per barrel quadrupled, so did the price of everything, from a suite at Claridge's to a greasy hamburger at the corner Wimpy Bar. 1974 London was no place to be a starving student; you would only get hungrier.

I didn't plan to be a student in London. I planned to be poshly employed at Sotheby's, the world's most famous auction house, a colossus that bestrode the art world from its venerable warren of offices in the heart of elegant Bond Street. The Galerie Kornfeld had paid me well for my apprenticeship and housed and fed me in relative splendor. I just assumed the gravy train would continue. I got a rude awakening, then, when I found there were no jobs at all at Sotheby's, and that even Ernst Beyeler could not conjure one up for me. The auction house had fallen on hard times. The oil crisis was killing the world economy, and the art market was collateral damage. There was high inflation and high anxiety. People weren't buying, and one expert after another was being made redundant, which was the English euphemism for "You're fired!" A job for some Swiss kid? Forget about it.

My resourceful mother leapt into the breach, searching for a hometown tie. She found one in a Basel banker named Richard Dreyfus (not the actor), who had gone to school at Eton with Peter Wilson, the current chairman of Sotheby's. Their friendship had continued in Egypt, where Dreyfus was doing business and where Wilson had made world headlines by auctioning what was called the Palace Collections of the super-accumulator King Farouk, who had fled to Capri on his royal yacht packed with gold following the coup d'etat by Major Gamal Abdel Nasser in 1952. That was the "auction of the century," whose biggest drawback was that Nasser and Egypt stiffed Sotheby's on the commission. Neither Eton nor Egypt could get Peter Wilson on the phone for my sake. Instead a minor assistant got in touch with Dreyfus and reiterated that a job was out of the question.

The only way this Swiss boy was getting into Sotheby's, the assistant said, was paying for the privilege. The house had just started a ten-month course called Works of Art, which the assistant described as a "training scheme" for aspiring gallerists and art-market professionals. Because of the tuition, then $2,000 a year (not including living expenses), and today nearly $50,000, my parents saw it as a "scheme" as well. My parents knew I was a flop in school. And now they were being expected to pay for more school? To teach me how to distinguish a Monet from a Manet, a Meissen from a Ming? The whole idea was for me to be gainfully employed, not to remain on the parental dole.

I begged and pleaded with them, pitching my enrollment in the course as a sort of union card that would get me hired, hopefully at Sotheby's, and certainly at some important gallery or museum. They were skeptical. *Sure. You can be a ticket taker at the Kunstmuseum.* I wouldn't even get a normal diploma. My mother's friends derided it as the height of dilletantery, a variation on a cooking class, like going to the Cordon Bleu in Paris. I made it seem like the Oxford of art, where only fifty students were accepted. *Fifty spoiled rich brats with rich indulgent parents, ne'er-do-wells who couldn't get into Oxford on a bus tour. Why not just go to Oxford? Why not get a scholarship?* They knew I had no comeback. In the end, though, what else could my parents do with this dead-end kid? They very grudgingly groaned their assent to the "scheme." I knew that this was the last chance they were going to give me.

To keep my expenses minimal, I found the cheapest flat I could, a share with three strangers on the Cromwell Road. The place was less Knightsbridge than nightmare. The tube roared under the house at all hours, shaking its foundations, and I wasn't sure which was more miasmic, the petrol fumes of the incessant buses and cabs, or the stench of the cats who populated the hallways. Again, Basel came to the rescue. I had a cousin who worked at the Swiss Embassy who put me on to his sister, whom I had never met but who was kind enough to give me a room in her lovely house near Regent's Park. Beyond the bed in the center of the large space, there were no other furnishings. I found it very Zen and tried to imagine I was back in Japan.

The Works of Art course was held, not at Sotheby's main headquarters in Mayfair, but rather in some generic office building on nearby Dover Street. My fellow students came from all over the world. There were few Americans, though the next year would see the attendance of America's First Daughter, Caroline Kennedy. That would have earned me credibility points with my parents, but sadly I was a year too early for those bragging rights.

There were indeed a lot of rich kids, about whom my parents might have said, "We told you so." It was estimated that at least a quarter of them came from families who were major art collectors. The elitism inherent in the program was underscored by the fact that while there were language classes in German and Italian as part of the program, there were none in French. It was assumed that *everyone* spoke French, just as it was assumed everyone knew the difference between baroque and rococo. There was no affirmative action here for the culturally deprived.

The sexes were equally divided. I would say at least half of the male students were gay, though that wasn't something anyone spoke about then. In Switzerland, which is odd in being extremely conservative but extremely tolerant, sexuality was only an issue if you were unable to keep your unconventionality under tight wraps. The art world that I was thrown into was the diametric opposite of, say, Swiss banking. There was zero prejudice. But even outside the art world, in the social world I never felt my masculinity questioned because of my interest in art, which might not have been the case in America in this era. I was always amused by the presumption that everyone in the art world was gay. Nobody I had met was gay, not Beyeler nor Kornfeld nor Berggruen nor Sam Francis. Who could have been less gay than Picasso? They were all very, very straight, albeit always open-minded.

The head of the Works of Art course was a diminutive thirty-something thrift-shop Beau Brummel with dyed hair and a Cockney accent who gave me a crash course in sexual awareness. He possessed the picturesque floral name of Derek Shrub, and he was anything but the Sotheby "type," which is to say Old Etonian or Old Harrovian, discreet and connected, pure Establishment. If Sotheby's was Bond Street, Derek was much more Carnaby Street. Maybe that's why they kept him up in this faceless building on Dover Street. Derek saw himself as a studly libertine. He had it, and he flaunted it. He was quite open that he was living in a ménage à trois, all men. Every comment he made had a hint of sexual innuendo. "I have no education," he would boast. "I'm purely *tactile*." Shrub had cut his teeth in the furniture department of the Victoria and Albert Museum.

When I first met Derek Shrub, I cockily asked him what I could learn from the course, given that my training at Kornfeld had already made me something of a junior expert. "You can't get married at seventeen without having slept around," Shrub shot back. He, along with his two fellow instructors, would teach us all about silver, furniture, jewelry, Asian art—everything, not just the Old Masters and Impressionists that brought in the big money, or at least had brought in that money before the current market doldrums.

Not everyone in the course was from a privileged background. There were two scholarship students, one of whom I would eventually marry. But that was a long way off. At the beginning, the emotion I had toward this woman was not lust but jealousy. She wasn't a prospective wife. She was a threatening rival, in a world of very scarce resources. Her name was Isabel Sloman, and she was the star of the course, already armed with degrees from University College London and the Courtauld Institute of Art. Her father, Sir Albert Sloman, was a World War II RAF fighter pilot turned distinguished academician, the founder and first Vice Chancellor of Essex University, one of the rising "redbrick" schools that were turning out sharp and hungry young graduates, educated versions of the playwright John Osborne's "Angry Young Men," who were ready to challenge the unmotivated toffs of the British Establishment.

Isabel's mother was French, from Cognac, where the family had a summer home. She was blond, slim, and smart, but not too square and prissy to dress in miniskirts. The bottom line was that any gallery or museum, or Sotheby's, for that matter, would be thrilled to hire Isabel—certainly ahead of *me*. In my weekly letter to my parents in Japan, my being threatened by her was readily apparent. I singled her out as a "fierce contender" for whatever I could do to win my family's approbation. Little did anyone guess that the enemy would eventually become my spouse.

Derek Shrub, in an indirect way, played Cupid for us, by taking us out of competition. Whenever anybody in the art world was looking to hire young talent, Derek was the first man they called on. During the term of the course, a distinguished Old Masters purveyor on Jermyn Street called Heim Gallery, owned by a Polish count, had an opening. The first person who came to Shrub's mind, naturally, was Isabel. At first I was angry that he hadn't offered this rarity of rarities, a paying position, to me. But when Isabel, who was overstocked with education and should have been a professor herself, took the offer, I felt a vast sense of relief. Now, in my mind, I had Sotheby's all to myself. Furthermore, now that we were no longer rivals, we could become friends. As long as she wasn't jeopardizing my future, I admired Isabel greatly. In time that admiration would morph into love.

Meanwhile a game we played in class put a new spin on my career aspirations. Derek Shrub asked who among us was interested in becoming an auctioneer. Even though Sotheby's was an auction company, the class had not taken us to a single auction. Maybe it was because the results were so meager that Shrub didn't want to depress us. In any case, the only auctions I had ever seen were those at Kornfeld. Eberhard Kornfeld, no mean auctioneer, always admired Sotheby's as the Promised Land in his chosen field. He kept a framed print of the Sotheby's entrance, with its mystical black basalt Egyptian sculpture of the lion goddess Sekhmet over the portal, on his desk to keep himself humble in the presence of the Big Time. The Sekhmet, which dated back to 1320 BC, had been Sotheby's "mascot" and symbol, like the Bern bears, since it was sold at auction there in the 1880s for the then-pharaonic sum of £40 and the buyer never came back to claim it.

Because I considered myself a relative expert given my Kornfeld experience, I boldly raised my hand. Only two others in our class of fifty, both men, followed my lead. One was an Austrian named Peter von Eltz, who became a successful Berlin auctioneer and has a castle in Austria. The other was a young Englishman with whom I long ago lost touch. What ensued was a series of simulated auctions, with each of the three volunteers taking turns as the auctioneer. When Shrub called me to the podium to auction some piece of furniture, china, a middling painting, whatever, I was very, very shy and intimidated. Shrub attributed my intimidation to my ignorance. If I truly understood what I was selling, I would do a far better job selling it. I needed to communicate my admiration for, and knowledge of, the object, to connect with the buyer in the most felicitous way. I also needed to remember that bidders are smart, informed collectors, who can see through any hype and catch you in any errors. In short, it was *selling*, something I, as a would-be European gentleman, had never done and had no reason to be comfortable with. But that was what Sotheby's was all about, selling, art as trade. Get used to it, and study harder, that was the lesson. The bait had been put in the trap for me.

My conviction that Sotheby's was mine for the taking proved to be pure hubris. The boot camp that was the Works of Art course, which I completed in 1975, had given me one thing, and that was confidence. Derek Shrub had been my drill sergeant, and he had made me learn and shaped me up. The only thing I found missing in the course was that I had not met a single artist through it. I remember David Hockney coming through one day. He was becoming hugely famous in California, and I wanted to meet him. But it never happened. All I ever encountered was dead artists. That was the part of schooling that Ernst Beyeler had warned me I would never take to, the reason I should stay away from art history. But I had had no choice. Now it was time to make that art history pay, to earn a living. And again, it was no room at the inn. I thought I had a possible score when I learned that still another attractive cousin of mine had become the mistress of one of Sotheby's top executives. Here love did not conquer all, specifically the issue of my unemployment. I didn't want to leave London and go home to Basel in defeat. So I ate the very humble pie of taking an unpaid job as a receptionist at the front desk on Bond Street. At least it got me past Sekhmet the lion queen and, finally, into the building.

7

MY ROLE MODEL

At Sotheby's front desk, at the same time I was "receiving" visitors, I was also acting as a kind of gatekeeper. It wasn't quite a snob thing, like the bouncers at Régine's in Paris or later Studio 54 in New York, who sized you up by your looks and decided whether you were cool enough to be allowed into the inner sanctum. No, I was too lowly myself to be an arbiter of anything. I barely belonged in Sotheby's, so how could I pass judgment? However, Sotheby's did have a reputation for English hauteur and arrogance. That "Bond Street swerve," the condescending look that made you feel you didn't belong, was what impelled the Detroit shopping-mall magnate Alfred Taubman to buy the place in 1983, just to show those snotty Brits a thing about the customer always being right and always being welcome. Although I never turned anyone away, I had to make quick decisions as to when I could refer a prospective client "upstairs" to one of Sotheby's experts, with whatever it was that client had to sell. There were many of these experts, in Old Masters, Impressionists, modern art, porcelain, jade and Eastern art, medals and coins, manuscripts, and so on. Talk about arrogant and short-tempered. These cranky experts did not suffer fools, and if I referred them anything that they perceived as a waste of their precious time, I was the fool who would be made to suffer.

One day an elderly couple walked in off Bond Street. They were carrying a box as carefully as if they were bearing a load of nitroglycerin that might explode with one false move. They wanted an opinion. Mine was the only one available, at least at this first stage of the screening process. They must have taken at least a half hour to unwrap the package. It was like those Russian dolls, boxes within boxes. Finally, they proudly presented their treasure. It was clearly a family heirloom, some piece of ceramic, which in all frankness I cannot recall. To them it was worthy of Windsor Castle. To my slightly tutored eye, it appeared more worthy of Portobello Road or Petticoat Lane, and one of the lesser stalls at that. I tried to be as complimentary as possible to sugarcoat my opinion that its only value was sentimental.

I felt like a cad raining on their parade, but I would have felt even worse after the excoriation our ceramics expert would have unleashed on me had I referred them upstairs. I couldn't pass the buck. The buck stopped with me, and there were no bucks at all to be made here. The couple were unfailingly polite and thankful for my negative assessment. However, when it became time to rewrap the treasure, their approach had changed completely. They simply threw the item in one box and left the prior wrappings, which could have done up a mummy in Luxor's Valley of the Kings, for me to clean up. The lesson for me was that people only care for things if they are worth something. When they thought they had a treasure, they treasured it. When the treasure turned out to be a dud, they were ready to dump it. Without value, care goes out the window.

After eight weeks at the front desk, opportunity knocked. The one virtue of being inside Sotheby's was access to gossip about job opportunities. A very junior expert in the Old Master prints department was leaving for Colnaghi's. That gallery, just down from Sotheby's on Old Bond Street, dated back to 1760 and was considered to be the oldest art gallery in the world. Specializing in Old Masters, it had recently been acquired by Lord Jacob Rothschild, one of the English Rothschilds, a man who could have anything. One of Sotheby's directors approached me at the front desk and took me aside with the golden opportunity. Would I be interested in "going upstairs?"

I would have been thrilled to go anywhere upstairs—except to this golden opportunity. I knew if I took it, I would be stuck for the rest of my life in a dead-end job. There were only about thirty collectors in the whole world interested in Old Master prints. This was not a growth segment; this was ancient history. And the area was highly technical, which I was not, in terms of evaluation and authentication. I said no. The director was insulted. Who was the coat-check boy to spurn Rembrandt, Raphael, Titian? I was lucky that in his pique, he didn't make me redundant. Since I was working for free, they would be saving nothing but ego by getting rid of me. I hung on.

I did my best to make myself useful. I befriended Duncan McLaren, a director of Sotheby's International, who was spearheading Sotheby's efforts to globalize its operation. After acquiring New York's Parke-Bernet auction house in 1964, Sotheby's had gone on a European tear, establishing offices in 1966 in Munich, Zurich, and Paris. Somehow I was able to use my Swiss art connections to do McLaren a favor, which he was kind enough to return, putting me on to the next job opening. On its surface, the opportunity, to become an English furniture evaluation expert, seemed far less prestigious than becoming an Old Master print expert. I knew even less about antique furniture than I did about Old Masters, far less. I also knew this was the last chance I would get at Sotheby's. This beggar could not afford to pick and choose.

I said yes with great alacrity. I was then issued a mid-range Renault, a detailed AA road map of England, Scotland, and Wales, and a list of clients to call on. Overnight, Sotheby's turned me into the salesman I never dreamed I would become. And the clients I was given were anything but the Rothschilds in Waddesdon Manor. I didn't go to castles or stately homes. I went to modest homes, looking for hidden treasures. The only people more disappointed than I was in my new position were the clients I would call on. Their faces dropped when they opened the door. They were surely expecting an English gentleman with gray hair and perhaps a walking stick. Instead they got a young foreigner with an accent who usually knew vastly less about their furniture than they did.

I never quite mastered motoring on what was to me the wrong side of the road, and I never quite recovered from the dreadful pub food I would pay for with the books of luncheon vouchers Sotheby's had issued to me. If I had assumed that Sotheby's was the most glamorous place to work, this assignment cured me of my grand illusions. Still, I held on for the next year and a half. At least I proved to my parents I could earn a living, albeit a subsistence one. What saved me was my growing friendship with Isabel Sloman, my archrival who had left me in the dust. She had a fancy banker boyfriend, and I had vowed never to take marriage vows before I was thirty-five. Nonetheless, our careers in art did give us a powerful common ground, which grew stronger and stronger.

Isabel was worth waiting for. So was Peter Cecil Wilson, the seemingly mythical chairman of Sotheby's who was supposed to give me my dream job through his Eton classmate, whose call he never returned. Finally, once I enrolled in the Works of Art course, he did summon me to his office for a sort of welcome, if only as a belated courtesy to Richard Dreyfus. That meeting was a disaster. Peter Wilson, for all his presence, was a very shy man. I was a very shy boy, and totally intimidated. When you put two shy people in the same room, the results are rarely Kismet. Neither of us knew what to say, so all I remember is the painful pregnant pauses between platitudes. I was never so relieved as I was to be out of that room, though I was worried for a time that he found me such a dullard that he would have me sacked from the course and barred from Bond Street. Little did I ever suspect that this aloof, godly character would become my friend and chief mentor.

Wilson and I eventually would bond over furniture. He, too, had started lowly at Sotheby's, in 1936, first as a porter, then a cataloguer, in the furniture department. He never suffered my ignominy of having to beat the hedgerows for business on the highways and byways of the British Isle. However, he loved beating hedgerows in search of any item of beauty. When I did get to know him and became his glorified chauffeur in the South of France, he would take detour after detour into the tiniest of villages looking for the local antique shop and then killing time, sometimes hours, looking at furniture, and whatever else they might have had, as if he had been unleashed in Windsor Castle. He loved art of all kinds. He also loved to sell. Before Sotheby's he had had a desultory career start as an ad salesman for *Connoisseur*, the glossy magazine of art and antiques.

But what a salesman Peter Wilson became, if "salesman" is the right word for his virtuoso performances in the auction room, a live show that gave me the same awe and pleasure as watching Jimi Hendrix play the electric guitar. He exuded aristocracy, elegance, and knowledge, and he never resorted to baleful looks to shame a buyer into spending more, or jokes, or any cheap tricks. It was said that the cunning of Peter Wilson was that there was no cunning. There, was, however, a great presence, and that he was born with. He exuded superiority. It didn't hurt his authority that he was a towering six-four, or that both his paternal and maternal grandfathers were barons; the portrait of one of those, Lord Ribblesdale, was painted by John Singer Sargent and hangs in the National Portrait Gallery.

It also didn't hurt that Peter Wilson was a star in foreign intelligence at MI6, cracking spy rings in South America and Japan. His close wartime friend Ian Fleming was said to have modeled James Bond after him. At the same time, Wilson, for all his pedigree, was *nouveau pauvre*. His parents had to sell their library, then sell their stately home when he was a boy. Peter's father, nicknamed "Scatters" for his profligate ways, made—and lost—more at gambling than he did as a stockbroker. Peter always knew he would have to work for a living, and that need for money gave him an edge, and a drive, that most of his fellow aristocrats lacked. That drive drove him to spur Sotheby's to greatness, from fusty institution to global juggernaut.

There were darker currents that contributed to Peter Wilson's edge as well, currents people at Sotheby's would whisper about. First, he was gay. This may have been par for the course for Derek Shrub, but for Peter Wilson, it was as unmentionable as the diabetes that forced him to inject himself with insulin all through the day. No one ever could recall seeing him "shoot up," though on occasion a syringe might fall out of the pocket of his bespoke suit. He handled this, like everything else, with characteristic aplomb, as if he had dropped a comb or a pen.

Wilson seemed far more James Bond than Noël Coward, though he obviously had a bit of both. Having divorced his wife in 1947, he had been roving discreetly for decades; his taste in men ran to rugged Sean Connery types. His main man was a retired soldier who was now a greengrocer in Kent near Wilson's weekend retreat. Wags at Sotheby's would call him "the country wife," à la Wycherley. That was Sotheby's— brainy, bitchy, literary, and sotto voce. The two men shared the same love of gardening that Wilson had with his ex-wife. In fact, Wilson always came across as a family man, bursting with pride over his two sons, Philip and Tom. Even his modesty had a hetero accent. When I gushed to him about what a wonderful auctioneer he was, and confessed my own anxieties about wielding the gavel, Wilson confessed in turn that he had been a nervous wreck before his initial ascent to the podium in 1938. He described how he had spent the entire weekend before the sale mock-auctioning off every piece of furniture in his house to his new wife and their baby nurse.

In addition to his illness and his gayness, the other chink in the Wilson armor, the flaw that made him as fascinating as he was, was the possibility that, rather than being the inspiration for 007, he may have been a spy for the KGB. Wilson fit the profile of the other high-toned, poshly educated, discreetly homosexual group of Russian agents—Philby, Maclean, Burgess, and Blunt, the latter being, like Wilson, a pillar of the English art establishment as Queen Elizabeth's official art adviser. Blunt, who was discovered after the betrayal of the others, was known as the "Fourth Man" in this Cold War spy saga. Unproved rumors that Peter Wilson could be the "Fifth Man" gave everyone a frisson of world-shaking ambiguity. In the business of illusion that he was in, a business of super-sophisticates who had seen it all and were jaded by the usual, this unwritten résumé item was good for business, and business, in the end, was where Peter Wilson was master of the game.

You'd never know it from his tiny, cluttered office, just off the main sales room on Bond Street. The place looked more like a storeroom than a command center, and was much smaller than the offices of the managing directors over whom Peter Wilson ruled. He was like a tall Napoleon who always insisted on wearing uniforms far less elaborate than those of his generals. Wilson never stayed put there for long. He loved roaming the mazelike halls of Bond Street, visiting every department to see what new treasures his experts had acquired. He was a man truly obsessed with objects, and the object of his affection at any moment could just as easily be some pillbill worth a few pounds as some Renoir worth millions. His greatest pleasure, both as a schoolboy at Eton and as a country squire in Kent, was roaming the local village antiques shops looking for undiscovered gems; hence the Riviera wild-goose chases he took me on. In addition to his greengrocer in Kent, Wilson's other

weekend companion was a burly salesman, whom he discovered peddling antiques from a wheelbarrow. In the most snobbish business in
the world, the ruler of that business was the least snobbish person you
could imagine. All that mattered was that an object be beautiful, *pace*
John Keats.

Peter Wilson was the most polite man I ever met. I never heard him
say a negative word about anyone, even anyone at Christie's. And he
never pulled rank, or ordered anyone around. Still, he got things done.
For example, when I was working for him in Monaco and we were in-
stalling exhibitions at the grand salon of the Sporting d'Hiver convention hall, Wilson would come in and see a table in what he thought was
the wrong place, whether in terms of lighting, position vis-à-vis other
furniture, whatever. He'd ask me, so softly and meekly, "Do you think
it might be a good idea to put that table over there?" Translation of
Wilson-ese: "Move that damn table this very second!" Peter Wilson
spoke softly, and you never saw the big stick, though you knew it was
there.

Aside from his personal charisma, what drew me to Peter Wilson
was his sheer brilliance in revolutionizing what was one of the world's
most unrevolutionary businesses. The two institutions that defined the
auction trade both dated back to eighteenth-century London. Even
though Sotheby's and Christie's have been neck and neck, tooth by jowl
now for centuries, Sotheby's to me had a far higher public profile and
resulting mystique, and all that was due to the flash-and-dazzle techniques of Peter Wilson, the most unlikely of great PR men. Commerce
apparently was in his blue blood.

As canny as a rug seller in a Turkish bazaar, Wilson had a sixth sense
for reading clients and was a master of negotiating, without even seeming to be trying. I first saw this mastery in action when I started work
in our new Geneva office in 1977. Wilson called me from London with
the bad news that one of our top targets had chosen Christie's over us
to conduct a "house sale" of the fabled contents of her mansion in Cologny overlooking Lake Geneva. Cologny and Vandœuvres were to Geneva what Greenwich and Bedford were to New York, the toniest of
suburbs, although "suburbs" fails to capture the rural splendor at play
here.

The seller was Rosemarie Kanzler, a beautiful ex-manicurist turned Berlin cabaret singer (very much like Sally Bowles in *Cabaret*) who had married a dizzying succession of some of the world's richest men, annexing to herself a series of fortunes, including Squibb Pharmaceuticals and Ford automobiles. Now able to marry for pleasure rather than purpose, she and her latest husband, a decorative younger Frenchman named Jean Pierre Marcie-Rivière, had rented one of the grand houses on the lake, which belonged to the Bodmer family, bibliophiles who owned a Gutenberg Bible. Now they were selling the contents in a "house sale," which was the finest way to showcase their enviable lifestyle and, because of the "stuff" involved, would reap huge amounts of publicity for Christie's. Everyone would attend, to see how the super-rich lived. Wilson was extremely put out that Christie's had "stolen" this from him, as he had cultivated Rosemarie for decades. Now he put me to the task of stealing it back.

It seemed impossible at first. Wilson had learned, through his well-cultivated grapevine, that Christie's had nabbed the sale by cutting its commission to 10 percent. "Call Jean Pierre and congratulate him and tell him we could have never done it for less than fifteen percent," he instructed me. "And remind him, subtly, of course, that to do the best, *our* best, anything less would have been impossible. If you want Rolls-Royce service, you have to pay the price." So I called Mr. Marcie-Rivière and talked Wilson's talk. In the process, I found out that the deal with Christie's had not yet been signed. Furthermore, that "best" thing seemed to work. Marcie-Riviere volunteered that he would dump Christie's for us, to get our Rolls-Royce service, for a commission of 12 percent.

I reported proudly this to Peter Wilson. But Wilson, like the most cunning trader in the casbah, always had to go one better. "Call him again and tell him we can't do twelve percent, but as a special favor, a very special favor to dear friends, we could go as low as thirteen and a half percent." The minute I mentioned that number, Marcie-Rivière jumped at it. As I was rushing to get the papers together and race out to Cologny for him to sign, Christie's called Marcie-Rivière and offered to slash its commission to seven percent. But the sellers refused this enormous bargain. Wilson, using me as his puppet, had used the psychology of class to get the deal. Marcie-Rivière was so under Wilson's spell that he even said things like "Seven percent? How can they possibly be so *cheap!*" The sale was a huge success, as thousands trooped out to Cologny to see how the one-millionth of 1 percent lived. Halfway through the auction, which Peter Wilson conducted in his usual seated style, at an antique table, he leaned over to me and said, "Why don't you take over. You made this happen." And, terrified as I was, I did my first auction and was written up—favorably—in the *Tribune de Genève*.

Peter Wilson made no secret of how strongly he felt about the nexus of art and money. "There are very few people who can appreciate art without wanting to own it," he told *The New Yorker* in 1966. "You have to covet art to really appreciate it." Wilson was highly amused by William Randolph Hearst, who, he often regretted, was not around for him to sell to. "Hearst had a real *need* to own those cloisters" and all the rest of the Old World that he brought to the New World at San Simeon, Wilson told the magazine. Even if Hearst never opened most of the crates of wonder he acquired on his European shopping sprees, the *need* was there, and that need to buy fed Wilson's equally compulsive need to sell.

In addition to being a closet diabetic and a closet homosexual, Peter Wilson was something of an out-of-the-closet Jew, an unabashed Semitophile. Despite the amazing achievements of the Jews of England, from the office of prime minister (Benjamin Disraeli) to the great emporia of Oxford Street (the Sieffs of Marks and Spencer) to the spires of Oxford and Cambridge (Sir Isaiah Berlin) to the banks of the City (the British Rothschilds), England has a notoriously long history of anti-Semitism. In the lead-up to World War II, London, like New York, saw a huge influx of Continental Jewish art dealers and collectors. Peter Wilson made it Sotheby's business to win their business, and take it away from the great private (and Jewish) dealers Duveen and Wildenstein.

Until Wilson, great masterpieces were usually sold privately, as all the parties were usually high leverage, low visibility, and extremely secretive. Not that Sotheby's and Christie's got the dregs, but the high-ticket items that would lead to a high profile for the auction house rarely saw the light of day. Coveting that profile, Wilson first went about establishing his Jewish sympathies and bona fides by hiring as his chief picture consultant a German Jewish émigré and ex-Heidelberg art professor named Hans Gronau. After Gronau had a heart attack lugging heavy paintings, Wilson tapped Gronau's Renaissance-scholar wife, Carmen, to become his right-hand woman. Rival Christie's was never perceived as offering a similarly safe harbor to Jewish collectors, and no one offered them larger guarantees than Wilson, who was willing to trade short-term profits, even if the works didn't sell, for the publicity value of having the privilege, the honor, the glory, of auctioning them.

Christie's wasn't the only competition that Peter Wilson had to battle to undercut. There was Parke-Bernet in New York, whose 23 percent commission, enough to gag any seller, gave Wilson a lot of bargaining room. He would often slash Sotheby's rate to 8 percent. Then there was New York's auction tax; London had none. This was another powerful bargaining chip, not only against the American house, but against the competition at Paris's auction collective, the Hôtel Drouot, which was also saddled with a lot of seemingly medieval French bureaucratic red tape. *Let the French eat cake* was the attitude of Wilson, who would cut any tape, and sometimes any corner, to get a prime commission. Sometimes art was war.

The Peter Wilson auction that first attracted international front-page headlines came in 1957. This was the sale of the great Van Gogh collection of the Amsterdam banker/philanthropist Wilhelm Weinberg, who had fled to New York in 1940 and died, without heirs, in Scarsdale in 1957. In the jet age that began in the late fifties with the Boeing 707s and Douglas DC-8s, Wilson could be considered the first Jet Set auctioneer. A man whose first move in the morning was to read the obituaries of both the London and New York *Times*, Wilson seized the opportunity and hied himself to Westchester County. There the Weinberg executor told him that all the proceeds would go to charity; he expected a huge splash.

Peter Wilson did the unthinkable. He hired the advertising colossus J. Walter Thompson to turn the auction into an *event*. Because it was a charity, he got his Mad Men to do it for nothing but the status of it. Then Wilson landed the biggest of all status "gets": Queen Elizabeth herself. Through his networking on the King Farouk auctions, Wilson connected with fellow Etonian Sir Edward Ford, who had been Farouk's boyhood tutor—alas, to no avail. Now Ford was Her Majesty's private secretary, and he thought it would be great fun for Elizabeth, who had been Queen for only five years, to get out of the palace and participate in something like this. Accordingly, Wilson set up a private viewing on Bond Street of the Weinberg art. Her Majesty brought along Prince Philip, Princess Margaret, and a huge retinue. The press went wild. Her favorite painting of the lot, it was rumored, was Degas's *The Wounded Jockey.* The Queen loved horses, and this was a wonderful horse painting.

The royal family did not attend Wilson's actual auction, which was televised around the world, but, again, Wilson's rumor mill ginned up the idea that Buckingham Palace was going to bid for it. In the end, the jockey went not to the Queen but to the king of Hollywood producers, Sam Spiegel, fresh off his triumph with *Bridge on the River Kwai.* He paid around $10,000, which was a princely sum in an England just past the era of postwar rationing. The high price that night was around $50,000 for a Van Gogh, and the whole sale grossed a record sum of close to $1 million, enough to get written up in *Life* magazine, the bible of 1950s America's upper bourgeoisie.

The public fascination with auction records had begun, and nobody set and broke more of them than Peter Wilson. Records and rankings were far easier for laypeople to deal with than taste. Money became the measure of art. "Is it beautiful?" was answered by the question "Is it expensive?" Art also began to be taken seriously as an investment, and not just a pleasure. Paintings, like stocks, could go up—and up, and this intrigued a world recovering from the rigors of war and newly obsessed with the joys of money.

In this new equation of art and money, Impressionist and Post-Impressionist art became the investment vehicle of choice for the high rollers. The main reason wasn't the colors and the romance but the fact that, unlike Old Masters, they were very hard to forge. These French masterworks were recent enough to be catalogued in great depth by modern dealers. A lot of this art was being bought by very new and sudden postwar wealth, particularly that of the Greeks. These people, lampooned by the old and newly poor Establishment as barely up from the mud, did not want to risk being played for fools by an art world in which they surely felt uncomfortable to begin with. A Van Gogh was a sure thing.

In 1958, Peter Wilson topped himself and got an even bigger *Life* spread when he auctioned off seven Impressionist masterpieces from the collection of another recently departed European Jewish émigré art connoisseur. This one was the late Jakob Goldschmidt, a Berlin turned Wall Street banking titan, who had died in 1955. This "Magnificent Seven" sale became the largest single-owner auction in history. Wilson pressed the bean counters at Sotheby's to guarantee the estate at the shocking amount of over a million dollars in reserves.

The sale, held late at night, in a London where the pubs closed at ten, was impossibly glamorous. It was the first auction where black tie was de rigueur. Television cameras were everywhere, and the big-name attendees included Kirk Douglas (who had recently played Van Gogh in *Lust for Life*; Wilson loved the Hollywood angle as a publicity hook), his costar Anthony Quinn (who had played Gauguin), Somerset Maugham, Margot Fonteyn, Mrs. Winston Churchill, and the Greek shipping tycoons Onassis, Niarchos, and Goulandris, once tough sailors, now refined art collectors. Bidding on a dedicated long-distance line from his home in Beverly Hills was Edward G. Robinson, Hollywood's preeminent collector, Little Caesar as connoisseur. If there was a big name to be dropped, Peter Wilson ensured that his PR battalion would drop it—everywhere they could. There had been articles about the sale placed in the press of over twenty countries. If at the time far more people around the world knew the name Sotheby's than Christie's, Peter Wilson is to be given most of the credit for making the name of his firm synonymous with the art auction.

There was also some high drama. Jesse Wolff, the preeminent New York art lawyer, who represented the Goldschmidt estate and, after the success of this sale, Sotheby's interests in America, was a fierce opponent of all things anti-Semitic. He had carved out a lucrative specialty in representing wealthy European Jewish émigrés and was a pioneer in restitution actions for Nazi art thefts. Wolff was what would be called in New York a "WASPy Jew," because he didn't fit in any way the derogatory stereotype of the frock-coated Delancey Street pushcart peddler. The captain of the Dartmouth ice hockey team and a star student at Harvard Law School, Wolff would have been right at home in the Brook or the Knick or any of Manhattan's toniest, and exclusionary, men's clubs, but he wouldn't have any part of anything with the vaguest hint of racism.

That fall night in 1958, when the black-tied and bejeweled swells assembled in the Sotheby's sales room, just before Peter Wilson took the podium, Jesse Wolff heard, from the corner of his ear, an anti-Semitic slur from the elite audience. Black tie or not, Wolff stopped the show. Never trusting the English to begin with because of what he had seen as their failure to act despite certain knowledge of the then-secret concentration camps, Wolff threatened to pull the paintings unless the aristo-bigot was ejected. The media took a long deep breath, as the sale of the century threatened to implode. Eventually, the bad-mouther was shown the door. A blow was struck against intolerance, and, once again, Sotheby's had shown that it was "the friend of the Jews." Wilson stepped up and the show went on.

What a show it was. The total auction proceeds were $2,186,000, a new world record. Every painting sold for above its reserve price, never less than $100,000, and the star of the night was Cézanne's *Garcon au Gilet Rouge (Boy in a Red Jacket)*, which went for $616,000 to Paul Mellon, double the world's previous record, set at a Paris sale of a Gauguin the year before, for a non–Old Master. When the bidding hit its limit, Peter Wilson put on his theatrical act. "What?" he pleaded, mock-poor-mouthing the rich crowd. "Will nobody offer any more?" The line, which became folklore, brought the stuffy house down with laughter.

"You stand in front of a picture like that, and what is money?" was Mellon's defense of his extravagance. Of the Magnificent Seven, only the cheapest painting, Renoir's *La Pensée*, which sold for $200,000, and the closest to its guarantee, went to an Englishman, Jack Cotton, a self-made property lord from Birmingham. The other six were sold to Americans. The whole auction lasted twenty-two minutes. "I've never sold so much so fast," Wilson declared, and added, with his typical modesty, "and I'm sure I never will again."

The sale had gone to Sotheby's of London, *The New York Times* reported, because Goldschmidt's son felt that Sotheby's was far better at attracting the big international buyers than Parke-Bernet in New York. The success of the sale was therefore a testament to the lure of Sotheby's, that it could bring both the art and the buyers across the pond. It blew Christie's, at least for the moment, into a distinct second place in their ancient rivalry. And it also spelled trouble for Wilson's next big target, Parke-Bernet. If Wilson could have the New York art and the New York buyers, why could he not have New York itself?

8

THE AUCTION HOUSE WARS

New York was a city of art dealers, with far more than London. Old-line Gotham *Social Register* types had been inculcated with the notion of publicity avoidance. You were supposed to get your name in *The New York Times* only thrice in a lifetime, at birth, at marriage, and at death. Not when you sold your art. Accordingly, New York had become a dealers' town, where selling at Sotheby's and Christie's was simply the way life was lived. However, after Prohibition was repealed, the descendants of the more discreet Gilded Age high society began going out at night and having fun on the town. Hence the rise of the more porous "Café Society" and its gossip columnists such as Elsa Maxwell and Igor Cassini. Now a high profile ceased to be a shameful thing, but rather became a badge of belonging.

Peter Wilson correctly sensed the rising egomania of New York's increasingly money-driven social elite and realized that, as in London, attending a big auction at Parke-Bernet for the property of a Morgan, a Vanderbilt, a Biddle, could give attendees a boost up the social ladder. If they actually bought something, not only were they buying a piece of the Fifth-Park Avenue elite, but also, if mentioned in a column, they felt they were being validated as an actual part of that elite, amorphous as it was. Thus in Parke-Bernet, Peter Wilson didn't see merely a good investment for Sotheby's. He saw Parke-Bernet as a work in progress that would enable him to Sotheby-ize and thereby glamorize the entire New York art scene, to his and his firm's everlasting profit.

Parke-Bernet had been founded in the 1930s by a duo of renegade auctioneers from the American Art Association, or AAA, which may sound like a twelve-step program (Art Addicts Anonymous) or an auto club, but was actually the American answer to Sotheby's during the age of robber barons, when the vast profits of Yankee ingenuity, in an effort to polish mercantile roots into the gloss of class, began pouring into art. The AAA catered to the kind of rich self-made plutocrats who went down on the *Titanic* and the *Lusitania*. Parke and Bernet did so well in revolt against their mother ship that they eventually took over the AAA and in 1950 built the modern museumlike monument to their virtual New York auction monopoly at 980 Madison Avenue. Over the entrance, in their version of Sotheby's lion queen, Parke-Bernet had a naked Venus, supposedly representing culture, seducing a muscle-bound mortal, presumably representing temporal, mighty New York.

Speaking of monopolies, if the entire auction business, Old World and New, seemed like a totally posh British affair, it was because the chairman of Parke-Bernet was a posh Englishman named Leslie Hyam. Hyam was a Cambridge physics graduate who stood, at six-three, eye to eye with his chief adversary, Peter Wilson. Like Wilson, he was a lover of objects, and a world authority on French furniture and Oriental rugs, among other *objets d'art*. Unlike Peter Wilson, Lesie Hyam was a lover of women and was known as one of the great rakes of Manhattan. Hyam had come to America to be a physicist. He was so inspired by the creative ferment in New York that he changed his mind and tried to become a novelist. And when that didn't work, he burned his manuscript and took a job at the AAA as a cataloguer. There he found his métier. His catalogues were considered the best in the business, up there with those of Kornfeld and Beyeler. They endeared him to Parke and Bernet and, when they retired, propelled him to the leadership of their now great firm.

Aside from sexuality, the one big difference between Hyam and Wilson was that Hyam was not an auctioneer. He left that task to his lieutenant Lou Marion, a hale and hearty Italian, né Mariano, who everyone thought was as Irish as a leprechaun, because of his flaming red hair and heroic St. Patrick's Day parties. Before auctioneering, Marion had tried to peddle insurance in New York's insular Irish precincts. He had changed his name to seem like one of the guys. He still had great connections at the Irish-dominated political machine of Tammany Hall that ran New York until the mid-sixties and could get done for Parke-Bernet things that the English Hyam could not. As an auctioneer, Marion had pulled off the biggest sale of them all, selling in 1961 Rembrandt's super-masterpiece *Aristotle Contemplating the Bust of Homer* to the Metropolitan Museum for $2.3 million. That was nearly four times Peter Wilson's finest moment in selling the Goldschmidt Cézanne.

Despite the Marion Rembrandt record, there were two areas where Sotheby's had a distinct advantage over Parke-Bernet. The first was the concept of the seller's guarantee, which Americans somehow regarded as un-American, a kind of secret price fixing. Americans liked the idea that every bidder had a chance to make a great bargain. A floor, which Wilson would set to lure the work to him, struck the Yankee mind as artificial and killed how great the bargain might be. The other Sotheby's advantage was its low sellers' commissions. Its 10 percent was half of Parke-Bernet's 20, which reflected its monopoly position in New York. The presence of Christie's in London kept Sotheby's honest, and its rates low.

What gave Sotheby's the biggest advantage it could have vis-à-vis Parke-Bernet, however, was the suicide of Leslie Hyam in the fall of 1963. He died of carbon monoxide poisoning in his car at his New Canaan, Connecticut, country home. He was sixty-one. The cause was said to revolve around romantic difficulties. Peter Wilson sent all proper condolences, then sprang into action to make the deal of a lifetime. Parke-Bernet without Hyam was like the Chicago Bulls without Michael Jordan, Facebook without Mark Zuckerberg, the E Street Band without Bruce Springsteen. He was the key man. In his absence, Parke-Bernet could be had for a relative song. Across the pond, Sotheby's key man used all his powers of persuasion to convince his board that acquiring Parke-Bernet would sully Sotheby's old-line purity, making it "less English." But the zeitgeist was on Wilson's side. In just a few months, in February 1964, the Beatles would appear on Ed Sullivan's show and

America would become a lot "more English." The music invasion paved the way for the art invasion.

The one person standing in Peter Wilson's way was his counterpart in Paris, the king of French auctioneers, Maurice Rheims. Wilson, Rheims, and Leslie Hyam in New York—these three men ruled the art world. Now, with Hyam gone, Rheims and Wilson would be having the biggest Anglo-French showdown since Napoleon and Wellington squared off at Waterloo. The two titans had clashed openly once before, in Cairo in 1953, when Rheims muscled into the King Farouk auctions and stole away a big cut of any items purchased by French collectors. Now Rheims, peeved that France was being overshadowed by England in the auction wars of the fifties and sixties, that Wilson was breaking all his records, wanted to take Manhattan, both for himself and for the glory of *la patrie*.

Rheims put together a consortium of French millionaires, including the Rothschilds, to whom his wife was related. This time, however, the elegant Old World Rheims was no match for the New World got-it-flaunt-it techniques of mass publicity and hype that Peter Wilson had mastered. Aiding Wilson was Stanley Clark, one of the great wizards of Fleet Street, who littered the world press with articles that Sotheby's acquisition was a fait accompli, when in truth the deal was a very shaky one. The chief obstacle was the department store heir Colonel Richard Gimbel, a World War I hero and an intense Anglophobe who owned over 20 percent of Parke-Bernet's shares, a tranche that could sink any deal.

The patriotic Gimbel equated selling to Sotheby's with surrendering at Valley Forge. The problem for Maurice Rheims was that Gimbel didn't like the French much more than he did the English. A pox on both their auction houses, was his position. Even though Rheims had jetted to New York with enough money to top the Sotheby's bid, his inability to speak English confirmed the Americans in their stereotype of the arrogant, superior French created by New York's haughty headwaiters. At least the Sotheby's predators speak *English,* the reasoning went. But Gimbel remained on the fence.

The person who did the most to save the day for Peter Wilson was his now-U.S. counsel Jesse Wolff, who used his charm and *Our Crowd* haut-Jewish fellowship to assure Gimbel that the new company would be a worthy repository of his nonpareil collection of rare books. The colonel's passion for the works of Poe and Dickens transcended his antipathy to perfidious Albion, and the deal was completed in 1965.

While Peter Wilson was the art man I most admired, Maurice Rheims was the art man I wanted to be. My impossible aspirations in that regard were initially generated by my mother's giving me a multiyear gift subscription to *Connaissance des Arts,* the voluptuous glossy magazine Rheims founded in the fifties. My mother was on her way to Japan, and she wanted to further my precocious interest in art in her absence. Since I was on the cusp of adolescence, I suspect Mother was also doing her best to keep my thoughts high and pure and to keep my nose out of other magazines like *Playboy.* As it turned out, one did not preclude the other, though I am sure I am the only teenager in the world who idolized both Hugh Hefner and Maurice Rheims. If there was such a thing as art porn, *Connaissance* was it, in the noblest sense, all redeeming social value.

In the mid-seventies, just starting my less-than-brilliant career at Sotheby's, I was given a new jolt of art adrenaline by reading Rheims's 1975 memoir *Haut Curiosité.* The book was later published in English, under the title *The Glorious Obsession.* Although few non-Francophones read it, I personally found it the most lively, entertaining, and inspirational primer anyone interested in art, and especially a career in art, could ever read. I realized early on that I could never hope to be anything like Peter Wilson. He was so British and at the same time so Byzantine. Maurice Rheims, on the other hand, was totally Continental. We definitely spoke the same language and had grown up in the same culture. Peter Wilson had too many secrets to ever write a book. Maurice Rheims was full disclosure, and because of his total candor on the page, I thought of him as a friend years before I ever had the privilege of meeting the man who was my idol.

What a privilege that was. In the 1990s, when I became head of Sotheby's Europe, based in Geneva, I inaugurated a lecture series featuring the great figures in the art world and its satellite galaxies of literature, fashion, music, and more. I presented a diverse portfolio that included Karl Lagerfeld, Anthony Burgess (*A Clockwork Orange*), the philosophers George Steiner and Bernard-Henri Lévy, Helmut Newton, and Jeff Koons before he became huge. But no "get" meant as much to me as Maurice Rheims, who gave a provocative lecture entitled "Apollo on Wall Street." He made a witty lampoon of our auction of the Elton John Collection, describing the catalogue as "promising Versailles but delivering a garage sale." I'll never forget his fabulous huge wandering eyes, framed by large glasses, darting everywhere, as entranced by beautiful women as beautiful art. They were the most alert eyes I'd ever seen.

How much wandering those eyes were capable of was brought home to me when I had the honor and privilege of calling on Rheims as a nonagenarian in his spectacular *hôtel particulier* on the Rue du Faubourg Saint-Honoré in the chic heart of Paris, near the Ritz. I had arrived too early. Maître Rheims greeted me at the door in a resplendent shirt and tie, over nothing but boxer shorts. Apparently he was always ready, ready for romance. He was besieged by constant visits from brainy female admirers, art groupies, if you will. In the entrance hall was a box of Old Master prints from which he allowed each of his distaff conquests to choose a priceless "party favor" on her way out the door. His distinguished daughters, photographer Bettina and filmmaker Nathalie, both toasts of Paris, were concerned that Father would give everything away. They needn't have worried. His collection was far too deep.

Rheims put his pants on and gave me a grand tour of a collection that ranged from Raphael to Limoges enamels to Balthus. The absolute highlight was a stunning painting by Klimt, which is now one of the treasures of my favorite museum in the world, the Neue Galerie in New York. Also unforgettable was a fin-de-siècle François Carabin desk whose caryatid figures supporting the frame were a precursor to Surrealism. As I spent time with Rheims I thought about him in comparison to Peter Wilson, who had died in 1981, far too young at seventy-one. Obviously Wilson didn't seduce young women, or men for that matter, with art as an aphrodisiac, the way Rheims did. Wilson was huge, imperial, the soul of *politesse,* an introvert who was totally self-deprecating, notwithstanding the obvious grandeur. The tiny (compared to Wilson), intense, extroverted Maurice Rheims, on the other hand, like most Frenchmen, would never self-deprecate, only self-aggrandize. What they had in common was the most discerning tastes and the deepest passion for art, whether in a flea market or a museum.

Rheims's motto was "Distrust objects," though he may have sold more of them than any other auctioneer, fourteen million, in his estimation. That included some of the greatest Old Masters and Impressionists, as well as such offbeat items as King Farouk's porno comic book collection, the guillotine blade that severed the neck of Louis XVI, and the hat worn by Napoleon at the Battle of Wagram. Small wonder Rheims didn't trust objects, which, in his estimation, only made great collectors on their deathbeds, surrounded by treasures that would outlast them, look that much more pathetic and powerless.

Maurice Rheims had grown up in Lorraine, as in the German border area of Alsace Lorraine, home of the quiche, the cliché of French gastronomy that was invading sophisticated circles of New York when I first came to visit. Rheims was the son of that rarity in France, a Jewish general. General Rheims was, shades of Colonel Gimbel, a major World War I hero, wounded at Verdun. Rheims was born connected. But he was also born in the dark shadow of the Dreyfus Affair. Jews, no matter how powerful, could never rest easy in France. Because of his roots, Rheims always remained a bit of an outsider, which made him highly sympathetic.

I also identified with Rheims as still one more dropout. He had tried studying art at both the École du Louvre and the Sorbonne. Neither worked for him. Nonetheless, he was the first and only auctioneer ever to be inducted into France's intellectual pantheon, the Academie Française. There were only forty members at any time, and they were known as *Les Immortels* (the Immortals, not a doo-wop group). Rheims the dropout joined the ranks of genius that included Victor Hugo, Louis Pasteur, and Voltaire. Not bad for a guy with a gavel.

It may have been easier for Rheims to get into the Academie than to get into the Hôtel Drouot, the Paris collective of around seventy auction firms, all housed in one vast Sotheby's-like emporium not far from l'Opéra. Founded in 1852 and possessing a monopoly on art sales in France for over a century, Drouot, never welcoming to Jews, was an even tougher door to break down when Maurice Rheims, born in 1910, tried to get into the art business in the mid-thirties, on the eve of Hitler. He not only broke the barriers and became a licensed *commissaire-priseur* (French for auctioneer/appraiser) at Drouot, but during the German occupation, he was the only Jew conducting auctions in the hallowed hall. This was notwithstanding the sign on the great doors, INTERDIT AUX CHIENS ET JUIFS: Off-limits to dogs and Jews.

Eventually the Nazis got wise to Rheims and sent him to their concentration camp at Drancy, outside Paris, which was a holding pen for deportation to Auschwitz. Connections saved him, namely his father's military friendship with Marshal Pétain. The two generals were both heroes at Verdun, and the blood they spilled together proved thicker than the *interdit* blood running through the Rheims veins. Maurice Rheims, once out of Drancy, joined the Resistance, smuggling Jews and Communists from France into Switzerland. Then he linked up with the Free French commandos in North Africa, and distinguished himself as a paratrooper with the Allies based in Algiers, where he became close to Charles de Gaulle. My little tour of duty in the Swiss army could hardly compare. As I said, he was an inspiration. Who could be his equal?

Back in Paris after liberation, Maurice Rheims quickly rose to become the top auctioneer in Europe. Just as Peter Wilson read the death notices of the *Times*, London and New York, Maurice Rheims devoured the "mourning" pages of *Le Figaro*, and became one of Paris's major buyers of flowers, as he never missed the funeral of an important collector. His first big sale after the war was auctioning the Hermann Göring estate, sweet revenge for Rheims. Because postwar Paris was in vastly better shape than postwar London, lots of rich Americans either had homes or permanent suites at the Ritz there. Accordingly, Rheims could access them to let him sell their treasures at Hôtel Drouot.

Rheims's biggest record came in 1956 with his auction of a Philadelphia Biddle's Gauguin's *Nature Morte aux Pommes* (*Still Life with Apples*) to Greek tycoon Basil Goulandris. The price was $255,000, which was the biggest of all non–Old Masters sales for about a year until Peter Wilson topped it in 1958 with his Goldschmidt Cézanne. What was said to have closed the deal was that the "apples" in the painting were actually oranges, and those oranges were Goulandris's favorite fruit. His chief rival, Stavros Niarchos, was right across the room at Drouot bidding as well, but the sentimental value of actual taste pushed Goulandris to take the prize. Hence the stuff records are made of.

After losing the battle for Parke-Bernet, Maurice Rheims went on to more great auctions in the sixties, most notably a vast Rothschild collection and the equally vast Bestegui trove. Don Carlos de Beistegui was a super-rich Mexican of Basque origins. He went to Eton, lived in a Le Corbusier penthouse on the Champs-Elysées whose terrace was designed by Dali, and had a grand château filled with authentic-looking fakes of the world's greatest paintings. Cecil Beaton copied the library for that of Henry Higgins in *My Fair Lady*. Don Carlos, whom everyone called Charlie, also lived in the Palazzo Labia in Venice, where in 1951 he gave what was surely the "party of the century," which inspired Truman Capote's Black and White Ball in 1966.

After the Beistegui sale, Rheims focused on advising the likes of Getty, Rothschild, and even the French government. When Picasso died in 1973, the Élysée Palace turned to Rheims to advise them on which of the master's paintings and other works they should accept to cover the familiy's gargantuan bill of death duties. No connoisseur was more up to the task than Rheims, and the result of his Olympian good taste is Paris's Musée Picasso, one of the greatest collections of art on earth. Until deep into his nineties he continued to seduce wonderful women and write wise and witty books like the one that steeled me in my desire to become an auctioneer and follow in intimidating footsteps that were like those of a dinosaur compared to those of a chicken. Still, his wit and unpretentiousness took the fear away and gave me a primer on how to deal with the sacred monsters of the art world that I was about to meet.

9

SIMON DE MONACO

The bank robber Willie Sutton famously said he robbed banks because that was where the money was. Likewise, Sotheby's opened its office in Monte Carlo because that was where the money was, especially in the mid-seventies, when they dispatched me there. The height of the Arab Oil Crisis seemed a dubious time to be expanding, certainly in London, where things had never been bleaker economically. When the new Monte Carlo office was formally announced in January 1975, the London stock exchange was at an all-time low. The Bank of England had to keep secret its efforts to bail out the colossal National Westminster Bank to keep it from going under. The only people in England who seemed to have any money at all were the Middle Easterners, who were buying all the best properties and were feared to soon be buying all the best companies. The one thing they were not buying, at the moment, was art. That day would also come. Nevertheless, there were still a lot of extremely rich people, and there seemed to be more of them clustered on the French Riviera than anywhere else.

My speaking French was probably my main qualification to be sent to Sotheby's new outpost. I didn't look for motive. I looked for an escape, from the gloomy weather, the gloomy economy, the gloom of driving on the wrong side of the desolate motorways looking for things to sell to people who weren't buying. Looking for a way out, I decided to make myself useful doing French translations for Sotheby's catalogues, which were bilingual. There was nothing like French for that touch of class that was the lifeblood of the British auction houses.

But this wasn't typical translation. There were countless terms of auctioneering jargon and technical terms of art that were way beyond me. My obsession with doing a perfect job that would get me noticed drove me to locate a brilliant student at the University of London and hire him to be my subtranslator. My investment paid off. Peter Wilson spotted the catalogues and enquired of John Winter, the catalogue majordomo, who was responsible for such perfect French. In time John Winter approached me with the accolade and said that Wilson wanted to send me to the new office in Monaco. It was like an offer from the Godfather, in this case the Godfather of Sotheby's. I could not refuse. Besides, it seemed like a great opportunity.

My title was *directeur des ventes,* director of sales, but like all titles, it implied a certain authority that was lacking in fact. I spent a lot of time hanging pictures and doing errands. The French term for gofer is *l'homme à tout faire.* The French have a great way with words. I also was assigned to call on people who might be interested in selling their art or their furniture, obviously not the super-collectors, but people who were a lesser risk that Sotheby's might lose if I put my foot in my mouth.

Peter Wilson had concluded a deal with Prince Ranier that gave Sotheby's the exclusive right to do sales in Monaco, right under the angry noses of the French across the border. To run the new shop he dispatched a dear friend, the dashing and distinguished Rear Admiral, John Templeton-Cotill, whose boyfriend was another admiral, the full Admiral Sir Richard Clayton. While a rear admiral is the lowest of the admiral ranks, both men were equally grand, with all the British naval spit and polish you could imagine. Together they owned the Château de Roaix, a converted fort of the Knights Templar near Peter Wilson's Château de Clavary. All three men were obsessive gardeners. On weekends the two retired admirals gadded about the Riviera on identical motorbikes; sadly, on one such jaunt Clayton was killed a few years later. There were obviously lots of jokes about Wilson and his high command, always quietly told.

Neither admiral knew anything about art, but "TC," as Templeton-Cotill was known to everyone, had served Britain all over the globe:

heading the Royal Australian Navy; working as Lord Mountbatten's chief economist, or cost-cutter, a position that endeared him to newly frugal Sotheby's; serving as naval attaché in Moscow; commanding the commando carrier *Bulwark*, the linchpin of the Mediterranean fleet; commanding Britain's Far East Fleet. However, TC's greatest value to Sotheby's was that he was a huge hit with old widows and spoke flawless French. No woman could refuse to consign to him her estate. After the Royal Navy he had run Sotheby's branch office in Paris (where, per French law, he could network but not sell), and he was Peter Wilson's first choice to run Monaco.

The Sotheby's headquarters were a splendid affair, as they needed to be to attract the clientele we were seeking. We were right next door to the two grand hotels where the kings and moguls stayed, the Hotel de Paris and the Hotel Hermitage, which sandwiched the Sporting d'Hiver, or Winter Casino, whose Art Deco main hall was surely the most spectacular auction room in the world. Our first sale more than lived up to its setting and, at a gross of $4 million, generated more money for Sotheby's than anything we did that year in London.

This was a furniture sale. I might have despaired that I was still a furniture salesman; I was just doing it in the sun instead of the fog. But this furniture was different from all other furniture. This was the joint furniture collection of the two great Jewish barons Baron Guy de Rothschild and Baron Alexis de Redé. We all know about the Rothschilds, but de Redé is an equally fascinating character. The occasion for the sale was that the two barons had become roommates, in the grandest sense of the word. De Redé had just sold Paris's finest home, the 1644 Hôtel Lambert, designed by Le Vau, the architect of Versailles, on the prow of the Île Saint-Louis, to Guy de Rothschild and his wife, Marie-Hélène, the Dutch-Egyptian queen of French postwar society.

De Redé was to Marie-Hélène what Jerry Zipkin would soon be to Nancy Reagan, the First Walker, a walker being an ambiguously gay, extremely stylish unmarried man who escorted best-dressed-listed women to exclusive French restaurants and expensive charity events. De Redé and Marie-Hélène couldn't be separated, so, despite the sale, de Redée stayed on at the Lambert in his own wing. It was an upperclass version of *Friends*. De Redé had the bulk of his Lambert furniture to sell, while the Rothschilds, having given their Château de Ferrières to the French government, had way too much furniture to fit into their new Paris residence. This was one of the rare times in the history of auctions when the sellers didn't sell for money. The barons didn't need money. They needed *space*. So they turned to Peter Wilson, not to Maurice Rheims, mainly to avoid the huge auction tax that would be levied in a Paris sale but not one in Monaco.

What a treat it was to meet these legends, who all seemed like characters out of another century, and out of Balzac. The Baron de Redé, in his fifties when we met, was beyond effete and beyond refined. We shared one thing in common: We were both Swiss. He had grown up in Zurich, on an entire floor of the Dolder Grand Hotel, surrounded with maids and servants. He was to the Dolder what Eloise was to the Plaza in New York. His actual name was Alex Rosenberg, which his banker father aggrandized into Von Rosenberg-Redé by doing certain favors for the eighty-six-year-old Austro-Hungarian emperor Franz Joseph on his deathbed in 1916.

The title referred to a barony in Romania, which wasn't exactly mainstream royalty, but a title was a title. By the time he was twenty, and World War II had broken out, Alex's father and brother had both committed suicide, and the money was gone. Dispossessed from the Dolder, the new baron dropped the Rosenberg and added a "de" to his title, becoming the Baron de Redé. He set off to America, first New York and then Hollywood, where being a baron went a long way. He worked in antique shops, trying to support his sister, who was brain damaged. Despite appearances, the baron wasn't all narcissism.

The baron's lucky break came in Manhattan in 1941, while dining in an East Side temple of gastronomy called the Brussels. He was nineteen. There he caught the eye of a gent two decades older who was dining with his wife, while staying at the St. Regis. This was no mere gent. This was the Chilean billionaire Arturo Lopez-Willshaw, one of the richest men on earth. His fortune came from fertilizer. Guano or not, it was still a fortune, just as the baron's Romanian title was still a title. What was love at first sight became one of the great sinecures and took being a kept man to new heights.

Lopez-Willshaw set his true love up in Paris at the Hôtel Lambert and put a million dollars in the bank for him. However, the baron was not a mere pretty-boy idler. He eventually used his Chilean grubstake (he inherited half the guano fortune when Lopez-Willshaw died in 1962; the wife got the other half) to buy an interest in a London merchant bank with yet another titled royal of Jewish descent, Prince Rupert Loewenstein. They would become the money managers of the Rolling Stones, and we all know how well that turned out.

A prettier version of *The Thin Man*'s William Powell who denied the aging process by dying his hair black and befriending the jet-setting Brazilian plastic surgeon Dr. Ivo Pitanguy, the baron had trademark eyes that were always half closed. You never knew whether he was looking at you or not, or if you were so boring, compared to the rest of his glittering life, that your very presence was putting him to sleep. The baron may have been the most connected man I ever met. The networking started at Le Rosey, the Swiss boarding school I was too hopeless a student to have attended, where his best friends were the future Shah of Iran and Prince Ranier; the baron often dined with him and Princess Grace at the palace in Monaco.

Baron de Redé was said to have discovered Yves Saint Laurent when he needed a designer to do the headgear for his 1956 *bal des têtes*, inspired by his buddy and fellow aesthete Charlie Beistegui, at which his other dear pal the Duchess of Windsor chaired his panel of judges for best costume. *Comme le monde est petit* was the name of the game. I felt lucky to remember a fraction of the big names that were bandied about, as I assisted Peter Wilson in planning the auction.

The sale itself took place over a week in the spring, the glory time in Monaco, and attracted bidders from everywhere in the world, some as eager to see Princess Grace, still a major tourist draw, as to see the furniture. But what furniture it was. Among the highlights of what were all highlights were two desks, one belonging to Napoleon, where he signed the Louisiana Purchase, the other an ingenious mechanical desk worthy of da Vinci belonging to Catherine the Great of Russia.

Monegasque regulations required that a local *huissier,* or licensed auctioneer, perform the actual auction. But that would not serve the crowd of collectors that had come to see Peter Wilson, who had become something of a rock star at this point. Accordingly, Wilson came up with the genius maneuver of enlisting the estimable Madame Marquet, who was duly accredited by the principality, to stand by his side and bring down the gavel. The gavel was the great part for Wilson, who felt strait-jacketed by the Monegasque restrictions. "It's all foreplay without the pleasure of conclusion," he told me. He also hated Madame's timing. He felt she banged the gavel too fast. By the end of the sale, he was basically holding her arm and bringing it down exactly when he wanted. He had turned her into his robot. Timing was everything.

The highest-ticket item was a three-foot-tall bronze Florentine model horse, which created a bidding war among English and Italian adherents but went to a Persian living in Paris for nearly $500,000. The French authorities were not pleased at Sotheby's brazen invasion of what they felt was Hôtel Drouot's territory and prerogatives, just across their borders. They scorned Monaco as a principality of whores. After all, didn't Ranier sell his famous casino to Onassis? Now he was selling the Sporting to Sotheby's. And selling out France. Accordingly, the French did what they do so well, bring out the red tape, blocking the export of any of the items that had been made, or partly made, in France, like Catherine's desk. Whatever the French tried to do wasn't sufficient. The sale put our office on the map, and the French couldn't take it off. Furthermore, our success gave the firm a boost from its doldrums elsewhere in the world. Monaco remained a beacon of profit, and of hope, for both London and New York.

Because Peter Wilson loved his Château de Clavary, he spent a lot of time at the Monaco office, and I, as his man Friday, had the pleasure of accompanying him on his assorted rounds. We usually traveled in a nondescript large Citroën chauffeured by his handsome Sean Connery–esque Cockney driver. Wilson seemed to have decorative tough Cockneys in tow wherever he went. This driver was more than discomfited by Wilson's habit of never having a penny on him. One day at a tollbooth on the new *autoroute,* we screeched to a dead halt. The driver refused to pay the toll. "You owe me seventy-eight quid, guv'nor," the driver barked. Wilson sheepishly turned to me to borrow the money. "Do you mind *awfully* paying for this?" he beseeched me helplessly.

The first American hired by Sotheby's after acquiring Parke-Bernet was Edward Lee Cave, a very Brooks Brothers/Madison Avenue type whose most memorable sartorial feature was the tie tacks he wore to keep his preppy rep ties in place. No one could keep Cave in place. He quickly rose to head the Decorative Arts division, and since that's what we specialized in in Monaco, he spent a lot of time at our office. And after he saw all the châteaus on the Riviera he realized there was even more money in selling the houses of the rich than just their contents. So he talked the firm into founding a real estate division, Sotheby Parke Bernet International Realty, which sold châteaux to Americans and Fifth Avenue co-ops to Europeans. Cave knew great houses not vicariously but firsthand; his wife, Pauline, was a Whitney heiress whose mother, Lady Baillie, grew up in Leeds Castle in Kent, surrounded by a fortune in eighteenth-century French furniture, which was ultimately auctioned at Sotheby's. Things somehow tended to be all in the family.

I was impressed with Cave in action. I once saw him prevent a sale from unraveling. Sotheby's was in a state of anxiety over an upcoming sale, fearing it would fail because the reserve prices for the seller were too high. Cave's brief was to get that seller, a tough American dowager staying in the Hotel de Paris, to lower her demands. Cave was literally on his knees begging her to give ground. His hair was a mess, he was drenched in sweat, and he fidgeted with his tie tack the way a pilgrim to Mecca might fidget with his worry beads. In the end, he got the job done, and went on to leave Sotheby's and find greater success as one of New York's top realtors.

In Monaco, I think I met every charter member of the Jet Set, a new social class defined by the glamour and mobility of its members, who could be rich, famous, titled, beautiful, or often all of the above. The rapid transit that made the Jet Set as fast as it was was created by the launch in 1958 of the first generation of commercial jet planes, the Boeing 707 and the Douglas DC-8, which halved the travel time from New York to Europe from twelve hours to six. By the time I got to Monaco in the mid-seventies, the Jet Set was already starting to fade, along with the new jets themselves, flying half empty because of fuel costs and a world of newly sophisticated voyagers who had cruelly been priced out of their travel fantasy by the current economic troubles.

Not so the Jet Setters, all Sotheby's clients or targets, proof that price insensitivity would always exist at the top end of the art market. Agnelli, the Aga Khan, Rothschild, Flick, Sachs, Niarchos, Thurn und Taxis, Thyssen. The only movie star I met was David Niven, who lived nearby at Cap Ferrat. There were few Americans, except for Oscar and Lynn Wyatt of Houston, she the perennial best-dressed Sakowitz department store heiress. These were all names in the world's gossip columns, mostly industrial-mercantile fortunes, some recent, some inherited, many playboys, all glamorous, and these were the names who came to our auctions in Monte Carlo. It was Billionaires 101, a course in consumption, though not always conspicuous.

My salary was low, my expense account lavish. I was issued a low-end Peugeot, better than my Renault in England but no match for the Porsches that some of the other young men in my office drove. I could see that, as in the Works of Art course, most Sotheby's employees came from wealthy families who underwrote their children's lifestyles. Like my parents, these families were surely thrilled their children had a job, some job, any job. Because my parents were not lavish with me in that way, I just had to work harder.

My job, as Peter Wilson charged me, was to "bring in the kit." That meant I was to call on clients, wherever I could find them, and encourage them to part with their treasures and do it through us. This led me into some awkward situations. One was with a lady pilot in her mid-sixties. She insisted on talking furniture while flying over the Alpes-Maritimes in her small propeller plane. She became so animated, she let go of the controls. I was terrified, but more terrified of returning to the rear admiral empty-handed. Then there was a ninety-three-year-old heiress who could do nothing but rant about how her husband had run off with his twenty-seven-year-old Cuban nurse. Because the money was all hers, she wanted to sell for no other reason than to teach him a lesson. That was reason enough for Sotheby's, though I found that my job was less being an art expert than being a social worker to the rich and famous.

After working hard dealing with the neuroses of my clients, the temptation was to play hard as well. I would have lunch at the Beach Club, where we had a cabana and I developed a permanent suntan, like George Hamilton. Dinner would often be at the vaunted restaurant of the Hotel de Paris, then dancing at Jimmy'z, which was the Monte Carlo branch of Régine's in Paris, and where I had my own private liquor locker with my own bottle of Johnnie Walker Black Label. The disco music of Donna Summer, who was just hitting it big in Europe, still reverberates in my ears.

My "big brother" and office mentor was a British jewel-box expert named Brian Ivon-Jones, who was a self-styled ladykiller. He had lived in Los Angeles, claimed to have dated starlets, and regarded me as a hopeless nerd. I was still waiting in the wings with Isabel, who was still in London at Heim and in thrall to a Belgian banker and still relegated me to "friendship." So here I was in this paradise of pleasure, all by myself. Hanging out with Ivan-Jones always made me feel worse. One night over cocktails at Café de Paris, early in my stay, we both were mesmerized by a bronze/blond Riviera goddess, the kind you might see in *Vogue* swimsuit spreads or Bain de Soleil suntan lotion ads.

"Let me show you how it's done, old chap," he said, admiring himself in the bar mirror. He left me alone and returned in a while, beaming ear to ear. "Dinner tonight, my boy," he boasted, grinning like a Cheshire cat. Feeling lonely and like a failure, I left and went by myself to a local soccer match. I was walking home afterward to my dismal tiny studio on Boulevard de la Grotte (where the word "grotty" may have come from) when there, alone and drunk in the square opposite the casino, was the playboy of the Western world, looking sad indeed. "Five hundred francs!" he said indignantly. "She wanted five hundred francs." That Riviera goddess, like so many other decorative objects at the Café de Paris, was a high-class call girl. Like Peter Wilson, she had come to Monaco for one thing and one thing only.

10

Our Man in Geneva

After about a year in Monaco, Peter Wilson decided to send me home to Switzerland. Sotheby's, on its expansion tear, already had started an office in Zurich in 1969 headed by Jurg Wille. Wille may have been the best-connected man in Switzerland, at least as far as art collectors were concerned, and art collectors were Peter Wilson's *only* concern. Wilson had his eye on the prize, and he had a great instinct for hiring people with connections, such as Rear Admiral Templeton-Cottill. Similar to TC, Wille had been a distinguished army man, from a long line of generals. His grandfather had been the commanding general of the Swiss army during World War I, and his father the equivalent of second in command during World War II.

The Willes were close friends with the Wagner music dynasty, and through the Wagners became the Zurich hosts of none other than Adolf Hitler. I always got a very creepy feeling, when I went to parties at the Wille mansion, that Hitler slept here. Our star client Rosemarie Kanzler, who was also from Zurich, but from the wrong side of the *Hauptbanhof,* had become a singer in Berlin on her way to wealth and had serenaded Hitler to sleep with Viennese lullabys. Rosemarie was a pet of Göring, Goebbels, and other Nazi top brass until she fled to the Western Hemisphere to conquer Wall Street's top brass. But Rosemarie was such a wild character, and so madly ambitious, you could never somehow fault her for her *sauve qui peut* romantic networking. On the less sinister German side, one of Jurg Wille's best friends was Robert von Hirsch, whose German family owned the titanic leather firm Offenbacher. That multitude of shoes and bags enabled him in his twenties to begin assembling one of the great art collections in Europe. Peter Wilson was also friends with von Hirsch, dating back to a schoolboy summer he spent in Germany.

When Hirsch died in 1977 at ninety-four, Wille "brought in the kit" for one of Wilson's biggest London auctions. Working in the long shadow of Jurg Wille would have been a very high bar for a novice like myself, so I was grateful Wilson sent me to the "farm team" that was the new Geneva office, a small warren of rooms in the city's Old Town, where I had briefly lived as a failed law student. Now I was worried about a repeat performance as a failed art seller. Peter Wilson was all confidence in the new enterprise. He dragooned a glamorously rugged English ex-paratrooper named Nicholas Rayner, a Peter O'Toole look-alike, from Wille in the Zurich office. Rayner was so handsome that Hollywood had come calling after Sam Spiegel, producer of *Lawrence of Arabia,* had spotted him at an auction. In Switzerland, Rayner added tobogganing to his sporting exploits and became a champion on the Cresta Run, a sport of kings in St. Moritz.

I was thus flattered that Peter Wilson hired me to be second in command, and announced the opening not in the typical spot of a pompous art magazine, but rather in French *Vogue,* with large photographs of both Rayner and me in the ad. I was amused at being in *Vogue.* I felt like a male model, and that was a big ego boost for a glorified errand boy. The *Vogue* ad was a radical move in a conservative business, but that was Peter Wilson, a PR man *malgré lui,* and way ahead of his time.

As I have said, Geneva wasn't really an "art town" but rather a jewelry town, the ultimate jewelry town, whose streets seemed to be paved with diamonds. But if I didn't want to be in the shadow of Jurg Wille, in Geneva our new office was in the equally ominous shadow of Dr. Géza von Habsburg. Von Habsburg headed the Geneva office of Christie's, which, in its endless competition with Sotheby's, had gone on its own tear of imperial expansion. At this stage of their rivalry, Christie's was always following Sotheby's lead. When Sotheby's opened its first branch offices, in Paris and Munich, so did copycat Christie's. The only independence Christie's had shown was not following our lead when we opened Zurich. Instead they opened Geneva. And since Geneva was a jewelry town, they had two of the best jewelry men in existence running that office. Not only was Géza von Habsburg the world's leading authority on Fabergé, but his young second in command, Hans Nadelhoffer, had just published the definitive book on Cartier. What a tough act to follow.

When I was accompanying Peter Wilson around the South of France, we often talked about opening a Geneva office. Because of Jurg Wille's deep connections, Sotheby's was beholden to him. He lived in Zurich, so Sotheby's went to Zurich. But at that time Geneva was a far more glamorous city, French, not German, with all the panache and joie de vivre that Frenchness implied. The idea of selling something as glittering as jewelry in unglittering Zurich seemed oxymoronic to me, and to Peter Wilson, who once declared, "Doing jewelry auctions in Zurich is like doing them in *Birmingham!*" The end result was opening our second Swiss office in Geneva. We knew it would be an uphill battle.

No one else in the jewelry world was as imperial as Géza von Habsburg. Who could match a name like his? Christie's loved to hire Continental aristocrats the way Peter Wilson liked to hire admirals. Von Habsburg was both an archduke and a prince. What a name! My boss in Geneva, Nicholas Rayner, knew, we all knew, we were no match for Géza, not in the genealogy department, not in the authority department. When I arrived, I tried to make a courtesy call on Géza, businessman to businessman. He refused to receive me. He saw himself as far more than a mortal businessman.

Not that I stopped trying to meet Géza. One day I thought I had my golden opportunity. Before the advent of high-speed rail, there used to be a Zurich-Geneva shuttle flight, and we both happened to be on it. Since it only took a half hour, there were no assigned seats. So I grabbed the seat next to the Archduke. Lucky me! Location, location, location. Then he cut me dead. "I'm terribly sorry, but I have no envy of sitting next to you," he told me, prince to pauper. I could have held my seat, but that never occurred to me. I politely (unlike the Prince) retreated to the back of the plane.

Geneva wasn't built in a day, or in the year and a half I was there. We had too big a mountain to climb, though scale we did. The real bright spot in my life was that I had finally won Isabel Sloman's heart. I proposed to her at Mentmore, the great Victorian Rothschild redoubt in England that was the scene of another of Peter Wilson's aspirational "house sales" like the Kanzler sale I did with him. Fancy real estate as a leitmotif of our courtship continued with our marriage at the cathedral on the hill next to the fairy tale Neuchatel Castle. A few months later we had our first son Alban on the way. With an imminent family to support, I focused hard on my work and the ongoing efforts to achieve credibility and clout in the local marketplace so dominated by the formidable Archduke.

To kick off our new office, Nicholas Rayner came up with the great idea to give ourselves a launch party, a *bal des têtes* modeled on the one given by the Baron de Redé, where Yves Saint Laurent did the headgear. Our gimmick was that our party's headgear had to be inspired by twentieth-century artists and art. I had no idea what to wear. Luckily my brilliant wife did. One day at the supermarket she saw a display of imported Campbell's soup. She bought all the cans and created a pyramid headdress of the cans as an homage to Andy Warhol, then at the pinnacle of Pop. Alas, the pregnant Isabel was terribly ill with morning sickness, evening sickness, you name it. So I went alone, and hung out with Peter Wilson, who wore the requisite black tie but no headdress.

The ball was held in the upper two salons of the Hôtel de Saussure, the finest building in Geneva. Our offices were in the basement, and we were able to charm the upstairs tenant, a flamboyant Bulgarian lawyer named Pierre Sciclunoff, into lending us his salons for our fete. People came dressed in Picasso sun hats; some wore de Chirico eggheads; others wore Magritte bowlers. Marc Blondeau, a Sotheby bigwig, dressed as the notorious, extravagantly bearded and behatted art forgery dealer Fernand Le Gros. In the amazing grand *salle de bain,* there were two enormous *bains,* marble tubs, side by side, that looked like sarcophagi. Men in their tuxes and women in their ball gowns couldn't wait to nestle into these tubs for posterity.

This great party was written up in the *International Herald Tribune* by its powerful fashion editor, Hebe Dorsey. For all the fabulous looks, only one of us got his picture in the *IHT.* Guess who? At age twenty-five, I had been seen in both *Vogue* and the *Herald Trib.* I was morti-fied! Unlike people today, especially art people, who love all the publicity they can get, I came from the old school of publicity avoidance. Even if I couldn't get Géza to acknowledge my existence, I tried to console my-self about my "indecent exposure" with the notion that he would read the papers, looking for clients, and notice that I had "arrived." Our *bal des têtes* was the first big party I had ever helped throw. It wouldn't be the last.

My best times in Geneva were spent going on the road with Peter Wilson. With no Cockney in residence as his studly chauffeur, I be-came Wilson's designated driver, and I drove him all over the country. There was a lot of great art in Switzerland, and Wilson seemed to know where every *objet* was located. For his chariot of fire, he didn't object to my downmarket Peugeot any more than he objected to his clunky Ci-troën in Monaco. He preferred to be low profile, lest prospective clients think he was living too high on *their* hogs. I was amazed at the tenacity with which he pursued clients, and their treasures. Peter Wilson was the Bulldog Drummond of art. Like the fictional detective who always got his man, Peter Wilson always got his art.

Illustrative of Wilson's single-mindedness was one of our earliest sor-ties, to court an Anglo-American couple, the Constable-Maxwells, who lived in a château on Lac de Morat. The husband, a Scottish baronet, was the stereotypical aquiline refined English gentleman abroad. The American wife was the stereotypical Marilyn Monroe ditsy blonde. Wil-son was there for one thing and one thing only: the Diatreta Cup. Made in the fourth century AD, the Diatreta Cup was considered the pinnacle of glassmaking, then and forever, the most important and most fragile piece of glass in the world. It was so intricate and perfect that how it was made remained a mystery. *Bibe Vivas Multis Annis* was the in-scription that ran around the cup: "Drink! Live many years."

To get the cup, Peter Wilson would drink and live many years, if that's what it would take. But to do so, Wilson never used pressure tactics, or even the aggressive reverse psychology that won us the Kanzler house sale. Instead he adhered to the Kiplingesque Ashanti precept from British colonial times, "Softly, softly, catchee monkey." He seemed to be flying to Geneva from London every other weekend for months to stay with his new best friends, the Constable-Maxwells, with whom he seemed to have nothing in common other than that Roman cup. As I would drive him there and back to Geneva, sometimes I would be invited for a meal. And during those meals, Peter Wilson would never mention the cup. Never! I never heard so much small talk. But not a word about the cup.

What the Constable-Maxwells enjoyed as much as their hallowed glass was playing croquet. I had no idea that Wilson was such an aficionado of the game until one afternoon I was forced to play, he and I on one team, the glass collectors on the other. Finally, the moment of truth was at hand. Wilson had a simple shot, a shoo-in, that would win the match (and let us escape back to Geneva). He spent what seemed like an eternity lining up what should have been a simple tap of the mallet. The giant man leaned over, trying to aim, to win, as if his life depended on it. Finally, he hit the ball. And completely missed. And seemed totally tortured that he had missed. The Constable-Maxwells couldn't have been happier if they had won the Tour de France. When the victors turned away for a second to savor their spoils, Peter Wilson caught my attention with a wink of his eye and whispered, "Sorry. But I had to do that to get the collection."

On the drive back to the airport, Wilson, reveling in our triumph with his guilty schoolboy grin, recounted the fable of the mountain walk of two contenders for a woman's hand with the lady's father. When the father slipped, one of the suitors leapt into the crevasse to save his life. They kept walking. Then the second suitor slipped, and the father leapt into the crevasse to save the suitor's life. Who got the lady's hand? The second man, the rescuee rather than the savior. The father, Wilson explained, had more invested in the man he saved than in the man who saved him. Likewise the Constable-Maxwells loved feeling superior to the man they had defeated in this high-stakes match. In time, their time, they consigned the Diatreta Cup to Wilson. There were, strange to say, no more croquet matches after the sale.

There was, however, one final catch. The cup was deemed too fragile for our shipper to be willing to transport it to London, so it fell on me to become a very glorified delivery boy, albeit one who was carrying the art equivalent of a load of nitroglycerin, like the truck drivers in the famous Clouzot film *The Wages of Fear.* "That piece of glass will break every record," Wilson promised the Constable-Maxwells. "Unless Simon breaks the glass itself," Mrs. Constable-Maxwell added ominously. Holding the treasure gingerly between my legs in the cab to the airport, on the seemingly endless flight to London, and then in the excruciating traffic jam to get to Mayfair, I found myself on what seemed to be the longest, scariest high-stakes journey of my lifetime. The records were indeed broken, though, thank heavens, not the glass.

One day in the Old Town, I received a most unexpected and unusual visitation in my humble basement office from three of the most important figures in the entire art establishment. I would call them the Three Kings. The first King was François Daulte, the world's leading authority on Renoir and Sisley, whose official catalogues raisonnés he had written. The catalogues were published by Daulte's close friend the art impresario Daniel Wildenstein. Based in Lausanne, Daulte was also a brilliant businessman, one of the rare scholars who turned his scholarship into a major living.

Daulte had created what would become the Japanese Gold Rush in the late-eighties art market by arranging, in the 1960s postwar recovery known as the Japanese "miracle," an annual series of Impressionist and Post-Impressionist art exhibitions all over Nippon. He hooked up with the Seibu Department Stores group to sponsor the exhibitions, very pleased to be linking commerce with culture. Two decades later the seeds planted by Daulte erupted into full (Impressionist) flower, as the Japanese, hooked on French art by Daulte's superb shows, bid the price of this art into the record books, to the great profit of Daulte and his backer Wildenstein.

The second King was Peter Zervudachi, an elegant and aristocratic Alexandrian Greek who fled Egypt with the fall of King Farouk. Based in exclusive Vevey, the lakeside home of Nestlé and Charlie Chaplin, Zervudachi was a private dealer to the most private millionaires of antique furniture, silver, and gold boxes. Because of his Mediterranean roots, he was the go-to dealer for the Greek shipping tycoons who cornerstoned the revival of the art market in the postwar era with their wealth derived from shipping oil in an oil-addicted world.

The third Magus was the biggest King of all, a major client of both Daulte and Zervudachi. This King was a "brand name" far bigger than Géza von Habsburg.

Baron Hans Heinrich Agost Gábor Tasso Thysssen-Bornemisza was the full name. His peers, and there weren't many, called him Heini. The Baron, which is what I called him at the beginning, was the greatest art collector in the world. And here he was, right here in my tiny office. I had seen him before in Monaco at the auctions there, maybe had shaken his hand with Peter Wilson or the rear admiral. But I had never really spoken to him before.

I had no idea why the Kings were here. Maybe the Baron, reputedly one of the world's great serial goddess-marriers, was interested in buying some jewelry for his latest wife. I had been working too hard to keep up with his amours in the gossip columns. I pulled up some hideous but comfortable very seventies industrial-looking white leather recliners and made tea for the Kings, while awaiting their frankincense and myrrh, or whatever they were here for.

Instead, here in this low-ceilinged cubbyhole that used to be the *cave*, or wine cellar, of the Hôtel de Saussure, we passed an hour of small talk, all in French, with no direction. Zervudachi did a lot of business with Sotheby's, so we talked about that. And Daulte's daughter, Marianne, had attended the Sotheby's Works of Art class with me. Now she worked in Paris at the Musée Marmottan, that great repository of the art about which her father was the reigning expert. That was the *realpolitik* of how plum museum jobs were come by. Daulte had often taken Marianne and me out to dinner when he was in London, and I suspected he might have been interested in playing matchmaker, but my heart was already taken by Isabel.

Because the Baron and I had no common ground, I can't remember what he said, other than that he had a great sense of humor and was as polite as Peter Wilson, whose impeccable manners made everyone feel at home. Whenever a woman employee would come into the office, the Baron would gallantly stand up to attention as if he were rising for the Queen of England, who was his only rival in terms of the breadth of their art collections. I suppose what we talked about was art, who was selling, who was buying, that sort of chatter.

Finally we ran out of chat. Everyone rose, and, still mystified, I walked the Three Kings to the entrance on the Rue de la Cité. There was a long moment of silence, as Daulte and Zervudachi just looked at each other, without saying a word. They seemed to be waiting for a cue from the Baron. Finally, he broke the ice. As we were about to part, the Baron himself turned to me and said, "Why don't you join us all for dinner later this evening at the Hotel Richemond." Wow! An offer I could not refuse. I was so excited.

I hadn't been able to stop admiring the Baron, who was in his late fifties, tall, and handsome in a movie-star version of barondom. He was perfectly groomed, razor-cut and manicured, and his eyes were kind of half closed in the manner of that other baronial collector, the Baron de Redé. But Heini, while not exactly rugged in the mode of the Cockney Connery types that Peter Wilson privately fancied, was much more masculine than de Redé. He was, at the same time, a ladies' man and a man's man, though not a sportsman.

He was for sure a modern Beau Brummel. The Baron was wearing the most elegant suit, which instantly made me feel badly dressed. Having learned from reading Maurice Rheims that clothes made the auctioneer, for whom it was essential to make the best possible first impression, I had spent all my meager Sotheby's wages in London on Savile Row, getting some bespoke suits at Gieves and Hawkes. These became my uniform. But the minute the Baron invited me to dinner, I felt I was in the uniform of a private and he a general. Savile Row was no match for the Baron's tailor. I wanted to go home and change. But change into what? This was the best I had, and I felt threadbare. I later learned that his suits were made for him by Caraceni in Milan, who one day would become my tailor as well. At that point, years later, I finally felt like I belonged.

I nervously arrived that evening at the Hotel Richemond, Geneva's top caravanserai, overlooking Lake Geneva and its famed *jet d'eau,* the Swiss waterspout counterpart of Yosemite's Old Faithful. The dining room was a bit bordello-ish, given the tasteful art crowd who filled it. The décor was dark red brocade, with plush gold seats and banquettes. An odd touch was the lounge singer at an electric piano, crooning classics like "My Way." All Swiss grand hotels seem to have such a lounge singer right in the restaurant, the entertainment equivalent of offering bratwurst next to foie gras on the menu.

Because it was summer, there were a lot of Arabs in the dining room. The Arabs, newly and wildly rich from the oil crisis they created, had settled on cool, Alpine, lake-y Geneva as one of their favorite summer destinations. The King of Saudi Arabia had bought one of the finest houses on the lake. He never came, but he did send his relatives and their huge entourages, who loved to dine *ensemble* at the fanciest spots, like the Richemond, music and all. The Arabs hadn't really started buying art at this point (their focus then was on jewelry and watches), but everyone at Sotheby's deeply hoped they would.

Creating a quintet with the Three Kings and me was a staple of the gossip columns, the stunning Princess Ira von Fürstenberg, who happened to be the niece of Gianni Agnelli and the ex of Prince Alfonso Hohenlohe, who had gone glamorously "into trade" by opening the Marbella Club, one of the prime haunts of the Jet Set. Princess Ira had married Prince Hohenlohe when she was a tender fifteen. She was a famous beauty. The French word for her was *pulpeuse,* or voluptuous, though the French word sounds sexier, to do her justice. When she arrived, the Baron stood and kissed her hand. I loved that Old World touch.

The Princess was the focal point of the entire evening. She was a nonstop anecdotalist, funny, ironic, and smart, the center of the table. I felt like I was in a living gossip column. The Princess, who had dabbled as an actress, was now dabbling as a jewelry designer. But why in the world was I there? The dinner provided no clues, but did provide the most expensive wine I had ever tasted. The Baron was a connoisseur of wine, women, art, everything, and price was never a consideration. I was thrilled to have met a legend.

The next day I got a call from Peter Zervudachi. "Are you wedded to Sotheby's?" he asked me. Then he went on to explicate the method in his madness. Heini Thyssen was looking for a new curator for his collection at his estate, the Villa Favorita in Lugano. He actually didn't have a curator, not in the art-history sense of the term. What he had was an elderly Hungarian man, more a concierge or caretaker. The Villa Favorita was open to the public, as part of a Swiss tax-exemption deal. What did he really need, a docent? A ticket taker? I had nervous flashbacks to my time at the front desk at the entrance to Sotheby's on Bond Street. I'd come a long way since then, from receptionist to the *Herald Tribune*. I thought of those American feminist Virginia Slims cigarette billboards. You've come a long way, baby.

Why me, I wondered, while Peter was pitching this golden opportunity. Maybe it was more golden for him and François Daulte than it was for me. Here I was, young, polite, and totally malleable. They surely saw me as easy to control. I was the perfect patsy, their inside man, that could only spell more business for them with Baron Thyssen. That was a cynical take, but business, big business like the Baron's business, can be a cynical affair. But then I stopped myself. Stop thinking what's in it for *them,* I scolded myself. Think about what's in it for *you.* Here was the greatest art collection in the world, and I was being given a chance to run it. Sotheby's was highly competitive. I was one of many there. Here I would be one of one. I turned from Italian cynicism to English opportunism, recalling one of Peter Wilson's aphorisms, "You've got to eat your cookies while they're being passed."

"I'm incredibly flattered," I told Peter Zervudachi. "Let me think about it."

As it happened, time—and Heini Thyssen—would wait for no man. The Baron didn't get his celebrated women without being a master of courtship. Mine was only about to begin.

11

A ROYAL COURTSHIP

─────────

I give a lot of coverage to Heini Thyssen in this book because Heini Thyssen not only changed my life, he *made* my life. Working as the curator for the greatest art collector in the entire world was an unmatchable résumé item. And it wasn't just on paper. Working for Heini, at the highest level of the art world, gave me an incredible self-confidence, both in my sense of taste and in my skills at diplomacy. If I could handle Heini, I could handle anyone. In terms of acquiring the ultimate Rolodex, being the Baron's right-hand man provided introductions to basically everyone on earth, in art, in politics, in finance, in society. The job was a networker's fantasy, and I was a novice at the connections game before I set foot in the Villa Favorita. Short of being Bernard Berenson to Peggy Guggenheim, being Simon de Pury to Baron Heini Thyssen was the ultimate job in art. Still, I came very close to not taking it. It took all of the Baron's charm and seduction to lure me to his highest of high tables.

As indecisive as Hamlet, I first sought counsel as to whether to say yes or no to Heini from the two women in my life, my mother and my wife. Stay at Sotheby's, my mother said, without missing a beat. Don't rock the boat. You have a family to support. My parents had paid for me to go to Sotheby's. They deserved some return on their investment. She urged me to put the Thyssen art out of my mind, to not look back at this Sodom of Old Masters, to avoid turning to salt.

My wife was far more open to adventure. We had actually gone to Lugano for our honeymoon in November 1976. We couldn't afford a real honeymoon, so we just started driving from Neuchâtel. Because of a freak blizzard that closed most of the roads in Switzerland, sunny Lugano was the only place that was not impassable. We stayed at a bizarre hotel directly overlooking the Villa Favorita, whose main attraction was that it featured a bridal suite with a round conjugal bed. We both would have loved to visit the Thyssen collection, but it was closed for the winter. I was too intimidated to call and try to use my Sotheby's connections to open the door. Now the door was wide open, and Isabel regarded that tacky honeymoon hotel as a good omen for a bright future.

Everyone else I spoke to tried to scare me off. Baron Thyssen didn't have the best reputation. He was known as an intimidating, eccentric autocrat who had only two interests in life, beautiful women and beautiful art. That was the good part. The bad part, or at least the most cited bad part, was that he was considered one of the most temperamental, mercurial super-rich men in the world of art, if not the entire world. I was a married man, a family man. I wasn't interested in the Baron's women. And Sotheby's surrounded me with all the art I could dream of. I had been at Sotheby's for five years, I was getting close to Peter Wilson, I imagined myself on a fast track. Why leave Number One?

I imagine Heini Thyssen thought *he* was Number One, because he didn't take my hesitation for an answer. He sent his plane to Geneva to bring me and Isabel to Lugano for a grand tour. Seeing would be believing. The plane was certainly a grand gesture. In those days no one had a private jet. Heads of state, maybe. Hugh Hefner. Howard Hughes. Thyssen's jet was a Dassault Falcon, which we boarded in the private Jet Aviation terminal in the Geneva airport.

While waiting I met for the first time David Nahmad, the Syrian-born dealer whose family seemed to buy art by the ton—great art, mind you, but art in volume. David was the cousin of the powerful Monaco banker Edmond Safra. The Nahmads had been based in Milan since the sixties, but now, with the rise of the Red Brigades in Italy and the risk of kidnapping, they had found the safest harbor to be New York. Basically, though, they lived on planes and in grand hotels, wherever the art was. These were the sort of person who flew in private jets, Goldfinger types.

The Baron was straight out of *Goldfinger,* and his current, fourth wife, Denise Shorto, who met us with him for the flight, was a Brazilian Pussy Galore. The radiantly blond Denise was a trophy if I had ever seen one. She was no gold digger. Her family was wealthy, her father a São Paulo banker, her mother a Scottish beauty, like the Baron's third wife, supermodel Fiona Campbell. The Shortos owned a major Coca-Cola franchise in a country addicted to all things sweet. Denise, in her early thirties, compared to the Baron's late fifties, looked like a perfectly coiffed society version of Brigitte Bardot. She had gone to the Sorbonne and spoke five languages without an accent. She loved art and seemed to know it. I guess she was the sort of woman for the man who had everything. While perfectly polite and charming, this petite blond lioness seemed to have little use for, or interest in, me.

Heini's subtropical, palm-shaded eighteenth-century Villa Favorita was the kind of place that went with owning a jet. It also reminded me, and it must have reminded Denise, of Rio de Janeiro. A large mountain that was a dead ringer for the Sugarloaf rose up directly across Lake Lugano from the villa, which was reached by a majestic mile-long avenue of cypresses, perfumed by blooming wisteria, evocative of Arnold Böcklin's *Island of the Dead.* Heini's father, "Big Heinrich," had bought the estate in 1932 from Prince Leopold of Prussia in a "house sale," taking the villa, its dozen *petits trianons,* its garages full of Bentleys and Isotta Fraschinis, and all its curated contents, all in exchange for one Watteau, the Baron told me: *The Clown,* now in Washington's National Gallery. In 1936 Thyssen *père* built a museum building here modeled after the Neue Pinakothek in Munich.

We had a baronial lunch, with too much wine, which was too noble to refuse, with the Baron and Denise, who spoke together in English, while he spoke to Isabel and me in French. Then he spoke to Sandor Berkes, his current curator, in German. Berkes bowed and scraped and addressed his boss as "Herr Baron," like in a bad movie. Berkes, an elderly Hungarian whom Peter Zervudachi had told me I would be replacing, clearly hadn't been clued in that his job was in jeopardy. He regarded me with an instant suspicion worthy of the gypsies in his homeland. We also met the Baron's private secretary, Dr. Joseph Groh, who spoke to the Baron in German and to Berkes in their native Hungarian. Then there was a very English-style liveried butler, a veritable Jeeves, except he was an Italian named Giorgio who spoke to the Baron in French. The Villa Favorita seemed like a Tower of Babel with a cast from the popular American TV show *The Munsters.*

After lunch, Denise vanished, and a seemingly relieved and more relaxed Baron gave Isabel and me a grand tour of the museum. I was breathless. This was Art History 101, the greatest hits from the Renaissance to the Post-Impressionists, the masterpieces we had studied in the Works of Art course. What paintings stayed in my mind? All of them. My mind was blown. Maybe the Ghirlandaio portrait of Giovanna Tornabuoni haunted me the most. Here was the quintessential Florentine Renaissance painting of a woman, who held the keys to the city and whose beauty embodied everything feminine that I was attracted to. Maybe it reminded me of Isabel.

There was also the unforgettable huge Carpaccio *Knight in Armour,* based on the legend of Charlemagne's chief general Roland de Roncevaux. And there was Holbein's *Henry VIII,* which would have hung in Buckingham Palace had the Thyssens not outbid the Windsors for it. Apropos of Buckingham Palace, the Holbein had been acquired by Big Heinrich from Lord Spencer, the grandfather of the future Princess Diana. The rumor was that Lord Spencer had used the proceeds of the sale to purchase a Bugatti. When John Spencer, Diana's father, came to visit the villa, I showed him the collection and couldn't resist asking him about the Bugatti story. With classic English self-deprecation, this Lord Spencer replied that the tale was not true. "He sold it to pay for my education," he said, setting the record straight, and then added, "But I don't think it was worth it."

Heini showed a lot of filial piety for his father, whom he described as a shrewd bargain hunter, picking over the spoils of great American collections in the aftermath of the Wall Street Crash in 1929. "I thought I could live my life without having to buy another painting again," he said about his father's vast collection of Old Masters. But when Big Heinrich died in 1947, Heini told me, it was easier to buy out his siblings' shares of the collection than to fight with them over money. "And then I got hooked." Hence his collection, in which he claimed to buy a new painting at least every week, and on some weeks, every day.

The Baron told us his father's philosophy was that "art stopped at the eighteenth century." And while his own philosophy of acquisition was to buy only works by dead artists, he described to us how he was able to kick his Old Master addiction. He owed his withdrawal to his third wife, Fiona, the Scottish supermodel, who, like Denise, had a love for art. She had dragged Heini, kicking and screaming, if you could imagine this grand seigneur ever complaining, to an exhibit in a Stuttgart art gallery of prewar German "degenerate art" that had been banned by the Third Reich. The dealer, Roman Norbert Ketterer, was a champion of such great "lost" German artists as Kirchner and Beckmann. Fiona was obsessed with the watercolors of another German "degenerate" master, Emil Nolde, and the Baron found her passion contagious and embarked on what would become his current buying rampage, which now included American artists from Whistler to Homer to Remington. "American art doesn't begin with Jackson Pollock," he said. He also seemed a little wistful for Fiona, especially given the tension we sensed with Denise. It was a vulnerability I found endearing

We had some more drinks before the Falcon took us back to Geneva. To women and art should have been added wine on the list of the Baron's connoisseurships. To say Heini drank a lot was an understatement. Over still another rare vintage, he confessed, with a self-deprecating wink in the style of Peter Wilson, that his father had died of alcoholism. Bornemisza, he said, referring to his Hungarian title, is translated "Doesn't drink wine." He said it should be "Drinks only wine." He liked to joke about his drinking, about his troubles with women, about his addiction to art. The Baron was a genuinely funny guy.

As we flew back to Geneva on the Falcon, all I could think about was the art, the wonderful art, and what a surprisingly likeable man the Baron was, contrary to all the negative gossip, mostly derived from people who had never met him. Those thoughts didn't cross my mind, only the art. Beauty was truth, truth beauty. Still, the downside for me was the prospect of being a *concierge de luxe*. Why would I be any different from Sandor Berkes, who must have also been young and ambitious when he signed on?

My mother's exhortation to not look my Sotheby's gift horse in the mouth was not only ringing in my ears but burning my eyes. Mother had written a long, serious letter reminding me of my new parental and conjugal responsibilities. The job with the Baron was for a young, single version of the Baron, someone footloose and fancy free, without dependent mouths to feed. She was living proof that you didn't have to be a Jewish mother to lay a guilt trip on your son. There was a Three Dog Night song of the era called "Mama Told Me Not to Come." That was shaping up as my theme song. I went back to the reality of my basement office at the Hôtel de Saussure.

Before I could compose my note of regret, the Baron was back on the phone. He invited me to come up to St. Moritz, where he had a chalet, for a mano-a-mano over our future together. Unlike my mother, Isabel urged me to go. She had no fear of making bold decisions. After all, she had made the bold move of marrying me. Also weighing on me was a call I received from Jurg Wille in Zurich telling me that if I didn't take the job with the Baron, he was planning to propose *his son,* who was also working for Sotheby's. That alone was proof of how covetable this job actually was; it also spurred my competitive instincts.

I got into my Peugeot and made the mountain drive to the most social of all ski resorts. I don't remember where I stayed, but it definitely wasn't the Palace Hotel, the ski lodge of the stars. I suppose I wanted to avoid taking the Baron's largesse and talk to him candidly about my anxieties. I didn't have to bring them up. The Baron had read my mind. He assured me that my position would in no way be anything like that of Sandor Berkes. He wanted me precisely because I was young, fresh, and unbiased. I would have immense freedom and liberty to find him the best art on earth.

Having undergone his baptism of fire into modern art through Fiona's embrace of the "degenerates," the Baron was no longer limited to Old Masters. He could buy *anything,* and he wanted *everything.* And I would be his truffle hound, his adviser, his right-hand man of art. Financially, not only would I be earning more than I was making at Sotheby's, but also I would have no rent to worry about. We would live for free in a satellite villa on the grounds of the estate.

So I crossed the Rubicon and said yes to the Baron and farewell to Sotheby's. Luckily for me, my *au revoir* was returned with an *à bientôt.* I received the kindest letter from Marcus Linell, a porcelain expert who had started as a porter and risen dramatically to become the firm's youngest director. He assured me the door to Sotheby's would always be open for me to return. Although it might have been sheer politeness, I took it to heart as a safety net.

Before I had made my decision, I had sought the counsel of Peter Wilson, though that was the equivalent of seeking the counsel of the Sphinx. He would never proffer a direct reply to such a momentous request for career advice. Yet just as Peter Zervudachi and François Daulte wanted to "plant" me with the Baron, it was logical that Sotheby's, too, saw the value of having one of their loyal subjects in-house with the world's most important collector.

I did not consult with my initial art adviser, Ernst Beyeler. The Baron was not a part of the itinerary he had set out for me. Beyeler was the one dealer in the world who did not pursue the Baron, yet as the Swiss cynosure, he might have expected to have been Heini's main art man. I think Beyeler was too grand to be pursuing anyone and probably thought that Heini should have been pursuing him. And because Heini rarely passed through Basel, their paths did not cross. As we know, the Baron only "pursued" women, so the two art titans never developed that expected symbiosis.

So off we went to Lugano. Because the Baron was having the gatehouse that would be our home redecorated for us, for the first few weeks we were housed in imperial splendor in one of the villa's guesthouses, with hot and cold running butlers and the most amazing food. I wish my first few workweeks had been as pleasant as our living arrangements. There was instant bad blood with Sandor, who had not been told about my arrival until all the locks were changed on his office.

My very first assignment was to accompany Sandor to Milan to courier a Thyssen painting on loan to the Brera Museum there. I rode beside a seething Sandor as we followed the truck bearing the painting on the *autostrada,* all the Grand Prix–style Italian drivers spitting and cursing at us for driving so slowly. I had flashbacks to *Annie Hall,* which had recently come out, and the scene where Woody Allen takes a white-knuckle ride with the insane Christopher Walken, who moments earlier had confided in him about thoughts of committing suicide by driving into opposing traffic. I feared Sandor, stripped of his position, might want to exit in a fireball of glory, taking his nemesis, me, with him. After surviving the trip, I was relieved to be alive, but still felt like a delivery boy.

Then Sandor began training me on how to open and close the museum. At four forty-five, right on the dot, he would bang a gong and then announce into his microphone that the galleries would close in fifteen minutes. He repeated this at five-minute intervals until all the visitors had been cleared out. I saw this as my duty for the rest of my life, and rued the day I didn't listen to my mother. But then the Baron, who often seemed clairvoyant, sensed my misery and put Sandor out of his, giving him a life estate in a small house on the property and a lifetime stipend as well. I never had to bang the gong again.

Meanwhile, Isabel seemed to spend what would be our entire seven-year tenure at the Villa Favorita bearing fruit. Our firstborn, Alban, we brought with us, but our other three children, Charles, Loyse, and Balthasar, were all conceived and born on the estate. We were deeply flattered when the Baron asked to be Balthasar's godfather, and even more flattered when he moved his secretary, Dr. Groh, out of his capacious life-estate viila to another residence, and moved us in to give us the room we needed. "You fucked yourself out of the gatehouse" was how the Baron put it to me. He may have been grand, but he was always funny.

The Baron, a born host who couldn't bear us as newcomers to be alone, and couldn't bear being alone himself, insisted we have every lunch and dinner with him in the villa, not in the main dining room, which was reserved for state occasions, but at a round table upstairs off a terrace overlooking the lake. At first Denise would sometimes join us, but quickly it became our own little ménage à trois. Denise and Heini may have looked regal as a couple, but they had totally different metabolisms. Despite her fair blondness, Denise had a totally Latin sense of time, *mañana*, to the tenth power. The Baron was scrupulously punctual, particularly to the many events given in his honor around the world. Denise would infuriate him by showing up two hours late to these highly scripted honoraria. Eventually she stopped coming altogether, much to the Baron's relief.

Soon after we settled in, the Baron gave us a demonstration of

F. Scott Fitzgerald's quote about the very rich: "They are different from you and me." It was a beautiful hot day, and after breakfast, apropos of nothing, the Baron said, "Let's fly to Venice today." There was a Canaletto exhibition at the Palazzo Cini he thought Isabel and I might enjoy seeing. He called for the plane, and off we went. Venice was brutally hot and humid, so after the art he took us to Harry's Bar, which the Baron said had the best air-conditioning in the city and where I tasted my first—and tenth—Bellini. I just thought this was a delicious little fresh peach drink to beat the heat, which it did. I had no idea how much the sweetness concealed the alcohol within, that is, until they had to nearly carry me back to the Falcon. The Baron would often live this way, breakfast in London, lunch in Amsterdam, a museum show in Paris, dinner in Rome. A lot of hedge-fund types and oligarchs and other big art collectors live this way today, but not then. Then the Baron was one of the few really huge art collectors, and he was one of the only members of the Jet Set with his own jet.

Back in Lugano, every meal, served by the butler and a retinue of waiters and stewards, was like eating at Maxim's or La Tour d'Argent, Michelin three-star gastronomy and noble wines with every course. I was lucky I didn't end up with gout. I did gain weight; how could I not. If I fucked myself out of the gatehouse and into the villa proper, I also ate myself out of Gieves and Hawkes and into Caraceni. These meals with the Baron might seem like a real-life Euro version of *Citizen Kane*. William Randolph Hearst, in his lonely dotage, would take similar young audiences captive at San Simeon and rant war stories at them all night, driving them crazy over Lucullan feasts. Or they might evoke *Sunset Boulevard*, with the Baron as Norma Desmond, reminiscing about a faded glory that she thought was still ongoing. But it wasn't like that. The Baron was at the height of his glory. There was nothing faded or senile or delusional about him. He was great fun, and the meals were an education in the worlds of power, politics, finance, and culture.

12

ME AND THE BARON

———————————

Without being the slightest bit defensive about his family's background and wartime activities, he addressed the notorious rumors head-on and turned them on their head, just as he had put me at ease about not replacing Sandor but becoming a new asset in my own right. His favorite joke, which was straight out of New York's Borscht Belt comedy circuit, was "My family's in iron and steel. My mother irons and my father steals." Heini went on, a bit more seriously, to tell us about his grandfather August Thyssen, the family patriarch, who was a Rhineland peasant who made his fortune in chicken wire and then traded up to coal, iron, and steel, until the only rivals he had in Europe were the Krupps, the *à clef* depraved Nazi dynasty in Visconti's *The Damned*. The Thyssens, by comparison, were as innocent as the Boy Scouts.

Although the Thyssen fortune—and its bad associations—came from Germany, the Baron's roots were elsewhere. His father, Heinrich, August's intellectual (as opposed to industrial) second son, had fled Germany to get away from his own father's long shadow and steel mills. He went to study in England, earning a doctorate in philosophy at the University of London. He then moved to Hungary and married a half-American baroness. Heini's grandmother on his mother's side was an American from Delaware.

Proud of his Yankee ties, Heini told us a great story how she and his grandfather had fooled each other into marriage. The Hungarian baron thought he was getting a Du Pont heiress, which she was definitely not. The American girl thought she was getting the Count of Monte Cristo, or some typically American Gilded Age fantasy of what a European aristocrat was. Alas, neither had a penny. All the family had to show for their misbegotten ambitions was a dubious hereditary title, which even Hungary had ceased to recognize. Nonetheless, Heinrich and now Heini were always "the Baron," and they invested that title with far more pomp and ceremony than it would have ever had without them.

When August Thyssen died in the 1920s, his empire was divided between his two sons Fritz and Heinrich. Fritz, the eldest, got the German steel mills, Heinrich the rest of the world. Heinrich set up his international headquarters in The Hague, at whose beach resort of Scheveningen Heini was born in 1921. The bulk of the non-German Thyssen fortune was concentrated in shipbuilding and banking; the bulk of Heinrich's true interests lay in Old Master collecting. For Fritz Thyssen, on the other hand, his pet avocation was kingmaking, and it was his influence, as the richest titan in post–World War I Germany, that propelled Hitler to the Führerhood. However, by the late thirties, Fritz, the Baron told us, had realized that he had created a Frankenstein.

When he expressed his horror at the treatment of Jews on *Kristallnacht* to his friend Hermann Göring, the reigning Nazi aesthete and art maven, Göring expelled him from the Nazi Party, nationalized his steel mills, and confiscated his art collection, which, like his brother Heinrich's, was one of the world's best. Fritz fled to Vichy France en route to Argentina, but the Vichyites betrayed him and delivered him back to the Nazis. In the cruelest twist of fate, he was sent to two concentration camps, Sachsenhausen and then Dachau, where he wrote a memoir that was published in America under the title *I Paid Hitler.*

After the war, Fritz's mea culpa wasn't culpa enough for the Allies. They had him tried. He was found guilty of being "a minor Nazi," as opposed to a "major Nazi" like Adolf Eichmann. The court didn't send him back to prison, but it fined him $100,000 as reparations for slave-labor abuses. He was perhaps the only high-profile German to be punished by both sides in World War II. In 1950 he finally made it to Buenos Aires, where he died of a heart attack the next year.

Heini had an older sister, Margit, who lived in a twelfth-century castle in the Austro-Hungarian town of Rechnitz. Margit had married the destitute Count Ivan Batthyany and lived a long, gay life raising Thoroughbreds, riding to the hounds, and hunting game. She was ten years older than Heini, so when I met her it was late in her life. At that time of declining health, she had fallen under the spell of a young doctor named Scheiffelbein. Just as Heini was a doppelganger for his father, Margit was the female double of both Heini and Heinrich, though that dominating pure patrician look played better in the masculine mode than it did in the feminine.

Heini and Margit had another sibling, Gabrielle, Baroness Bentinck, whom I also met, and who did not overly resemble her brother or sister. Gaby, as she was known, was the widow of the Dutch ambassador to France. The Bentincks were a grand family with royal branches both in Holland and Britain. Gaby had a unique way of being a great patron of the arts without having a clue who the artists were. One night at a Paris party, she sat next to a man who was introduced to her only as a "painter." She then went on about her father and brother and the Thyssens as the best friends of art since the Medicis. She assumed the man was a struggling artist. "Maybe we can help you," she suggested. "What's your name?" "Marc Chagall," the man answered. Having heard that story from Heini, I was very amused when Gaby, sitting next to me at a London party, asked me who the elderly gentleman on the other side was. I whispered in her ear, "Balthus."

Every year as head of the family concern, Heini would prepare and publish an annual report on the family business. Knowing how deadly dull these reports could be, Heini printed a footnote on the bottom of page 20 to the effect of "If you've read this far, call me and I will send you a case of Krug champagne." None of his family ever called him, but that was typical of Heini's dry wit. What I liked most about him was that he didn't take himself seriously at all. He appeared to stand back, away from himself, and watch his crazy, singular, stranger-than-fiction life unfolding and laugh at its soap opera aspects as much as the rest of the world.

Heini's father fared far better in the reputation department than his uncle Fritz. Seeing the rise of Hitler and the vulnerability of his Dutch assets, Big Heinrich stayed as far away from Nazis as he could, finding Swiss refuge in the Villa Favorita and focusing on his art as the world burned. Heini seemed to go overboard in sharing his art. He hated the idea of paintings being *stored*. He wanted his art to be *shared,* even if that sharing was with a single individual.

A case in point here was Heini's fabulous painting by the Russian avant-gardist Natalia Goncharova, which he lent to Paul Volcker, to decorate his office as President Ronald Reagan's chairman of the Federal Reserve. So here was the most important man in capitalism, in a conservative Republican administration, with a radical Russian Communist painting in the place of honor on his office wall in Washington, D.C., donated by a baron whose uncle had put Hitler in power. This was the power of art to build bridges.

The Volcker loan came as part of Art in Embassies, a program instituted at the State Department under the administration of John F. Kennedy, prodded by the art-obsessed Jackie, who believed that sharing art could be a powerful form of diplomacy. Because no one had more art to share or was a bigger sharer than the Baron, he became a mainstay of the program, and a good part of my job was to oversee the Thyssen art that hung in American embassies and consulates all over the world. Perhaps our proudest moment in this regard was in 1985, when Reagan and Gorbachev held their second summit in Geneva (after the first in Reykjavik) to end the Cold War, and Art in Embassies came to us for the "right" paintings to set the mood at the rented villa of the Aga Khan, the locus of the peace talks.

Heini had assembled during my tenure a major collection of American art from the nineteenth century, from Winslow Homer and Childe Hassam on the East Coast to Frederic Remington and Henry Farny in the Wild West. It was a long leap forward from Old Masters, but where the State Department was concerned, when it came to Americana, Art Was Us. Notwithstanding Heini's generosity, he was still a businessman, a big, big businessman who had resurrected his family's shattered empire in the postwar era and made it a colossus once again. Art was a pleasure for him, but it was also an investment. Nothing could valorize a painting more than being on the front page of every paper on earth with the two biggest leaders posing in front of it.

My very first major assignment from the Baron was to travel around the world creating a complete inventory of all his paintings. He had offices in many cities—Bremen, Zurich, Monte Carlo—plus homes in London's Chester Square, St. Moritz, Sardinia, Marbella, Jamaica, and more. Everywhere he had major art. Including the Art in Embassies loans, I had a lot of traveling to do. My first stop was the Baron's new English stately home, Daylesford House, in the Costswolds in Gloucestershire, which he had bought at the urgings of Denise, who loved the world of the English aristocracy. Denise had just had the house redecorated by *the* interior decorator of the moment, Renzo Mongiardino, an Italian former theatrical set designer who had been discovered by Stavros Niarchos to redo his Kulm Hotel in St. Moritz. Once Niarchos "discovered" Mongiardino, so did the rest of the Jet Set. He also had the Kennedy imprimatur, through Lee Radziwill, so he was unstoppable.

Daylesford had been the estate of Warren Hastings, the Viceroy of India, and the home, topped by an onion dome, had an exotic subcontinental aura and décor. I arrived there by myself. Mongiardino had de-Indianized things somewhat, with touches like leather tapestries. The house had a full staff of servants, gardeners, whatever, all there to serve only me and one other guest, a French Jesuit priest named Edouard Gueydan who was enrolled in Fribourg University in Switzerland when Heini had gone there to study law, about as enthusiastically as I had at Geneva. Interestingly, as a young man Heini had no interest at all in art, until his father died and bequeathed him all the Old Masters.

Father Gueydan was tall and cut a striking figure in his clerical collar and black garb, always walking around with a large leather-bound Bible in his hand. He did not practice any form of ascetic renunciation, at least not during our stay at Daylesford. Instead we followed what my friend photographer Mario Testino has called the see-food diet. You see food, you eat it. And oh, what we saw: lobsters, caviar, foie gras, truffles, Scottish beef and salmon, and on and on. Father Gueydan further amused me by taking out the Baron's priceless collection of Augsburg silver and using it for an impromptu mass for the staff.

After my Jules Verne of an inventory, I was barely back in Lugano before the Baron insisted that I accompany him on a series of trips that would have exhausted a Pan Am stewardess. We went to Prague with

Ira von Fürstenberg and her brother Egon, who had gotten divorced from Diane after the global success of her wrap dress. This was Cold War Iron Curtain Prague, before the city became the Paris of the East. We met the writer Václav Havel, before he became president, and his best friend and adviser, Prince Karel Von Schwarzenberg, who would become Havel's chancellor following the Velvet Revolution in 1989. The Prince was a distant cousin of Princess Ira and Prince Egon, and it was amusing seeing such a scion of the most ancient European aristocracy so wrapped up in radical changes. After Prague, we went to Vienna and stayed (where else?) at the Palais Schwarzenberg.

Then Heini took me on two major museum tours of the United States. First he sent his collection of Old Masters to nine cities, starting with the National Gallery in Washington and ending with the Met in New York. I think Denise may have showed up in Washington, arrived fashionably and infuriatingly (to Heini) late, then vanished until she did a repeat performance in New York. More fun was our American heartland tour to six "provincial museums," including those in places like Oklahoma City, Omaha, and San Diego. Heini loved the local color, even though he looked the odd man out in his travel uniform of blue blazer, gray slacks, white shirt, red and blue striped tie, and black loafers.

Heini didn't need to be wearing the colors of Old Glory to endear himself to Americans. People in this land of capitalism were dying to meet one of the richest men in the world. In Oklahoma City, we went to a club called Cowgirls at the height of the *Urban Cowboy* mechanical bull craze. The lovely local girls couldn't seduce Heini onto the bull, but they did teach us how to square dance, which in time would result in one of his most memorable parties, for Henry Ford, where the Villa Favorita was transformed into the Little House on the Prairie.

We had a different sort of adventure in Omaha. As soon as we arrived, we got a distressed call from our American organizer, Fred Cody, that we had " a serious problem." A large protest was being planned in front of the Omaha museum against this exhibition of "Nazi Art." Heini was the epitome of grace under pressure. "Just call my friend Simon Wiesenthal," he instructed Fred. "He'll take care of it." And Fred called. And Simon did. Wiesenthal, the famous Nazi hunter, issued a press release that Omaha had the wrong Thyssen in their sights. Fritz was the ex-Nazi, Heinrich the anti-Nazi, and Heini the great friend of the Jews. The protest turned into a virtual parade and a hero's welcome for the Baron, and long lines to see the show.

I can't thank Isabel enough for tolerating my gypsy life with the Baron. Even in Lugano, I was working night and day, though we did have those countless meals together, if not to ourselves. The Baron, whose motto was "Work Hard, Play Hard," was the embodiment of it. Although there were some nights that Giorgio and I literally had to carry him back to his room, the next morning at 7:00 A.M. he was up and completely sober, his razor-sharp mind perfectly focused, eager to buy some more art. The doctors had warned him to stop drinking, but he had paid them no heed. That is, however, until he had a stroke in his early sixties that ended the use of his left arm.

The Baron somehow managed to keep his routine of swimming for hours in the villa's pool or off his yacht, *Hanse* (German for medieval trade guild), which was the only exercise he would countenance. But abstention did not suit this man of profound pleasure. Instead he found a new doctor who told him that the best cure for his hardened arteries was endless amounts of raw garlic, spread on toast. I'm not sure if the doctor was a Transylvanian vampire hunter or not, but the Baron liked the prescription, and the villa—and ourselves—ended up reeking of garlic like a Korean kimchi restaurant.

Stroke or no stroke, nothing could quell the Baron's quest for paintings. He would dog-ear the pages of the books and catalogues in his vast art library whenever he saw something he liked. He assumed that he could acquire anything he wanted. There were countless dog-ears, and it was my task to track these paintings down. This was long before the Internet; the only way to evaluate the paintings, aside from in person, was Ektachrome slides, which were very expensive, $300 each. Every morning we would receive in the mail huge packages of Ektachromes from dealers everywhere. We knew, as Buyer Number One, we had first crack at everything. I then had to do plenty of homework on prices and provenance. Today I'd log on to Artnet. Then it was endless legwork, but very thrilling to be at the center of the market.

It was also very gratifying to be the one person the Baron could trust.

Yes, he knew all the dealers, Daulte, Zervudachi, everyone. But they all had something to sell, they all had an angle. I did not. The closest thing the Baron had to a real Bernard Berenson super-expert to counsel him was his father's Old Masters adviser, Rudolf Heinemann, a Jewish émigré art dealer who fled from Berlin to New York in 1935 and became a leading scholar at the NYU Institute of Fine Arts.

Heinemann had died in 1975 before I arrived at the villa, but when I accompanied the Baron to New York, we would always visit Rudolf's widow, Lore, in her apartment at Fifth Avenue and 72nd Street and luxuriate in her collection of Old Masters, Degas, Cézanne, and other classics. When I returned to Sotheby's after my time with the Baron, I would visit Lore by myself. In her seventies and still very sexy, she would invariably emerge with the back of her dress wide open and ask me to zip her up. Heini would always joke that if I had *unzipped* the dress, I could have gotten her incredible art for Sotheby's to auction.

Now that the Baron was no longer limited to Old Masters, it fell to me to be his eyes and ears in the brave new world of modern art. The Baron's modern collection was sometimes criticized by art critics as not up to the level of his Old Masters. What could be? Besides, the Baron was critic-proof. In his way of standing outside himself, he could only look and laugh at all the fuss. Bad reviews were what happened to someone else. Buying art was Heini's best revenge. He simply loved to buy. If he went to an auction and couldn't get what he had come for, he'd just purchase something else.

Heini was single-minded in his pursuit. Once we were at a dinner party at the American Embassy in Paris given by Reagan's ambassador Evan Galbraith. I had just located a Mondrian that I thought would be a perfect fit for his collection. He agreed. The only catch was that the painting was being auctioned in London at Sotheby's that night. "Let's buy it!" Heini decided over cocktails. He asked Ambassador Galbraith to set up a room with a hotline to Sotheby's. The painting came up for auction in the middle of the dinner. Heini and I left the dinner table and came back with the Mondrian, and a huge smile. Aside from the breach of protocol, Heini changed the dinner's entire agenda by rhapsodizing for the rest of the evening—to a table of art agnostics—about the treasure he had just acquired.

Whatever Heini bought last was precisely what he loved most. After dinner at the villa he'd go up to his office, where his latest *achats* were hung, and stare at them lovingly for hours until he nodded off. With his embarrassment of riches, his own personal inventory system of last in, first admired was what worked for him. In that sense Heini was an artistic serial monogamist. I, on the other hand, was perpetually in love with everything I helped him choose. Playing favorites among master-pieces was too dizzying. Continuous ecstasy was an enviable state of grace. All in all, the Baron's collection, to me, is pretty amazing, a panoramic view of art from the twelfth to the twentieth century with every major painter represented. What other private collector could match that?

Contemporary was still out of the question, with the single exception of Lucian Freud, long before he became the multimillion-dollar man. The Baron had met Freud through Denise's brother, Roberto Shorto, who had a wonderful eye, albeit a terrible nose, given his unfortunate overuse of cocaine. His nickname was Roberto *Snorto*. Roberto con-vinced Heini not only to buy several Freud paintings but also to sit for his own portrait by Freud, who had gambling debts and needed the money. Freud was a terribly slow and deliberate painter. Heini calculated that he did 160 hours of sitting for the portrait, which depicted the Baron with a Watteau in the background that Freud had never seen but copied, in color, from a black-and-white photo I had found and sent to him. A Watteau, remember, had been what Heini's father had gotten the Villa Favorita in exchange for. The worst part for him wasn't the time but rather the climb, up five long flights to Freud's studio in London's Hol-land Park. Heini did enjoy Freud, who, despite his deep associations with England, was actually born in Berlin. Heini would tease Freud for being "more German" than himself.

Another of Roberto Shorto's commissions of a Heini portrait went the way of all flesh. Roberto, who was the quintessence of à la mode, had become friends with Andy Warhol and brought him to Lugano to "do" both the Baron and Denise. This was before I started work there. Denise loved Andy and posing for the photos, which he would then silk-screen into his trademark images. However, one night at dinner, the Baron noticed Andy fiddling with something under the table. What is that, the Baron demanded. Only my cassette recorder, Andy told him. Andy may have recorded everyone, as part of his approach to art and fame, but the Baron would not stand for it. The Baron rarely lost his temper, but this time he exploded and threw Andy out of the villa. The episode confirmed the Baron in his determination to avoid all living artists, on his walls or at his tables.

Heini loved to joke that he preferred paintings to women. "You put them on the wall and they stay silent." He also liked to say that he likewise preferred Old Masters to old mistresses. Feminists would not have been amused, though Denise was no feminist.

She was, however, a shrewd operator in the art world. In the eighties, when she and Heini embarked on one of the most acrimonious divorces in the annals of conjugality, it was alleged that Denise and her close friend the recently departed Italian art dealer Franco Rappetti conspired to shake down galleries who sold to the Baron for commissions as high as 50 percent, secretly added to the sales price. After all, the Baron's wallet, as economists would say, was infinitely elastic. What was money, when you had it all, where beauty was concerned?

The New York dealer who somehow managed to charm Heini the most was the louchest of the lot. His name was Andrew Crispo. As the lover of a pantheon of important homosexuals ranging from Liberace to Henry McIlhenny, the chairman of the Philadelphia Museum of Art, Crispo had hustled his way from a Philadelphia orphanage to a deluxe gallery in the Fuller Building at 57th Street and Madison Avenue, the Tower of Babel of the uptown New York art world. No commission kickback was too large to pay to get the Baron as a client. In 1978, just before I started with the Baron, Rappetti was found dead on New York's West 58th Street, impaled on the roof of a Volkswagen camper eleven stories below the window from which he was said to have jumped. Arrangements with the society undertaker Frank E. Campbell were made by Andrew Crispo, who would be tried for murder in the eighties, for the S&M torture and execution of his handsome Norwegian assistant. He was acquitted, leaving another assistant as the fall guy, only to later go to prison for tax evasion.

After Rappetti's death, the Baron continued to deal with Crispo, if only because he had the goods. With the Baron as his top client, Crispo had no trouble getting great paintings to sell. The death of Rudolf Heine-mann in 1975 in some ways freed Heini up and opened his mind to new art. Heinemann would have never countenanced a lot of the work he bought through Crispo. That was precisely why Heini continued buy-ing from Crispo, playing the rebellious son against Heinemann's stern father/authority figure.

Nevertheless, the Baron still found himself other dealers. The prime qualification of one of them was that he wasn't even a dealer. Marco Grassi was a young Italian who had studied at Columbia and Princeton before returning to Florence to become an art restorer. Heini had met him there and asked him to restore a Renaissance bust; Grassi identified it as a fake and refused the commission. That endeared him to Heini. Then there was Heini's backup New York dealer, Larry Fleisch-man, who was Duveen compared to Andrew Crispo. Fleischman, head of New York's Kennedy Galleries, and Crispo despised each other. Each wanted to be Heini's main man and only man.

Fleischman was the master of the gimmick. He founded something called the Friends of American Art and Religion as a way to get Heini to show his art at the Vatican. And it worked. Heini showed his American art there, although it had absolutely no religious content. Whatever, Heini and Fleischman got an audience with Pope John Paul II. How-ever, Fleischman was shocked and horrified when he went into the papal chambers and found himself face-to-face not only with Satan incarnate, Andrew Crispo, but also Satan's lawyer, the New York demon fixer Roy Cohn. Surprise! I still recall being around when a photo of Archbishop Marcinkus, the head of the Vatican Bank and a key figure in the Banco Ambrosiano scandal, was taken with his arms around Crispo and Cohn. Marcinkus was a towering figure. Crispo and Cohn were half his size. It was an unholy trio if ever there was one.

Eventually, the Baron finally decided to rationalize his purchasing decisions, and that's when I entered the picture. Given this turbulent entry into modern art, the Baron clearly needed someone knowledge-able and aboveboard to oversee and objectify the purchasing process. If anybody needed a curator, to protect him from himself, it was Heini. He probably needed more than a curator; he needed a combination of Sigmund Freud, Superman, and the Pope. I was blissfully ignorant of all the Denise-related Sturm und Drang. If I had known, I would have probably heeded my mother's advice. But here I was, in medias res. The madness was supposedly behind Heini, but it was definitely ahead for me.

13

THE MERRY WIVES
OF HEINI; OR, THE MAKING
OF A COLLECTOR

I was not much more of a sportsman than the Baron. My main exercise was walking the long cypress-shaded mile from the Villa Favorita main house to our gatehouse abode. I needed at least that to walk off some of the haute cuisine I was eating as a steady diet that might have been conjured up by Escoffier himself. One day my promenade was interrupted by a taxi whose driver pulled up beside me and stopped. The back window was rolled down, and a stunning blond woman in her forties, and perfectly so, asked if she was on the right path. This woman, who was a cross between Catherine Deneuve and Susan Sarandon and had a Spanish accent, didn't introduce herself. She didn't see the need. She was on a mission, and she had her eyes on the road and on the prize. This was my first encounter with the lady of Spain—Miss Spain, in fact, 1961—Carmen Cervera, who would win the prize and become the next Baroness Thyssen.

There was no shortage of beautiful women who came to see the Baron. No man was a bigger catch. This was around 1984; he was still married to Denise, but as she was wife number four, hope sprang eternal in the aspirant category that there could likely be a number five. He could have hired a retinue of fancy call girls from Madame Claude, who indeed supplied such short-term fantasies to a lot of the Jet Set playboys I had catered to at Sotheby's in Monte Carlo. But call girls were not the Baron's style. He was an old fashioned *vert-gallant* who thrived on chivalry, courtship, and the thrill of the chase. If he hadn't, Madame Claude might have saved him hundreds of millions of dollars.

I had been at the Baron's fifth wedding, to "Tita," as Carmen was known to all, in 1985. It had taken place in the little town hall of Moreton-in-Marsh, the nearest constabulary to the Daylesford stately home. There was a horde of paparazzi, a veritable swarm of locusts with cameras. You would have thought they were staking out Paul McCartney or Mick Jagger rather than a sixty-something Swiss art collector. A week later in Lugano, I had walked to the Villa Favorita's nearest newsstand to get the Sunday papers when I was stopped dead in my tracks by the cover of a German news magazine. There in living color was a large photo of Tita basically naked by a swimming pool, with a garden hose wrapped around her lush torso like a serpent in the Garden of Eden. The headline: "Ooh! La La! The New Baroness." I bought the magazine as a sort of souvenir, but I had no self-destructive intention to show it to the Baron. Back at the villa, however, the Baron was way ahead of me. He welcomed me proudly holding the magazine. "Doesn't she look *amazing*?" he exulted.

How did Carmen Cervera, a middle-class girl from Barcelona, win the conjugal version of the Irish Sweepstakes? Yes, she was indeed a beauty contest winner. But that was two decades before. Yes, she had been married to a movie star. But that star was Lex Barker, the tenth *Tarzan,* back in the early fifties. He wasn't Clark Gable or Cary Grant. He wasn't even Johnny Weissmuller, the Tarzan *par excellence.* The Baron could have had the current Miss Universe, or any number of Hollywood starlets, or top models, or society trophies, or real princesses. He'd already had all those.

What did Carmen have? The real question is what did Heini want, in women and in art, and the best answer is to meet the prior Baronesses to see what made Heini run. Aside from his second wife, who was no longer alive, I had met all the wives. What impressed me most was what exemplary women all of them were, and how different each was from the next. In love and in art, Baron Thyssen could never be accused of being a slave to convention or to type. He knew beauty could take a thousand forms. His wives took five of them.

Heini's first marriage, in 1946, when he was twenty-four, was the one that might have been expected of a handsome young aristocrat. He married an equally decorative young aristocrat, at the time a student in Lausanne, with a pedigree far deeper and sturdier than his own. This was the Princess Maria Teresa of Lippe, a fellow Catholic and the holder of an Austrian title that went back to the Holy Roman Empire. Born in Vienna, the tall and stately Princess was related to many of the great titles of Europe, including her uncle Prince Bernhard of the Netherlands, where the Thyssen shipyards were located; they had been all but destroyed in the war and would need influential local patronage to be rebuilt. Heini got it both through Teresa and through his sister Gaby, who married a dynastic Dutch Bentinck.

That Teresa's noble family was, like so many others in Europe, on the precipice of poverty was an impediment only to Heini's fortune-hunter-phobic father, Heinrich. But Big Heinrich was getting increasingly senile and soon died, in 1947. With Uncle Fritz also in declining health, the Thyssen empire fell into the hands of young Heini, whose mandate was to pick up the pieces, which, notwithstanding meager expectations, he would do brilliantly.

Heini quickly got away from the Nazi-stigmatized iron, steel, and armaments business and focused on shipping and banking, as well as taking a large stake in the Heineken brewery colossus, which greatly appealed to the drinker in him. He also diversified into other investments, widely ranging from American real estate and glassmaking (Indian Head) to the Rotterdam harbor to a Japanese cardboard factory to Australian sheep farms. Eventually his Thyssen-Bornemisza Group, which he headquartered in Monaco, would employ over ten thousand people and become one of the first global conglomerates. Heini was no mere heir, no mere art collector. He was a tycoon.

As a swashbuckling captain of industry, Heini may have felt constrained by the marital bonds of his young princess bride, who had quickly borne him an heir, Georg Heinrich. When I met Teresa, she was the Princess Fürstenberg, a cousin by marriage of Ira and Egon, whom I had traveled with. She was regal, but she felt like family at the same time. She had stayed friends with the Baron, in the most civilized way. Whatever her age, she was a great beauty with great allure. Who could have asked for anything more in a woman? Heini Thyssen, that's who.

By 1951, it was wild oats time, and not just for Heini. This was the heyday of the postwar playboy, and Heini joined a crew of rich bon-vivant lady killers that included the Italian auto heir Gianni Agnelli, the Dominican serial heiress-marrier Porfirio Rubirosa, the Russian count and Hollywood costume designer Oleg Cassini, the Brazilian in-dustrialist "Baby" Pignatari, the Ismaili Muslim holy man/racehorse breeder Aly Khan, and other staples of the gossip columns that vicari-ously fascinated the world of the fifties the way reality shows do today.

Heini Thyssen met the first sexy serpent in his Garden of Eden in 1951 in Paris. This was the beyond-gorgeous Nina Dyer, a twenty-one-year-old model who had used her looks and polymorphously perverse sexuality to propel herself from Liverpool to the Côte d'Azur to become one of the poster girls for the proto–Jet Set. Nina Sheila Dyer's beauty was high cheekbone exotic. A kinky version of the Anglo-Indian movie star Merle Oberon, Nina was born in Ceylon (now Sri Lanka), her father an Englishman who worked on a tea plantation, her mother Indian. At twenty she moved to Liverpool, where, hoping to be an actress, she attended drama school. Those hopes unrealistic, she moved to London and began modeling bathing suits. Because of her Indian half, the snooty, imperial Brits refused to appreciate her beauty and barred her from magazine covers. She wasn't "pure" enough.

Across the Channel, however, Paris embraced her. She became a top model for Pierre Balmain, then a design superstar, which led to invita-tions to all the right yachts and villas on the Côte d'Azur, and inevitably to the rightest of the right, Heini Thyssen. By the time they met, the Baron was bored stiff with the *Almanach de Gotha* castle set of his wife Teresa. He was ready for a walk on the wild side, and here was Nina to take him for it.

After a lavish three-year affair, in which he was forced to compete for Nina's favors with the French actor/auteur/lothario Christian Marquand, the best friend of Marlon Brando and namesake of his son, and the con-sort of such screen gems as Brigitte Bardot and Jane Fonda. Proving his commitment despite Nina's infertility, Heini, who didn't need an-other heir, divorced Teresa and flew to Colombo, Ceylon, in 1954 on a

BOAC de Havilland Comet, the first commercial jet, for his wedding to Nina, in what were literally the first Jet Set nuptials. Teresa, who stayed happily grounded in the Old World, soon remarried one of her own, a von Furstenberg cousin of Heini's good friend Princess Ira. Even before he needed a wedding gift, Heini had made the grand gesture of buying Nina her own Caribbean paradise, Monkey Island, off Jamaica, where he already had a mainland villa, Alligator Head. He also gifted her with two black leopards, which Nina insisted live with their six large barking dogs in their Paris suite at the then-luxe Queen Elizabeth Hotel off the Avenue George V. The animal gift was the gift that kept on giving, in the worst possible way. The older servants at the Villa Favorita would regale me with stories of Nina walking those leopards on diamond-studded leashes on the villa grounds. The Baron, who had been raised in the most controlled environment of peace and quiet, was driven nearly as crazy by the pets as he was by Nina's continued affair with Christian Marquand. He also spent a fortune at Harry Winston to sate Nina's jewelry addiction.

The excitement of being married to Nina and the competition with the actors and artistic types that she favored may have helped turn the Baron into being an art collector. Being an industrialist had cachet but no sex appeal. Wealth and power may have been an aphrodisiac, but, after all, how sexy was J. Paul Getty? Heini, unlike most low-key money men, relished getting his name in the columns, not to mention on the front pages, which he did for his 1955 exhibition at the Metropolitan Museum in New York of a group of his Old Masters, including his Holbein *Henry VIII*. That in turn triggered his first independent purchase of a major work, outside of buying up his siblings' inherited Old Masters. This was Francesco del Cossa's world-famous 1473 *Portrait of a Man with a Ring,* which got him still more favorable publicity. Women seemed to the Baron to love art, and the Baron, who loved women, would use any catnip he could.

Unfortunately in Nina's case, the art may have been necessary but it was not sufficient. After getting into a fistfight in a Paris nightclub with Christian Marquand, and after Nina ran up couture bills of hundreds of thousands of dollars at Balenciaga, Jacques Fath, and Christian Dior, the Baron had had enough. He filed for divorce in the summer of 1956, settling over a million dollars on Nina and letting her keep the millions' worth of large stones, a château outside Paris, and an El Greco for good measure. The main thing Nina had to sacrifice was her title as baroness.

Nina proved resilient. Within a year she had married Aly Khan's son, Sadruddin, who, like the Duke of Windsor, gave up his succession to become the Aga Khan by marrying the divorced woman he loved. Heini was invited to the Geneva wedding. He did not attend. Nina switched from Hungarian baroness to Muslim princess, and took the Muslim name Shirin, or "sweetness." After three years, things turned acrid, and the royal couple divorced. In 1965 Nina committed suicide by taking an overdose of sleeping pills. The night before she died, Heini told me, Nina had telephoned him. He was nowhere he could get the message, and he told me many times, in his cups, how awful he still felt that he might have been able to save Nina's life had he been near a telephone. He genuinely loved her, and felt she also cared for him, citing to me her thoughtfulness in the middle of their divorce. When Heini showed up in court with a terrible cold, Nina berated her lawyer for giving the ailing Baron such a hard time while he was feeling low. That small gesture of kindness was never forgotten.

Heini Thyssen had a thing for models, far more than a thing for princesses. Three months after his divorce from Nina, Baron Thyssen married still another top model, and this one was top of the tops. Even at the dawn of the celebrity-model era of Suzy Parker and Dorian Leigh, Fiona Campbell-Walter, a mainstay of *Vogue,* was the rare fashion model to appear on the cover of *Life* magazine (January 12, 1953), which was the ultimate validator of people in the fifties and sixties before television made it obsolete. Unlike Nina Dyer, whose colonial bloodline made her unsuitable for English taste, the ultra-patrician Fiona Campbell-Walter, the favorite model of "court photographer" Cecil Beaton, was the Platonic ideal of what the Queen herself ought to look like. Plus she had the right pedigree. Her father was one of those rear admirals who seemed to cross my path as if the Royal Navy were full of them.

This Scottish rose was actually born in Auckland, New Zealand, during one of her father's tours of duty. She had met the Baron on a holiday in St. Moritz, and their engagement was said to have lasted all of twelve hours before they wed at the little town hall of Castagnola, a picturesque village on the shores of Lake Lugano. She was twenty-six, he thirty-five, and a press photo that circulated on the front pages of the globe showed him carrying the supermodel in his arms. What no one suspected was that Fiona, not the Baron, had the handful.

Fiona didn't need the money. She was the most highly paid model of her time—and in her most classic photograph, standing on a beach, makeup-free, wrapped only in a Givenchy bath towel, you can see why. Her daily rate was as high as $5,000, which was more then, adjusting for inflation, than what Giselle Bundchen and Kate Moss get today. She *deserved* the cover of *Life*. She was the first mannequin to make modeling socially acceptable. That was why she was all the more a trophy that Heini had to have, just like he had to have that Francesco del Cossa masterpiece. There was no price tag too high for beauty. Luckily for the Baron, Fiona's price tag turned out to be far less than Nina's. She gave him two more heirs, a daughter, Francesca, and a son, Lorne. And, even more important for this story, in her own passion for the German "degenerate" school, she gave him one further push into the art collecting that would make this industrialist an aesthete beyond all others, a unique identity that would last an eternity.

Part of the credit did belong to Fiona for encouraging the Baron in new directions, and playing on his chivalrous commitment to give his wife everything she desired. On the other hand, the Baron was highly competitive. His spending spree on eighteenth- and nineteenth-century paintings was an adjunct of his shipbuilding wars with the golden Greeks, Onassis, Niarchos, Goulandris, all of whom had become major art collectors in the fifties. No Greek spurred Heini to action more than his rival Stavros Niarchos, who made huge headlines in 1957 by buying Edward G. Robinson's Impressionist collection for $2.5 million. Suddenly Heini decided that he, like the Greeks, must have Impressionists. He was as competitive with his art as with his ships, which he was proud to boast were built from scratch in Rotterdam, in contrast to the war-surplus tubs that Niarchos made his fortune shipping oil in. It also didn't hurt Heini's quality image having the world's top model as his wife christening his new ships with the finest champagne.

At the Stuttgart auction that Fiona had dragged him to, Heini ended up setting a world record for a modern German work by buying the Emil Nolde watercolor for $10,000. The Baron was amazed how cheap such record setting could be, and the allure of similar publicity hooked him on auctions and on modern art. He liked Nolde so much he bought a dozen more of his works. In fact, Big Heinrich had owned a large trove of German and other European art of the 1800s. But when he died in 1947, Heini, no connoisseur at this point, sold off all of it.

Now he began buying modern art at a rapid pace, which would accelerate under my watch to the Baron's purchasing a painting nearly every single day. But back in the Fiona years, when his buying began, he bought on average only about ten paintings a year, great paintings for sure, but nothing like the volume to come. Once Heini went out on his own, as opposed to being the prisoner of his father's precepts, he went wild, and he made some highly unlikely acquisitions. One of these was the Jackson Pollock *Brown and Silver I* from 1951. Although Pollock was technically a dead artist and hence allowable under Heini's rules, he was awfully avant-garde for the classical Baron. Heini liked him, however, because of the urban legend surrounding Pollock's East Hampton death: that he took his eyes off the road while dead drunk and getting a blow job in the driver's seat of his Oldsmobile convertible from his girlfriend and fellow artist Ruth Kligman. That was the kind of artist Heini could relate to, so he bought into the legend.

When Fiona and Heini divorced in 1965, the press-baiting Baron told one journalist that if Fiona had just been more unfaithful, that would have spurred him, ever the competitor, to try harder. The reality was that Fiona, just like Heini, had been plenty unfaithful. It was proof that all the beauty and all the money were insufficient glue to keep a perfect couple together. The object of Fiona's straying affection was the object of her secret ambition to become a movie star. You might have thought she would have fallen for a megaproducer like the art collecting Oscar winner Sam Spiegel. But she was looking for love at the same time. Hence she fixated on a dashing but second-tier Hollywood television producer, at a time when television was totally steerage class compared to cinema.

His name was Sheldon Reynolds. He was a rarity at the time, a Hollywood producer operating in Europe long before the jet age made Europe affordable and accessible to the mass of middle-class Americans. Until then, they would have to get Europe from TV, and Sheldon Reynolds catered to that market. He had a hit series, *Foreign Intrigue,* that ran from 1951 to 1955 and spawned a feature film of the same title starring Robert Mitchum. The film was well reviewed but flopped in theaters. Why buy tickets to what you could get for free at home?

When he met Fiona, Reynolds was producing an American situation comedy filmed in England, called *Dick and the Duchess,* starring Patrick O'Neal and British cult horror-film queen Hazel Court. The quintessential non–Ugly American abroad, Sheldon Reynolds was handsome and sophisticated, an epicure, a skier, and a noted dresser who could give the Baron in his Caracenis a run for his money.

The whole divorce from Fiona was something out of an American sitcom about the idle rich, or maybe *The Philadelphia Story.* The non-battling Thyssens announced their upcoming split over cocktails at the bridal suite of the monument to Americans abroad that was the Castellana Hilton in Madrid. As for terms, Heini got off for a song—a million-dollar song, but that was a bargain compared to Nina Dyer's haul. Fiona also got jewels worth another million or so, as well as a Goya and a Monet, as well as custody rights over both children, whom Heini was of course allowed to visit, which he loved to do. And, as a final civilized fillip, Fiona, unlike Nina, was allowed to continue to use the baroness title.

True Greek revenge ensued four years later, in 1969, when Fiona began a front-page affair with Alexander Onassis, the only son of Aristotle Onassis. Alexander was sixteen years Fiona's junior. Alexander had met Fiona when he was twelve, and what adolescent could recover from being smitten by the world's most beautiful woman? By eighteen Alexander had matured into a Greek god who could have anyone. The one he wanted was Fiona.

The age gap wasn't the main problem. Ari Onassis wanted his son to marry a Greek virgin, preferably the daughter of one of his Greek shipping rivals, not the supermodel older ex of his German adversary. Ari did everything in his enormous power to squelch the romance, which included mobilizing the disapproval of his new wife, Jacqueline Kennedy. The Ari-Jackie romance already had a world of detractors to contend with. Sadly, what ended the affair was a fatal seaplane accident in

1973. Fiona never remarried. Sheldon Reynolds eventually married a Hungarian playgirl, who, as Andrea Reynolds, left him for Claus von Bülow in the midst of the murder trial that Reynolds was trying to re-create as a miniseries. As Claus was a pal of Heini's and a fellow bon vivant, I got to meet him and Andrea. While she was lively, highly sensual, and a great storyteller, as a beauty Andrea had to have been a let-down for Sheldon Reynolds after his affair with Fiona.

I met Fiona, too, and still continue to see her. She remains one of the great beauties of all time, with that thick lustrous hair and that face that launched a thousand ships, admirals at the helm. Before I signed on with the Baron, she had asked to meet me to give me some maternal advice. The encounter took place at the Geneva office of Peter Zervu-dachi, who was the prime mover to begin with of my employment by Heini. Meeting Fiona was meeting a legend, and it certainly helped seal the deal. If a woman this fabulous could fall for the Baron, so could I.

When it came to his wives, the Baron let little grass grow between his marriages. Fiona was out in 1965. Denise was in in 1967. They were wed in Lugano in December of that year following an engagement of twenty-three days. Aside from their both having Scottish mothers, Fiona and Denise had virtually nothing in common. Born in 1940 and thus in her late twenties when she met Heini at a Jet Set soirée in Gstaad, Denise was too petite to be a model, but she was sexy enough to be constantly compared to Brigitte Bardot. "Sex kitten" was the term of art, and art was the term of Denise. During their marriage, which ended formally in 1983, Heini had bought over eight hundred paintings, at a staggering velocity of nearly a hundred a year.

Denise was not to the art world born. Her native Brazil was not known as a country of art collectors. When it came to high culture, Rio was not Basel. Having attended a number of fancy finishing schools and women's colleges in both America and Europe, Denise was by far the most educated and cerebral of Heini's wives. Though no one would think of calling her a bookworm, she was totally au courant and clever as a fox. Denise, along with her sisters and her brother, Roberto, were the quintessential international jeunesse dorée. They got around. They knew rich people everywhere, and some of these rich people had art, sometimes great art. They also knew the art dealers who catered to these rich people. Without being especially cultured, the Shortos, because of their great looks and glamour, had privileged access to culture. They were cutting-edge, and Heini, nearing sixty, thrived on their youthful energy, rather than feeling exploited by it.

There was also the financial angle. Heini continued to buy art from Andrew Crispo, who got along well with Roberto and understood how to incentivize this baby brother. Denise had a far bigger picture in mind. She appreciated the fact that great brand-name art could appreciate more than any other assets, and her goal was to maximize the value of the Thyssen estate, which she hoped would one day devolve on her son by the Baron, Alexander Thyssen-Bornemisza, who was born in 1974.

Denise also knew Heini's track record of failed marriages. She was anything but a Pollyanna who thought their love would last forever. Denise may have had fantasies that the Baron might make their little tabula rasa Alexander his sole heir. And after all, hadn't all of Denise's fantasies come true? Why not this? Inheriting the biggest and best art collection of them all would be the greatest legacy she could create for her son. I got to know Alexander, too, who was a shy boy, perhaps somewhat overly protected by his mother, but full of surprises. Once, when he was around ten, we were all in the Lenin suite of the Hotel National, hard by the Kremlin. There was a grand piano in the room. Out of nowhere, Alexander sat down and began playing, like a young Van Cliburn, living proof that culture did indeed run in the Thyssen family.

Being young and "cool," both Denise and Roberto naturally gravitated toward the new, West Broadway rather than Madison Avenue. However, even Madison Avenue itself was gravitating toward the new, the tipping point here being the 1973 Sotheby Parke-Bernet auction of the contemporary art collection of Robert and Ethel Scull, who owned a taxi fleet called Scull's Angels. The fifty paintings, by Johns, de Kooning, Warhol, Rauschenberg, Barnett Newman, et alia, went for a record $2 million. The Scull sale was the first post-sixties auction "happening"; it made Pop Art both chic and hip at the same time and validated it as collectibly respectable for the Jet Set. Peter Wilson, never the snob, couldn't have been more delighted at how the market had expanded, and exploded. Naturally, Wilson himself had planted the bomb, establishing a new Contemporary Department at Sotheby's a few years after taking over Parke-Bernet.

The commercialism deeply offended at least one of its prime beneficiaries, Robert Rauschenberg, who protested the sale outside on Madison Avenue, waving a placard that read SCULL'S A PIG. He was outraged that the Sculls and Sotheby's were reaping hundreds of thousands of dollars for works they paid as little as hundreds for. Of course, he and the other artists soon got over it and got comfortable with being rich. Andrew Crispo, who would have sold Heini his mother, was as happy to commission a Rauschenberg as a Renoir. By the time I arrived, the Baron's collection of modern art was deep enough to enable me to organize a great show of "Modern Masters" that we took on the road to New Zealand and Australia. The Baron enjoyed our antipodean odyssey to the land of his sheep farms every bit as much as showing fifty-seven of his Old Masters at the Met in New York.

After I met Tita for the first time in the villa's driveway, she quickly became a key part of the Baron's life, replacing Denise at "state functions." Again, these people were very "sophisticated," or "European," which were the words, I suppose, for such open marriages. If Denise was a sex kitten, Tita was a sex lioness, a big cat indeed. I'll never forget an early-in-the-affair lunch for twelve Heini gave at the Plaza Athénée. All the eyes of *tout Paris* were on Tita, who was wearing a skirt so short that I thought all she had on was a belt. All those eyes widened when Father Guydon, dressed in his black cassock and wielding his Bible, asked Heini's "dirty dozen" to rise, as he said a long prayer to bless the table. The gourmets of Paris society had surely never seen such a combination of the profane and the sacred at one exclusive table before.

Heini had met Tita through another great character, Manfredo Horowitz, who was the most successful jewelry salesman in the world. Harry Winston's main man in Europe, "Fred" Horowitz was a Polish Jew and a ski champion who had escaped Hitler for Switzerland, where his skill on the slopes and charm with women made him nearly as rich as the Jet Set playboys he sold gems to for their wives and mistresses. With his trademark ski tan and his preternaturally thick blond curls, Fred had his own yacht on the Riviera called the *Diamond D*. Fred's specialty, and his unparalleled talent, was finding goddesses like Tita and introducing them to gods like Heini, sealing and memorializing their love with precious stones, which he of course commissioned. He was Europe's top matchmaker for the rich and famous.

Fred's pièce de résistance where Heini was concerned was the 170-carat Star of Peace, a gargantuan rough diamond; Heini had Fred cut and set it for Denise, then took it away from her and gave it to Tita. The tug-of-war over the gem was fought in the courts in the midst of Heini and Denise's three-year divorce battle. The winner of the contest was Tita, who had a whole photographic series of her wearing the Star shot by Helmut Newton. She would not leave home without it. "You need a strong neck to wear this," Tita joked to me.

A fiery but devout Catholic Catalan from Barcelona, Tita was born not to money, but to ambition. Her father was an engineer. Her parents separated when she was five, and her mother gave her the perfect education for a beauty-pageant aspirant: singing lessons, dancing lessons, English lessons in London. She even had a teenage romance on the Costa Brava with the French Elvis, Johnny Hallyday. Her mother then entered the eighteen-year-old Tita in the Miss Catalonia contest, which she won, and then Miss Spain. Armed with that title, she went on the foreign circuit, peaking when she placed third in a third-rate pageant called Miss International.

Tita did not place in Miss Universe, but that pageant did get her a trip to Miami Beach, where she caught many celebrity eyes, including those of Bob Hope, Dean Martin, and Frank Sinatra, from whom she was "saved" by Marilyn Monroe, who was there attending a cocktail event as Frank's date. When she heard Frank telling Tita off-color Rat Pack jokes that, given her inexperience with English idioms, left her clueless, Marilyn interceded in loco parentis for young Tita and shamed the Chairman of the Board as a dirty old man.

Back in Europe, Tita began doing advertisements for Swiss watches, among other products. On a plane trip to Zurich in 1962, she was thrilled to spot Lex Barker, who, after his Tarzan career fizzled in Hollywood, had resurrected himself as a huge star in Germany, much as would be the case decades later with *Baywatch*'s David Hasselhoff. Unable to contain herself, Tita boldly approached the erstwhile king of the jungle and asked for his autograph. Her courage was rewarded; they were married in 1962. As with Heini Thyssen, Tita would be Lex Barker's fifth wife. Also as with Heini, all of Lex's previous wives were goddesses. One was an heiress and the next three actresses, including two major stars, Arlene Dahl and Lana Turner. Tita, who shared Heini's wicked sense of humor, liked to joke that it was better to be the fifth wife than the third or fourth, because you were far more likely to be the *last*.

There was a lot more to Lex Barker than the iconic looks he displayed from the African jungles to the Via Veneto, the latter as Anita Ekberg's fiancé in Fellini's *La Dolce Vita*. The scion of a prominent Wall Street family, Lex attended Exeter and Princeton before chucking the Establishment first for Broadway, then Hollywood. When Lex married Tita, his wedding presents included roles in two of his less notable German films, *Killer's Carnival* and *Die Slowly, You'll Enjoy It More*. Having studied architecture at Princeton, Lex designed their striking home in the historic Catalan village of Girona, Mas Mañanas (More Tomorrows), where Heini would seek refuge during his divorce battle with Denise.

When Lex died of a sudden heart attack in New York in 1973, Tita assuaged her sorrows by pursuing her unrequited acting ambitions. Yet somehow, she could not elude the stigma of B pictures. Her next husband was a hustling Venezulan producer named Espartico Santoni, whose most notable effort was the 1963 *The Castilian*, starring himself, Frankie Avalon, Cesar Romero, and Broderick Crawford. Subsequent, and even lesser, titles included *Feast of Satan* and *Exorcism's Daughter*. Marrying Santoni in 1975, Tita was the second of the playboy-producer's seven wives. While they were married, she got minor parts in such subminor films as *Night of the Howling Beast*, also entitled *The Werewolf and the Yeti*.

Santoni achieved more success with his nightclubs than his films. He owned two hot spots in Marbella and one called Espartico, in West Hollywood's Boys Town, in the 1980s. Tita's marriage to Santoni ended when it was invalidated on grounds of bigamy. Santoni briefly went to prison for fiscal shenanigans. Nonetheless, Tita landed on her feet. Her looks and charm served her well. She moved in power circles, befriending such Thyssen-level tycoons as Las Vegas's Kirk Kerkorian and English corporate raiders Lord White and Lord Hanson. And then came Heini.

When they met in 1981 in Sardinia, through Fred Horowitz, Tita had just had a son, Borja, with a Spanish film publicist. Heini confounded the gossips of Europe by embracing the boy. At age five, Borja was given a lavish baptism at St. Patrick's Cathedral on Fifth Avenue. He got some of his very fancy friends to step up as godparents: Ann Getty, the art-collecting daughter-in-law of Heini's richest-man rival J. Paul Getty; Alexander Papamarkou, the Greek investment banker; and the Duke of Badajoz, the Spanish aristocrat and brother-in-law of the King of Spain and mainstay of the Prado Museum in Madrid. The next year Borja at five was given the surname Bornemisza-Cervera, and after the Denise divorce, Heini finally adopted him as one of his heirs. Borja eventually became a little baron. What mattered to Heini was love and loyalty, not paternity.

Heini's infatuation with Tita ultimately led to her sharing, or catching, his infatuation with art. How could she not? As Tita displaced Denise as Heini's official consort and escort, she could see how art had gotten him received like a head of state. She had known many rich men, but none had been art collectors. She saw how art was the great validator, saw the huge difference in respect it engendered, far more than money or property alone. When she went with Heini and me on our grand world tours of his exhibitions, she could see firsthand art's ambassadorial qualities. And as time went by and stock markets crashed, and real estate markets, like the ones on her Spanish Costa Brava and Costa del Sol, also crashed, she could see how art kept going up and up and up. Small wonder she got hooked on art.

14

FOREIGN INTRIGUES

You meet the most amazing people in the art world, though not always over caviar at fancy openings in palaces. One day, early in my tenure, before I was certain that I was more than a docent in Caraceni, the Portuguese gatekeeper called me about someone at the entrance to the villa wanting to see the collection. It was winter, and the villa was closed to visitors until April. "He says his name is Hockney," the gatekeeper said to me. "Hockney the painter?" I asked. I then heard the gatekeeper ask the man, "Are you a painter?" Mr. Hockney said yes. "Hockney the painter," the gatekeeper confirmed. "Let him in," I insisted. The gatekeeper thought he was a *house*painter and let him pass.

I, on the other hand, was thrilled that the great artist had dropped by on the spur of the moment. He had been in Milan doing the set decoration for *The Magic Flute* at La Scala. In appreciation of the grand tour I gave him, he invited Isabel and me to the premiere and seated us in the very best box, the Verdi Box. On another occasion, Heini excitedly showed me a letter from Leonard Bernstein, who was coming to Switzerland from New York and was asking for a tour. Heini, disappointed that he would be away and unable to meet the musical genius, graciously gave me his lost opportunity to play host to the man behind *West Side Story*. Full of anticipation, I arranged what amounted to a state visit for Mr. Bernstein. But when the great man arrived, he didn't seem anything at all like the wild-haired, flamboyant conductor/composer I had read about all my life. And in fact he was not. He was Leonard Bernstein, indeed, but not *that* Leonard Bernstein. Instead he was a sedate New York lawyer with a love of art. For me the thrill was gone, but Attorney Bernstein got the tour of a lifetime.

Two important legends I got to know were, on the other hand, cases of what you see is what you get. These were J. Carter Brown and Philippe de Montebello. I doubt that any employee anywhere short of some nation's foreign service, or maybe a Pan Am pilot, had a more globally itinerant job than mine. I was constantly on the road, or more likely in the air, accompanying Heini to meet either heads of museums or heads of state, although often one could not tell one from the other.

If anyone said that America lacked a native aristocracy, Carter Brown would have been Exhibit A of the rebuttal argument. A Rhode Island blue-blooded Yankee, Carter was of the Browns for whom Brown University was named. He was at the top of whatever class he entered, whether at Groton, at Stowe in England, at Harvard, where he headed the glee club and then got one of the first MBAs in "arts administration," an early indication that art was capable of becoming the big business Peter Wilson was hell-bent on making it.

Topping all this, Brown got a master's in art from NYU, apprenticed with Bernard Berenson at I Tatti in Florence, and married a niece of Paul Mellon, the great collector and chair of the National Gallery. Brown was one son-in-law who didn't need nepotism to get his job. His second wife, the daughter of a Cuban sugar baron, was also the granddaughter of the Marquis di Marconi, the Italian nobleman who invented the wireless. It was only fitting that the couple wed, as they did, in Westminster Abbey. Brown loved Heini and wanted as many of his paintings for shows at the National as Heini could spare.

Philippe de Montebello was the French aristo-version of Carter Brown. His father was a count, but his most distinctive bloodline was his consanguinity to the Marquis de Sade, though you'd have never known it from his courtly charm. Almost the same age as Brown, de Montebello also went to Harvard and NYU before making his career at the Met, which he doubled in size and turned into a big business of its own.

The one major collector major directors were courting with the same zeal they did Heini was Armand Hammer, whom I also got to meet at the Villa Favorita. Hammer, the Los Angeles–based chairman of the colossus Occidental Petroleum, was as egomaniacal as Heini was self-effacing. He and his wife arrived in Lugano with their own photographer. Hammer didn't seem like the omniscient connoisseur he was supposed to be. When I showed him our one Caravaggio, all he could say was that the guy who ran the garage in Westwood that fixed his car was also named Caravaggio, Joe Caravaggio, to be exact.

No one could deny what Hammer had accomplished. A doctor, who had barely practiced, and the son of a doctor, Hammer, who insisted on being addressed as *Dr.* Hammer, made his first fortune selling drugs (pharmaceuticals) to the nascent Soviet Union. He and his brother, Victor, alchemized some of this drug money into oil money and, eventually, the classiest money of all, art money. They owned the powerhouse Hammer Galleries on 57th Street. With the possible exception of Norton Simon, Dr. Hammer was the preeminent art collector in Los Angeles.

While Heini liked the idea of building bridges and using art for diplomatic ends, Armand Hammer wanted nothing less than to end the Cold War all by himself, or at least get the sole credit for it. What he really wanted was a Nobel Prize, which was one of the rare accolades in life that ultimately escaped him. Heini (and I) had spent nearly a year engineering a historic exchange of art between the Baron and the Kremlin. Now Carter Brown wanted to show what the Kremlin had let us show in Lugano, and Dr. Hammer had come to see us to, forgive the pun, hammer out a deal to collaborate. When Heini balked, Dr. Hammer seized the credit and headlines by lending his priceless codex of da Vinci drawings to the Russians, who only then would allow the show to come to America. In the end it was all Hammer and no Heini, whose name did not appear in the show's catalogue.

Credit or not, the Russian exchange was one of my proudest moments in working for the Baron. The genesis of the idea was at a dinner party—when was it not?—when the Russian ambassador to Germany, who was a rare Communist art aficionado, told the Baron about the treasure trove of Impressionist paintings in the Pushkin and Hermitage museums. Maybe, the ambassador said, a trade could be worked out to exhibit Heini's Old Masters in Russia in return for the Russians sending an equivalent cache of their wonders to the Villa Favorita. It was an "I'll show you mine if you show me yours" sort of proposal. Heini loved proposals like that and dispatched me to Russia to see what they really had.

My investigative mission had a babysitting component. I had with me Roberto Shorto and the teenage Lorne, the Baron's son with Fiona. This was 1983, long before perestroika and long before oligarchs and the conspicuous consumption of today that had then gone the way of the czars. There were no phones, the tap water was brown, the smell of cheap disinfectant filled the corridors, and the food was inedible, even the borscht. The only good stuff was the caviar and vodka, but I had a minor with me to keep in line. I also had to keep Roberto in line, in view of the one surprise—the superbly beautiful women who were everywhere, offering foreign exchange on the black market, offering themselves on the sex market. In Leningrad we did go to an unexpected futuristic Studio 54–style disco in a factory in the suburbs. All pleasures were secret, by law. The few phones I could find I was certain were tapped. In these Brezhnev days, paranoia was the way of life.

Almost everyone was dubious that the paintings we would see were anything but fakes. There was not a lot of trust between East and West in those days. But I confidently charged ahead. The collection we were targeting had been assembled by two Moscow-based rival art-collecting textile oligarchs who had caught the art bug in Paris at the turn of the twentieth century. Both men were in the "rag trade": Serge Shchukin was a cloth merchant; Ivan Morozov was a textile manufacturer. Both were early adopters of the Impressionists and Post-Impressionists when they were still rejected by the Establishment of the day.

Shchukin became the close friend of Matisse, who also decorated his Moscow town house. Like Heini, Shchukin liked to sit alone in his office, for days at a time, and contemplate his newest purchases. Shchukin's friends didn't "get" Matisse, particularly the huge canvases that would one day become so famous. Shchukin was undeterred. "A madman painted them, and a madman bought them," he said. Also like

Heini, both Russians bought in volume, though Morosov was not a sharer like Heini was, keeping his huge collection to himself. His patronage of Cézanne paralleled Shchukin's of Matisse. Both garment men were victims of the Russian Revolution. As the Bolsheviks seized their collections, the collectors fled to Paris. At least the revolutionaries allowed the art to be shown, in Morosov's confiscated mansion. In 1948 Stalin closed the museum down, for being "bourgeois and cosmopolitan." Under Communism those qualities were crimes against the state. They seemed to remain crimes, from what I could see. Whatever, the art was divided between the Pushkin and the Hermitage.

Our hostess in Moscow was the regal czarina of Russian art, Madame Irina Antonova, who, after five decades, just retired in 2013, at ninety-one, as the director of the Pushkin Museum. She had been placed in this august position in 1961 by Nikita Khrushchev. In her youth she had been romantically involved with pianist Stanislav Richter, and later founded a music festival in his honor at the Pushkin. She spoke perfect English, French, German, and probably more. If you met her, you would never think imperialism was dead in Russia. She was as steely as Catherine the Great.

We also went to the Hermitage in Leningrad, now St. Petersburg, where we were received by the director, Boris Piotrovsky. Piotrovsky was a famous archaeologist specializing in Caucasus, Scythia, and Nubia. He had helped analyze the tomb of King Tut. We needed to be archaeologista to dig up the Shchukin and Morosov works that had been buried in his museum for decades. When Boris died in 1990, his son, Mikhail, an Arabic languages scholar, succeeded him, in a display of nepotism that was anything but Communistic.

I was thrilled to be allowed by Madame Antonova and Dr. Piotrovsky to discover many of these "decadent" paintings in the dark halls and basements of the museums and "liberate" them by bringing them into the sunlight of freedom at the Villa Favorita. I was terribly nervous when the crates arrived. I had been warned by so many paranoid experts that the Russians would try to trick us and send us fakes. But as I set about authenticating the works, my results proved that all such paranoia should have been left back in Moscow. The paintings were all real. The four-month show was the most successful in Swiss history. Nearly half a million visitors came to the villa to see them, not to mention the millions more who saw them after Dr. Hammer appointed himself as their American impresario.

We had an amazing party to celebrate the closing of the exhibit. On the first floor of the villa we had a seated dinner, with all the Gauguins hung on the walls behind the guests. The part of Heini's Hungarian heritage that he loved most was Gypsy music. To that end, we had a favorite Gypsy orchestra led by a wildly demonstrative violinist named Dr. Suscz. Heini may not have been athletic, but you wouldn't know it from the spirited way he danced to Dr. Suscz's wild mazurkas. It was highly amusing seeing the inebriated aristocrats of the world dancing like Hungarian peasants and having the time of their otherwise stuffy lives.

My only fear was that Dr. Suscz's flailing with his violin bow would pierce some of the priceless Gauguins and we would have a Steve Wynn disaster on our hands, plus an international incident with Russia. Fortunately, Dr. Suscz was able to curb his enthusiasm just enough for Lloyd's of London not to have to be called in. At the dinner Heini gave an inebriated toast to the visiting Soviet ambassador, vowing that if the Berlin Wall ever came down, he would gladly donate his entire art collection to Russia. That was how out-of-this-world inconceivable the notion of Communism's fall was at the time. When it happened in 1989, no one reminded Heini of his promise, though his role in uniting East and West through art was a major step on Russia's road to capitalism.

Heini had done so well with the Russian Impressionist show that he responded positively to my latest brainstorm, which was to do a Fabergé egg exhibition with publisher Malcolm Forbes. Forbes had recently bought his eleventh Fabergé egg, which had given him bragging rights for owning one more egg than the Kremlin, which had ten. Forbes was a tough customer who had, in addition to his love of art, a passion for hot-air ballooning. I thus came up with the idea to make a balloon to resemble Forbes's new Fabergé egg. Forbes and Heini both loved the notion. There were two catches. The first was that the master balloon-maker in England that Heini found was too expensive even for Heini. The cost was around $30,000; even billionaires have their limits. But not Malcolm Forbes. Forbes, despite his business magazine, was anything but economical. I tried to negotiate with Malcolm's son Kip, but Daddy held firm. No balloon, no exhibition. I had to yield. The Baron couldn't risk being seen as a cheapskate.

The second catch was that Forbes wanted Heini to go up in the balloon with him, a prospect that Heini could not stomach. The compromise here was using very long ropes to anchor the balloon to earth. The Baron would go up, up, but not away. Back on terra firma, the Baron assuaged his vertigo with Forbes's then-inamorata Elizabeth Taylor. No one was more outwardly conventionally masculine than the star-dating, Harley-riding, balloon-flying Forbes. Hence I was surprised, when I visited his magazine's New York headquarters, to be shown his very private collection of nineteenth-century paintings of naked young men.

The romance with Tita was not just a one-way street in the Baron's direction. Tita was happy to introduce Heini to some of the moguls who had pursued her, and some odd friendships developed. One was with Tita's pal Kirk Kerkorian, the successor to Howard Hughes as the most powerful man in Las Vegas. The only thing I could see that the two men, Kirk and Heini, had in common, aside from their wealth and their affection for Tita, was that both of them were rumored to have dyed their hair. Talk about red carpet. When Kerkorian invited Heini, Tita, and me to Wolfgang Puck's Spago in 1982, when it had just opened atop the Sunset Strip and was by far the most exclusive and star-filled restaurant to hit Hollywood since the Brown Derby, no star (and there were many) got a better table or more fawning reception than the wiry Armenian aviator. Kerkorian graciously gave us his jet to fly to his MGM Grand in Las Vegas. On the flight, we were trying to bid in a phone auction for a Max Beckmann, but we had a bad connection. Kirk made sure the jet landed at the nearest airport so we could play the art game. From the tarmac, we were finally able to get on the line with Sotheby's, but we ultimately decided not to bid when we saw that no one else had and the painting would be "bought in," auction-ese for left unsold. Then we took off again for Vegas. Such was the way the Jet Set played the game of art.

The divorce from Denise was as ugly as those Russian Impressionists were beautiful. Just for the jewelry he had "loaned" her and was attempting to retrieve, Heini was suing Denise for $80 million. At one point Heini had the phone lines at Daylesford disconnected so Denise could not call anyone. At another he had Denise arrested in Vaduz, the capital of Liechtenstein, by charging that she had filled a truck with art and jewelry and absconded across the Swiss border. After a few days in jail, the Liechtenstein authorities let Denise go. Heini's next move to protect his assets from Denise was to establish a Shorto-proof Bermuda trust, under the control of his firstborn son, Georg, whom we all called Heini Junior. He was something of a Mini-Me of the Baron.

The two men may have looked alike but couldn't have been more different. Junior was as retiring as Senior was flamboyant. No Gypsy mazurkas for Georg, who loved only business. He collected art, but only Swiss artists, lived in an austere apartment in Monaco, traveled on commercial flights with only a tiny briefcase, and never tried to emulate the grand-scale social role his father loved playing. In short, he was the perfect steward of his father's financial interests, a bulwark against the rapacity of Denise, and, theoretically, her successor, Tita. Little did anyone realize that in two decades the Bermuda trust would turn into a Bermuda triangle where countless millions of Thyssen dollars would disappear into the coffers of lawyers in one of the biggest family feuds in the annals of aristocracy.

The offspring most the chip off the old block was Heini's daughter, Francesca, by Fiona. Ebullient, outgoing, the life of any party, "Chessie," as she was known, was the toast of the post-Beatles "Swinging London" in the late seventies when she was twenty and I began working for her father. She had dropped out of Le Rosey, the ne-plus-ultra Swiss finishing school, alma mater of the children of usually divorced royalty, which had recently begun admitting women. Roberto Shorto had also attended Le Rosey, in the sixties, and had been expelled for blowing up a campus fountain.

Chessie gave up Switzerland for her mother's London and enrolled at Central Saint Martins, the future alma mater of Stella McCartney, John Galliano, and Alexander McQueen. She quickly became the Paris Hilton of her era, notorious for flashing body parts at drug-filled discos, such as the glam-rock Blitz in Covent Garden, where she met her boyfriend, Blitz majordomo Steve Strange. The Blitz crowd included Boy George, David Bowie, Pete Townshend, and Prince Andrew. Only the latter would have been welcome on the guest list of the Villa Favorita. Chessie and Steve and Prince Andrew and his soft-porn girlfriend Koo Stark would escape the paparazzi for private weekends at the Rottweiler-protected, reporter-proof Daylesford. They also flew to India with Ringo Starr and Barbara Bach to play elephant polo.

Steve Strange was not exactly eligibility material. He was openly bisexual. That was perfectly appropriate for those androgynous times. He was also a heroin addict, fitting those times as well, though Chessie, like Heini, was anything but judgmental. After all, who could have been kinkier than Nina Dyer, whose kinks were Heini's aphrodisiacs? Bitten by the acting bug that had also infected her mother, Chessie later got involved with Michael Douglas. But eventually, her heart belonged to Daddy, and to art, in Chessie's case, contemporary art, of which she became a great champion. She was seven years younger than I, but the closest thing I had to a contemporary in the entire Thyssen entourage. Notwithstanding my conventional exterior, Chessie divined my inner glam rocker, and we became fellow travelers and have stayed close for decades. No one is more fun. It was not an understatement to say that Chessie and Tita were not the best of friends, nor was she chummy with Denise, or even Roberto, with whom she shared an eye for new art but little else.

Once the Shortos were finally dispatched and Tita took her pride of place as the official Baroness in 1985, our travels, and our purchases, went into high gear, so much so that the Baron's beleaguered accountant, Riccardo Guscetti, was becoming apoplectic in trying to keep current with the Baron's bills for art. The idea that the Baron could be a deadbeat seemed preposterous, but the ledgers did not lie. He was millions of dollars in arrears in his payments, and playing for time with his creditors was totally unbaronial. Guscetti advocated selling off many of the lesser works, but Heini loved all his works, probably more than his children, and he could part with nothing. After all, on paper he was a billionaire. Why worry about something as petty as cash flow?

We made some stabs at economy, though these were the economies of princes, not mere mortals. For example, we found ourselves at the Okura Hotel in Tokyo doing a joint telephone bid in a New York Sotheby's sale for a major Gauguin. Heini and Tita were in their bathrobes eating room-service breakfast. Our bidding partner, Jaime Ortiz-Patiño, was on the line from Sotogrande, Spain. The grandson of the Bolivian "tin king," who was richer than the "sun king" Louis XIV, Jaime was a major developer of golf courses and a major collector of golf and bridge memorabilia. He also collected art. Neither man was known for frugality. Still, a recent precedent had been set for joint ventures when Norton Simon had joined forces with the Getty Trust to acquire a Degas pastel from the reboubtable Havemeyer Collection of New York's fin-de-siècle "sugar king." So Heini and Jaime decided to make love, not war, and not bid up the price. They would each take the Gauguin for two and a half years at a time. We got the work for $4.5 million and topped off our Okura breakfast with celebratory champagne. Five years later, Jaime decided to sell, and Heini got the Gauguin all for himself for $22 million. But since he got $11 million as the co-owner and had only paid $2.25 million, he made out like a bandit.

Nevertheless, it would have taken hundreds more of these great deals to balance Riccardo Guscetti's books. Feeling his oats, Heini commissioned a second portrait from Lucian Freud. Tita declared it made Heini look twenty years too old, which was precisely the right criticism to doom that art. As a measure of her distaste, Tita invoked the story of the portrait of Winston Churchill commissioned by Parliament and painted by the modern artist Graham Sutherland. Sutherland's idea was to make Churchill seem more "real." Preferring the legendary, Churchill hated the painting. The word he used to describe it was "malignant." His wife, Clementine, hated it even more.

In Parliament, Churchill damned the work with the faintest of praise, calling it "a remarkable example of modern art." Instead of being hung in Parliament, which was the intent, the painting went home with Clementine to Chartwell, where she burned it. Tita threatened to follow Clementine's violent example with the Freud. Meanwhile she commissioned a Spanish painter named Macaron to do another portrait. Despite Heini's preternaturally long fingers in the portrait, which gave him the appearance of having eagle's claws, I happened to love the Freud. Don't burn it, I begged Heini, offering to take it off his hands. I even offered to buy it, but he wouldn't let me.

Instead the Baron *loaned* me the painting, which I hung first at our lake house at the villa and then in our new home in the countryside outside Geneva. Every year Sotheby's did a valuation of the Baron's collection, including the Freud, which kept going up and up. When the value hit $500,000, I decided that it would be far safer to move the Freud to my office in Geneva, where there was lots of security, compared to the zero in our isolated hamlet. I probably looked at that painting, hanging on my office wall, more than any other in my life. I grew very attached to it. Unfortunately for me, the painting that Tita wanted to incinerate was soon worth upwards of a million dollars. "I think I am beginning to like it, " Tita said with with her sly smile. She then proceeded to repossess it from me, in the nicest way, of course. There was never any love lost between Lucian Freud and Tita. She might change her mind; he would never change his.

One of Heini's favorite new friends during the time I worked for him was Alfred Taubman, the Detroit realty mogul. They were an odd couple, the Old World baron and the New World shopping-mall king, but, like Peter Wilson, Heini Thyssen thrived on the shock of the new. We gave a great square-dance party at the Villa Favorita in honor of fellow Detroiters Henry Ford and "Big Al," as the tall and imposing mall man was known, and his wife, Judy, a former Miss Israel whose perfect command of many foreign languages would have made her a perfect translator at the United Nations. Judy used to work at Christie's auctions as a jewelry presenter, or "show girl," as presenters are known in the trade (as opposed to Vegas "showgirls"). There is a classic picture of her in this period holding up a diamond necklace. Soon the show girl would be the boss lady of Christie's archrival. In 1982 Al Taubman would come in as a white knight to rescue Sotheby's from an unfriendly takeover bid by two New York investors, Marshall Cogan and Stephen Swid, who had swooped down on a disarrayed Sotheby's following the unexpected death of Peter Wilson in Paris, from diabetes, in 1984. Wilson was only seventy-one. I was in shock myself, so I can imagine how the company was turned upside down.

I hadn't seen Wilson that much following my involvement with Heini. That job was the most jealous of mistresses, though Wilson was always in the back of my mind in almost every decision I would make. What would Peter do? How would Peter handle it? Those were my guiding lights. The idea of Peter retiring from Sotheby's, as he did in 1980, at sixty-seven, was a concept I couldn't ever get my head around. Peter *was* Sotheby's, or certainly the modern Sotheby's. But Peter loved art even more than he loved the company, and he was delighted to repair to the South of France to tend his gardens, his paintings, and his antiques at Château de Clavary. Still, he was never more than a moment from the telephone, and Sotheby's relied on his wisdom in all matters, up to the Taubman takeover just before his death, just as much as I did.

I went to London to bid a very sad farewell to Peter at his memorial service. There, at St. George's Church, around the corner from Bond Street, a who's who of both the peerage and the art world came to sing hymns and pay tribute to the man who transformed Sotheby's—and me. In fact, the assemblage at the church was almost identical to that of a big evening's sale of art at the auction house. Wilson had appointed as his successor his cousin Lord David Westmoreland, who was even more old school than Wilson and, on the surface—and what a smooth surface—had none of his cousin's eccentricities.

Leading the service was a fellow aristocrat, Lord Jellicoe, the son of a famous admiral and a war hero/commando who himself was Britain's last First Lord of the Admiralty (how Sotheby's loved admirals, front and rear). But even Lord Jellicoe was something of a symbol of the sun setting on the British Empire. In the seventies he had to resign his leadership position in the House of Lords when he and a fellow peer, Lord Lambton, were both exposed as being clients of the notorious call girl/madam Norma Levy. It was the biggest English sex scandal since the Profumo Affair. Sotheby's seemed to be going the way of the Lords, and it was not surprising that it was soon taken over by the Lord of Malls.

One rumor was that Al Taubman's motivation to control Sotheby's was revenge against the English snobs who always gave him the bum's rush when he attended auctions. There was no snobbery to rail against where Heini was concerned. The only one to rail at was me, when I was unable to find an authentic square-dance band in Europe to play the country music that would be the party's theme. Despite Heini's love of Dr. Suscz and his Gypsy violinists, this time the Hungarians just wouldn't do. Proving my resourcefulness (and saving my job), I called the U.S. Army base in Heidelberg, Germany, and located a genuine American square-dance band and had them flown to Lugano in a troop transport plane. Al and Judy, and Heini and Tita, do-si-do'ed the night away. I would have thought the two beauty queens might have bonded more than they did. Judy's bookishness and Tita's earthiness were more like oil and water.

As soon as Big Al took over Sotheby's, he put Heini on his advisory board, a stellar crew that included Detroit auto mogul Max Fisher, Turin auto mogul Gianni Agnelli, Viscount Petersham, of the *Financial Times,* the Duchess of Badajoz (sister of the King of Spain), Ann Getty (both women Borja's godparents), and Seiji Tsutsumi, who owned the Seibu department store chain whose art exhibitions fueled the eighties Impressionist craze in Japan. At the board's twice-yearly meetings, always in splendid venues, such as a black-tie dinner in the main hall of the Frick Collection to which I accompanied the Baron, I rarely heard Big Al discuss art. He seemed rather phlegmatic until the subject of space came up.

Not "space" in terms of Saturn and Uranus, but "space" in terms of traffic flow and store placement, as in shopping malls, about which no one knew more than Al. He was the Einstein of malls, the wizard of flow, the flow of human traffic. Heini was thinking of expanding the Villa Favorita with a new museum to accommodate his ever-expanding collection and had set me to the task of arranging a contest among famous architects for the commission. Al Taubman, fascinated by the challenge of creating the ultimate art showcase, using shopping-mall precepts, liked to whip out pen and paper and begin drawing his dream space for Heini. I noticed that Al, in his furious sketching, was left-handed, like a seeming disproportion of the geniuses that I have encountered.

It was in the midst of this burgeoning friendship between Al and Heini that I found myself in the extremely awkward position of being approached by Sotheby's to "come home." The initial call came from Michael Ainslie, Al's CEO, a courtly Tennesseean with a southern drawl and a Harvard MBA. Ainslie reminded me very much of George Bush (the father). This former property developer's previous job had been heading the National Trust for Historic Preservation. Ainslie wasn't purely a numbers guy; he dealt in culture. His charm rebutted the

European stereotype that American businessmen were a bunch of cowboy parvenus, a presumption that Al Taubman also had the burden of rebutting. All the charm in the world, however, could not have pulled me away from the Baron, at least at first blush.

Ainslie persisted. Given that Sotheby's had given me my education and my start in my career, and without them, I would have never met the Baron, it would have been ungrateful of me to refuse them flat-out. It would have also been ungracious to refuse Ainslie's invitation to come to New York to hear him out. So I flew over, though not on the Concorde, which was "Heini class." Sotheby's, in the midst of fiscal straits, was far more frugal. They did put me up at the Carlyle, and gave a dinner for me at the Upper East Side home of their new chief financial officer, Dede Brooks. Combined with Sotheby's brand-new and cost-conscious institutional-modern headquarters (derided as the "People's Palace") in the terra incognita of York Avenue, the bottom-line-focused American-ness of that dinner party gave me a crash course in how much and how quickly Sotheby's had changed since I'd been gone.

Dede Brooks was a dynamo, tall, preppy, sporty. If they ever make a movie about Dede, the queenlike Helen Mirren would have to star. Dede was figuratively and literally from the same school as George Bush (Yale), though her elbows were perhaps less padded. She had a similarly preppy, sporty husband, who I believe worked in finance (who on the Upper East Side didn't?), but he barely made an impression compared to her. Dominating the room, she bombarded me with a million questions, none of which I can recall.

Also at the dinner, providing some levity amidst all the business chatter, was the Sotheby's auctioneer Robert Woolley, who famously walked around at his own parties with a parrot on his shoulder, like the pirate Long John Silver. Woolley was British, as were two other guests, the married power couple David Nash, head of Impressionists, and Lucy Mitchell-Inness, head of contemporary. I think the Brits were invited to make me, as a "Euro," feel more at home. Yet the change was clear: The mood and the center of gravity of Sotheby's had clearly shifted across the Atlantic.

Still, Sotheby's was Sotheby's, and the more Michael Ainslie pursued me, the more I realized that this was an offer that I might not be able to refuse. What I really missed was auctioneering, and in the position Ainslie was discussing with me, I would get my moment at the podium, something that I could not do with the Baron. Going into Hamlet indecisive mode again, I realized the best person to talk to, in the interest of full disclosure, and in the interest of our friendship (I felt like a part of the big, crazy family), was Heini himself. Gracious as ever, he told me to do what was best for my career, whatever I wanted it to be. He would never stand in the way of a golden opportunity. My chief sage counsel, Isabel, who had told me to be bold in leaving Sotheby's, now advised me to be bold in coming back.

With one exception, Michael Ainslie, who had come to meet with me in Lausanne, couldn't have been more generous. I would be returning to Sotheby's as chairman of Switzerland (Jurg Wille had retired), as well as managing director, Europe, based in Geneva. The titles sounded grander than the tasks, but in a business of images, grandeur counted. Another wonderful concession was that Ainslie agreed to let me continue to work for the Baron one day a week. If that was getting to have my cake and eat it too, it was also a cake that Sotheby's would like to have a slice of.

The only sticking point in our negotiations was my request for a portable phone. In 1986 a portable phone was something out of James Bond, not Steve Jobs. They were huge, cumbersome affairs, used mostly by law enforcement, and maybe a few secret agents. At a time where Sotheby's was working at frugality, there was no room for fantasy. I tried to explain that this was no request for Concorde tickets, but a very practical mode of communication for someone who was going to be on the road almost all the time. I tried to evoke the movie *If It's Tuesday, This Must Be Belgium* to show what a moving target I would be. Eventually Ainslie gave in, and I was saddled with this leviathan piece of low technology to lug all over the Continent in a giant suitcase. I looked like a traveling salesman.

Just as I was about to seal my fate with Sotheby's, fate intervened in the worst possible way. Heini and Tita had gone to New York for a Sotheby's advisory board gala. The problem was that it wasn't gala at all for them. Heini woke me up in the middle of the night in Lugano in a drunken rage, railing that he and Tita had been given the worst seats in the house for the dinner, hard by an endlessly swinging kitchen door. He was going to quit the advisory board. He also wanted to never have any dealings with Sotheby for the rest of his life, plus the life of his foundation. In short, Sotheby's was damned for all eternity. The corollary of that was that I must have nothing to do with them, either. There went my brilliant auction career.

I spent the rest of the night drafting my abashed "regrets only" speech to Michael Ainslie. But before I could call him, I got another call from Heini, who never even mentioned the night before. It was as if it were a bad dream for me and reminded me of a reverse take on the running joke in Chaplin's *City Lights,* where the Tramp befriends a drunken millionaire, who loves the Tramp at night when he is drunk but denies even knowing him the sober morning after. I was able, after all, to pack up my borrowed Lucian Freud and begin my move back to Geneva and back to Sotheby's.

Not that I needed any reminder of the Baron. My efforts to find an architect to redesign the Villa Favorita to accommodate the enormous volume of art we had acquired in our seven years together had hit the brick wall of Swiss bureaucracy, frugality, whatever. Heini felt that because of all the tourists he had brought to Lugano to see his art, Switzerland should pay for the expansion. Switzerland said no. So Heini, smarting at this Swiss slap in the face, let it be known that his collection could be available to the country that would show him the respect Switzerland had not. This would set off a massive international competition worthy of Machiavelli, Richelieu, and Metternich combined. The biggest move of the Baron's life, and the biggest transfer of art in history, lay ahead of us.

IF I HAD A HAMMER

My reentry into the Sotheby's office in Geneva was as fraught as my entry into the Villa Favorita. Just as my predecessor at the villa, Sandor Berkes, was not thrilled to see me, my old boss at Sotheby's, the paratrooper/auctioneer Nicholas Rayner, was equally unenthusiastic at my return, now as his superior. At first he told me regretfully that there was physically no room for me at Sotheby's headquarters. The company had an outbuilding far across town. Rayner graciously offered me space there, in the equivalent of Siberia. I graciously refused. The collision of the immovable object and irresistible force resulted in a brief standoff, followed by eventual equilibrium. Jewelry was Rayner's bailiwick. Paintings were mine. We learned to get along, for the greater good of Big Al, and the spirit of Peter Wilson.

I also owe Rayner a debt of style for being an inspiration in my development as an auctioneer. The auctions, of which Peter Wilson had given me a delicious taste in my first round at Sotheby's, were a major incentive for me. Since Geneva auctions were mostly jewelry, I began recutting my teeth on auctions in Monaco, my first one of rare books. There were built-in problems, namely the Monegasque law that a local had to bring the hammer down. I thus had to play puppet master with the eternal Madame Maquet, manipulating the *huissière*'s arm up and down to close a sale. That definitely cramped my style.

Cramping my ego was my first evaluation by Peter Batkin, Sotheby's one-man Michelin rater of auctioneers. Batkin had created a system of judging the performance of the gavel-wielders, with categories of style, speed, and control. I had thought I was doing pretty well after not being at bat for seven years. Not so Batkin. "We have to talk," he said to me gravely one day. He took me aside and showed me the dreadful marks I had received in every category. I felt awful, a dismal failure.

That didn't stop me. I tried harder, emulating the masters, thinking how the Big Boys would do it. My first role model was, of course, Peter Wilson, who had so much soul force and authority that his near whispers from the podium compelled everyone to listen closely and hang on every word. My second model was John Marion, in New York, who was following in his father Lou Marion's elephantine footsteps. Watching John Marion do an auction was like watching John Wayne in the saddle. Again, total authority, but with a cool, casual Wild West swagger. Years later I went to Dallas to do an auction for the Beaux Arts Ball there. Sharing the podium with a genuine and highly colorful cattle auctioneer (we alternated on lots), I tried to channel John Marion.

My third role model was Nicholas Rayner, who was theatrical, the Laurence Olivier of the podium. He was very dramatic, changing his tone and pitch in the middle of bidding to create Hitchcockian suspense. His sales were all fun, sheer entertainment. You didn't have to be a buyer to love them. I realized from him that I needed to become more *vivacious,* that was the word, and I set about to do so. Rayner was great, and I wanted to be great like him, so I made it a point to make him like me.

My first big splash in Geneva, or rather *our* (Rayner and I) first splash together, was the April 1987 sale of the Duchess of Windsor's jewels. The Duchess had died in April of the year before in Paris and had left her treasures to the Institut Pasteur. The decision of how to monetize the jewels was left to the Duchess's humorless iron-lady lawyer-executrice Maître Suzanne Blum, upon whom Nicholas Rayner unleashed his considerable charms to win the rights to do an auction.

Luckily for us, my haughty nemesis Géza von Habsburg had left Christie's, depriving it of its royal advantage. Running the show at our archrival was its Cartier genius, Hans Nadelhoffer, who tragically would succumb to AIDS the next year. This was before the nineties era of elaborate presentation competitions, with mocked-up catalogues, sample

1.

2.

3.

4.

1. FAMILY JEWELS. Jürgen Teller made this photograph of his young son wearing jewelry when I asked him to jazz up the jewel auction catalogues of Phillips de Pury. **2. NIGHT CAPS.** On the occasion of the birth of our daughter Diane Delphine on January 1, 2011, a Swiss banker friend gave us these nineteenth-century embroidered nightgowns and night caps. **3. EVERY LITTLE BREEZE SEEMS TO WHISPER LOUISE.** In Paris with Louise Blouin MacBain at the private residence of the Ojieh family, on the occasion of a Phillips, de Pury & Luxembourg auction preview. **4. LITTLE EINSTEIN.** Albert Oehlen took this photograph of Michaela, Diane Delphine, and me when we visited his studio in the Appenzell. Our daughter tried on an Einstein impersonation.

5. LOW PROFILE. This photograph of me, sitting in the cellar that was my original office at Sotheby's Geneva, was commissioned by the *Tribune de Genève* for the first profile that ever appeared on me. **6. BARONIAL.** Hans Heinrich and Tita Thyssen-Bornemisza. "You need a strong neck for this!" Tita was joking when she was wearing this 100+ carat diamond. **7. THE TWO HEINIS.** Georg Heinrich and his father Hans Heinrich Thyssen-Bornemisza, or Heini Jr. and Heini, as friends would call them. **8. HECTOR *EN FAMILLE.*** Isabel and me, with our children (from left to right) Charles, Alban, Balthasar, and Loyse, as well as our dog Hector in Corsier near Geneva.

9.

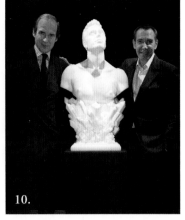

10.

11.

9. HEAVY HITTERS. With Baron H. H. Thyssen-Bornemisza; Sir Hugh Casson, President of the Royal Academy; and Norman Rosenthal (before his knighthood) in front of works by Edward Hopper and Pablo Picasso at the opening of the exhibition Modern Masters from the Thyssen-Bornemisza Collection at the Royal Academy, London 1984. **10. CAPTAIN MARBLE.** With Jeff Koons and his self-portrait in marble during the preview exhibition at Phillips de Pury, May 2008. **11. THE ENABLER.** Ulla Dreyfus, the widow of Basel banker Richard Dreyfus, who was very helpful to me at the time when I was trying to get into Sotheby's, together with Baron Lorne Thyssen-Bornemisza. **12. TEAM PLAYERS.** With the full team of Sotheby's Geneva celebrating the success of the sale of the Duchess of Windsor's jewelry auction.

12.

13.

14.

15.

13. LIVES OF THE PARTY. Two royal originals: Baroness Francesca Thyssen-Bornemisza (now HIH Archduchess Francesca von Habsburg) and Princess Gloria von Thurn und Taxis, who was then known as the punk princess. **14. JUDY AND BIG AL.** Judy and A. Alfred Taubman at the country-and-western-theme party given at the Villa Favorita on the occasion of the opening of American Masters from the Thyssen-Bornemisza Collection. **15. HUNGARIAN RHAPSODY.** Baroness Francesca Thyssen-Bornemisza and Dr. Szücs, the leader of her father's favorite gypsy band. **16. RUSSIAN ROULETTE.** In full action during the historic 1988 Sotheby's auction in Moscow. Next to me is Lord Gowrie, who was then chairman of Sotheby's Europe and previously minister of the arts in Margaret Thatcher's government. On the far left is Peter Batkin, Sotheby's Russia man.

16.

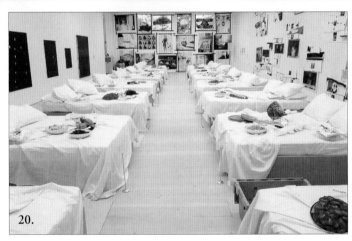

17. HAVE YOUR CAKE AND EAT IT. Witnessing Heini and Tita cutting their wedding cake in Daylesford, 1985. **18. SEX AND THE CITY.** On the set of Bravo's *Work of Art—The Next Great Artist* reality TV show with the coproducer Sarah Jessica Parker. I was trying to make a point while I was clearly mesmerized by her oozing charm. **19. WILDLIFE.** In Saint Tropez during the summer of 2015 with Leonardo DiCaprio conducting the benefit auction for his environmental foundation. Four shirts later and four hours later we had raised 40 million dollars. **20. BEDHOPPING.** Charles Saatchi generously lent us his gallery for Michaela's and my wedding party in 2010. When the guests tried to find the tables they had been assigned to, they found 69 unmade beds with food on them, in homage to Tracey Emin in an installation done by Jennifer Rubell. In order to eat, the guests would hop from bed to bed.

21.

22.

21. MERCURY RISING. With Leonid Friedland, the brilliant cofounder of Mercury, Russia's leading luxury retail company, to whom I sold Phillips de Pury. The photograph was taken on the magnificent polo grounds of Peter Brant in Connecticut. **22. REALITY BITES.** From left to right, with Jeanne Greenberg Rohatyn, China Chow, Bill Powers, and Jerry Saltz on the set of Bravo's *Work of Art—The Next Great Artist.* **23. LAP OF LUXURY.** With Anh Duong sitting on my lap in the painting Eric Fischl did of us. **24. PARTNERS.** Helmut Newton did this photograph of Daniella Luxembourg and myself for the announcement card of our business dePury-Luxembourg Art. Meret Meyer, the granddaughter of Marc Chagall, told me after having received the announcement, "My piano nearly collapsed when I put your card on it!"

23.

24.

25. GREETINGS. Tina Barney did this photograph of Daniella Luxembourg, Olivier Berggruen, David Breuer-Weil, and me at the Metropolitan Museum of Art. It was used as a seasonal greeting card for our company de Pury & Luxembourg Art in 1989. **26. FOUNDING FATHER.** Peter C. Wilson, the chairman of Sotheby's, whose vision was at the origin of the art market as we know it today. **27. OLD CHUMS.** June Newton took this photograph at 3 a.m. in the bar of the Four Seasons Hotel in Berlin. Helmut Newton, Benedikt Taschen, and I were recovering after a benefit event for the Mentor Foundation, at which Newton's book *SUMO*, published by Taschen, became under my gavel the most expensive book of the twentieth century. **28. MODEL OF PERFECTION.** Fiona Thyssen-Bornemisza, seen here in 1962, is in her eighties today and is still one of the most attractive and stylish women I know.

29. MAN OF ART. Thanks to Maurice Rheims, Chief Auctioneer of the Hotel Druout (the French equivalent of Sotheby's and Christie's), Paris was in those days an auction center of equivalent importance to London and New York. **30. MONSIEUR.** The visionary owner and head of LVMH, Bernard Arnault. It was at his initiative that Daniella Luxembourg and I merged our business with Phillips at the start of 2001. **31. THE LAST CZARINA.** Irina Antonova, the determined director of the Pushkin Museum, has been in charge of that institution through all the big changes, from Stalin to Putin, that took place in Russia. **32. ART PATRON.** With the art obsessed owner of Christie's, François Pinault, in front of a painting by Michael Chow.

advertising, and the like. Then it just came down to lunch, and nobody gave better lunch than Nicholas Rayner. I was good for dessert, and the stone-faced Maître Blum thankfully came our way.

Once the sale was ours, we both tried to channel Peter Wilson in mobilizing public relations, and I must say we succeeded beyond our wildest dreams. Our angle was the sheer romance of the collection, how the man who gave up the throne of England for "the woman he loved" expressed that love in the form of jewelry, the most lavish collection of all time. Every paper in the world picked up on the theme. They put aside all the unromantic counter-tales of the sexless marriage, of the Duke's homosexuality and his sympathies for Hitler, of the Duchess's narcissistic calculations, and focused solely on love and style.

We highlighted the sapphires, the Duchess's favorite stones, because they matched her eyes, the animal brooches, particularly the Cartier panthers, and the 31-carat Golconda diamond that had previously belonged to Mrs. Evalyn Walsh McLean in Washington, who also had owned the Hope Diamond. We had more stories than there were magazines to tell them. In March before the sale we did a "live show" at Sotheby's New York of the hundred-plus pieces that drew enormous lines at York Avenue. We had heat.

We also had drama. We were expecting a triumph; at the same time we had to expect trouble. Because the salons at the Hotel Beau-Rivage adjacent to our Geneva offices were too small for the anticipated crowds, we got permission from the city fathers to erect a huge tent beside Lake Geneva. Michael Ainslie, alert to the risk of a power cut, whether by accident or sabotage, insisted that we install a backup generator, which I arranged. The power demand was indeed heavy; there were TV crews from all over the planet. A thousand bidders joined three hundred reporters under our big top, and another six hundred privileged American customers joined the auction from York Avenue via closed circuit. The mood was that of a heavyweight championship fight, and the good part was that Sotheby's had won before the gong sounded.

I was pleased to be seated on the dais next to Lord Gowrie, Margaret Thatcher's minister of the arts and my immediate boss as the new Chairman of Sotheby's Europe. The Dublin-born Gowrie had a touch of the poet in him, having been a literature instructor at Harvard and an assistant to the poet Robert Lowell. He wasn't the typical Dede Brooksian bottom-line efficiency expert in any way, though we did know that Big Al's mandate was that winning was everything. All couldn't have gone better, until, all of a sudden, per Michael Ainslie's worst nightmare, the power failed. Everything died. After what seemed an eternity but was only seconds, our generator kicked in and the show went on. We found out the next day from the police that there had indeed been sabotage, that all the regular power lines had been cut with an axe, but we could never find anyone from Christie's to pin the blame on. Now that would have been a story.

The big story of our sale was that that greatest of all Hollywood jewelry aggregators, Elizabeth Taylor, had been on the phone herself by her Bel-Air swimming pool to bid for, and buy, the Prince of Wales Feathers, a diamond brooch in the shape of the Prince's heraldic sign. It was the king of royal pieces that should have been in the Crown Jewels, belonging to another Elizabeth, the Queen of England, rather than the Queen of Hollywood. But "ET" got vastly more publicity than "QE II," particularly when the hook here was a feminist one. This was the first piece of jewelry that Elizabeth had actually bought by herself, for herself. She paid nearly $600,000. She didn't need Nicky Hilton or Mike Todd or Eddie Fisher or Richard Burton to buy it for her. She had done it herself, one big step—into Sotheby's—for womankind. Whenever I see Helmut Newton's iconic photograph of a bronze ET resplendent in those "feathers" in the pool whence she had called in her bid, I am reminded of our big night in the tent.

The sale paid off in more than mere publicity. Many pieces generated over ten times their estimate. Our gross was over $50 million, a record for Switzerland and a record for jewelry. I was on my way—to Moscow, for my next big triumph. Working for Baron Thyssen on our one-day-a-week arrangement, I had gone with him to Moscow to have lunch with Mrs. Gorbachev. It was early 1988. At the airport I sadly discovered that I had left my passport back at the hotel's front desk. Heini Thyssen would wait for no man, so he left me on the tarmac to retrieve my papers and fly home commercial. The official from the Ministry of Culture, who was with us, was kind enough to drive me back into the city. On the way, I suggested to him how exciting I thought it would be to have an art auction in Moscow. It hadn't been done since before Lenin. To my surprise, the culture man said he thought it was an interesting idea. Of course, he had no idea of the full madness to my method.

Let's explore it, he said. On another recent trip to Moscow, I had accompanied my friend Paul Jolles, the ex-chairman of Nestlé and a global art hound, to the secret studios of a number of Russia's "unofficial" artists—Erik Bulatov, Ilya Kabakov, Oleg Vassiliev—all of whom would eventually develop global reputations. This was a kind of underground railway of art, usually in brutally run-down, primitive peasant housing on the outskirts of Moscow, sprawling slums reminiscent of Bombay or Calcutta. But this was the only place where art, *real* art, was being made in the Soviet Union. "Official" art, the stuff that got you in the Artists Union, was state-approved PR for the Party—busts of Lenin, portraits of Stalin, images of happy workers and happy farmers. All fake, just like the all-powerful USSR would soon be exposed to be. Still, the official artists were the only ones who got supplies, paint, brushes, canvases, whatever, and they got paid. The unofficial artists got nothing, except in the really bad old days when they got shot. Once they held a counter-exhibition in a forest. The Party and the KGB found it and bulldozed the plot out of existence. These artists were classic Stalinist "non-people."

My auction brainstorm would bring these artists out of the closet and into the world of collecting. I had seen them. Their work was great. It would sell, certainly to real collectors, ones without an ideological axe to grind. That's why, on that long ride back to my hotel, when I let that cat out of the bag, I was certain that the minister would shoot me down, if not just shoot me. But when he still said let's explore it, I realized that the times in Russia, they were indeed changing. Perestroika and glasnost were not mere propaganda but were reflecting an actual thawing of the Soviet iceberg.

In New York, when I pitched the auction to the powers there, I was pessimistic, given the logistics and lack of obvious profits. This was before there were oligarchs and private fortunes. If we auctioned the unofficial art, who in Russia would buy it? There was no money. Still, Al Taubman, who had Russian blood, and CEO Michael Ainslee, the Tennessee good ol' boy who didn't have a drop, both encouraged me.

They provided a green light to my red scheme. His Harvard MBA training let Michael see the enormous publicity value of having Sotheby's be
"first in Russia, first in the world." Take that, Christie's!

The production was worthy of Cecil B. DeMille. We set up the show
to include the art of the descendants of the Russian avant-garde, works
by Rodchenko, Stepanova, Udaltsova, and more, to provide a historical
context for the new kids, like Ilya Kabakov, an oppressed Jewish artist
forced to support himself doing illustrations of "official" children's books.
We had previews in New York and London, and organized charter flights
of collectors to come to Moscow to provide the money to make this a
real auction. We rounded up seventy-five high rollers, major players from
Europe and America, and more press than at a Hollywood wedding—
or divorce. The works were exhibited in the huge international Hyatt-
atrium-style hotel complex called Sovintsentr, which was for foreign
visitors and off-limits to most citizens.

I conducted the auction at the Sovintsentr. I was nervous. Who
wouldn't be? Three thousand people were assembled. As I was walking
to the podium, I could see that the phone bank didn't work. All my colleagues were dialing madly, to no avail. That was like a long walk to the
guillotine. However, just as the blade was about to fall, I could see the
phone people's faces light up with joy. The phones had begun to work,
a split second before I began the auction. Miracle in Moscow! There
was always the vodka for backup courage, and, while I'm normally stone
sober for these events, a little "when in Moscow, do as the Muscovites
do" had seemed in order. Usually artists do not attend auctions. They
dread bad news. But for our artists, the event was a coming-out party.
With each sale, they all jumped up and embraced each other, socialist
style. Everybody wins. It was the only auction in my entire career where
the audience applauded wildly after every single fall of the gavel. That
applause created euphoria in the room, and I never before or since
have encountered anything like it.

I felt a little like Lenin on that podium, doing my part to redistrib-
ute the wealth. That was a very powerful feeling, aside from the normal adrenaline rush of selling art for money. I loved seeing smiles on
those dour Russian-winter faces. I also loved simply doing the auction,
out of Nicholas Rayner's shadow, using the best of his flamboyance, a

soupçon of John Marion's high-in-the-saddle Western sass, and as much of Peter Wilson's true Brit cool as this poor Swiss pretender to the Sotheby's throne could manage to muster.

For the first time in their hard lives, these Russian artists I was selling were making money for their work, more money than they had ever dreamed of. One of the artists. Grisha Bruskin, lost his glasses, and I found him, after I had banged my final gavel, crawling on the floor looking for his specs. "Don't be a fool, Grisha. Stop it," his wife exhorted him. "You can buy more glasses. You're rich now." His work had just sold for over $400,000. The estimate we had given was a mere $12,000, and we were being sanguine. It was a harbinger of the art binges in the decades to come. "Stop it, Grisha. Get up. You're rich," his wife kept repeating. Grisha stayed on the ground searching. It seemed too good to be true.

Grisha Bruskin wasn't the only unofficial artist to become a star that night. Another was Igor Kopystiansky. Before the auction, he had tried to trade one of his canvases to an American collector visiting his studio for the top-of-the-line Nikon camera dangling like a priceless icon from the American's neck. The camera probably cost around $2,500, which seemed like serious money to the artist. The collector said no. At the auction, that painting Kopystiansky wanted to swap went for nearly $75,000. The buyer? Elton John. There was surely no vodka in Moscow that night potent enough to drown the American collector's non-buyer's remorse.

It soon became clear why Grisha Bruskin was loath to give up on the glasses and stayed on the floor. All the auction money—nearly $2 million—went to the Ministry of Culture, to be distributed to the artists. They never got a cent. It's Chinatown, Jake. Who gets paid in Russia? Soon, however, the letters started coming out of Russia, and what started as a PR coup for Sotheby's quickly threatened to become a coup de grace. It would take Margaret Thatcher to save the day. Lord Gowrie, her former minister of the arts, complained to her about the Russians' having become Indian givers. Gorbachev was coming to London to meet with the prime minister. Somehow she let it be known that she was not amused by the Russian bad behavior. One day before Gorbachev was due to arrive, Sotheby's was informed that every artist had been paid. Aside from the money, the auction was nothing less than a turning point in the cultural history of Russia. Soon afterward, the repressive Artists Union collapsed, as did Communism, and the "unofficials" went on to be allowed to buy supplies, travel, and in some cases become global stars.

The Russian auction revolutionized not only the Russian art scene but also my career. I quickly developed a reputation, and my auctions acquired a mystique. The world was entering an Age of Publicity, which continues to show no signs of abating (*pace* Kardashians), and I was in the right place with the right vehicle. My gavel became my passport, my motor of career mobility. I did a series of high-profile auctions for Swatch, the new low-budget, high-style Swiss watch company that had been founded in 1983. Because of its wild colors and radically cool multiplicity of designs, the Swatch (for "Second Watch") models became collectible very early in the company's young history.

When, early in my new tenure at Sotheby's, I presented the reverse-chic idea of including at one of our auctions some of these revolutionary timepieces of the people, the watch experts in London were aghast. That would be infra dig, beneath the dignity of haughty Sotheby's. I persisted and somehow got my way. At the auction, in 1986, the great jeweler Gianni Bulgari swept up all the Swatches at five times the asking price. A reporter asked if he was mad. Bulgari told him to ask him the same question in a few years and he would see how mad he was.

Bulgari was no fool. I held my next Swatch auction, exclusively Swatches, in a top-model-packed Milan nightclub. All proceeds went to the Red Cross, which scored the auction serious charity points and even more good publicity. The auction ignited a worldwide Swatch fever, which, like so many fashion trends, was kindled in Italy. I was thrilled to be part of the Swatch movement, transforming a cheap timepiece into Pop Art for a cult of collectors and transforming this little Swiss start-up into a billion-dollar giant.

Like all crazes, from Dutch tulips on, the Swatch-as-collectible fad abated—but only for a while. I helped start things up again at Phillips in 2011, by holding in Hong Kong, at the Four Seasons Hotel, a Swatch auction for mainland collectors. For the sale, I was allowed by the company to design my own Swatch to be auctioned with two gavels as the hands of the watch. The pièce de résistance, another one-of-a-kind that I saved for Lot 8, which is the Chinese lucky number, went for a staggering $6.5 million. Even Cartier, the traditional watch king, had to have been impressed.

While I was becoming known for being able to cross-fertilize the high and the low, I didn't dare lose sight of the high, which was where Sotheby's bread was buttered. My timing was good. I had come back to Sotheby's just as the eighties bull market in art was exploding, and the bull riders were the Japanese, the free-spending kings of the art world. Hooked initially on Impressionists and Post-Impressionists, the Japanese now seemed to be buying *everything*, from the skyscrapers of Manhattan to the film studios of Hollywood. My parents' life in Japan and my art studies there now came in handy and gave me something of a cross-cultural gimmick. I had the pleasure and honor of conducting the first auction of Japanese prints in Tokyo, which I did in tandem with Kazuko Shiomi, the formidable Japanese woman who headed Sotheby's Tokyo office. We were quite a tag team, me taking bids in English, she in Japanese, but my struggling efforts in the Japanese I had learned as a student were accepted with grace and appreciation.

The big story of the times remained, until the art crash of the early 90s, the Japanese love affair with European art. Van Gogh's obsession with Japanese woodprints was reciprocated a century later by Japan's obsession with Van Gogh. Whether boom or bust, I was flying wherever Sotheby's had offices to do unique auctions. I managed to acquire my own identity on the auction circuit, which only served to promote my identity within the company. In 1992 I was promoted to chairman of Sotheby's Europe, replacing Lord Gowrie. I soon also became chief auctioneer of Sotheby's worldwide, succeeding John Marion, who retired to enjoy his brilliant marriage. Marion burnished my John Wayne super-cowboy image of him (coincidence: Wayne's real name was Marion [Morrison]) by marrying a super-cowgirl, Fort Worth debutante/rancher/philanthropist/art collector Anne Burnett Windfohr. Marion was living proof that there was indeed life after Sotheby's.

I wished that I could have said the same for my own brilliant marriage, which became a casualty of my suddenly brilliant career. In my new position I had to move to London, which was the headquarters for Sotheby's European operations. I also would be spending one week a month in New York, which was where Big Al lived and the nerve center of the company. Isabel did not join me. I must take full responsibility for my endless absences. I felt terribly guilty that I had taken Isabel out of a great career of her own and trapped her in a gilded cage that eventually would be the ruin of our marriage. Isabel did go back to school, in psychology—she could have given a course in the Baron alone—and devoted herself to working with the blind. But our marriage seemed beyond repair. Having come from my own tradition of absentee parents, I found a slight consolation from the guilt by calculating that even with my continuous absences from Geneva, where my family remained, I was still seeing my kids more than my Tokyo-based parents had ever seen me. Our four wonderful children were doing well in school and getting along brilliantly. I was as amazed at their resilience as I was at my own.

My New York counterpart was my onetime hostess during my recruitment, Dede Brooks. She was the head of Sotheby's, Inc., the North American "better half" of the company. A product of Oyster Bay, Miss Porter's School, Smith, and Yale, Dede was the embodiment of the "Long Island lockjaw" Wall Street WASP, and an unlikely candidate to run a business of art. She knew little beyond what she had picked up in her college art-history courses, the ones where résumé builders like herself could rack up A's far more easily than in math or the hard sciences. After Yale, Dede had begun her career at Citibank as a lending officer, after which she joined Sotheby's on the financial side.

Dede was great at bringing Sotheby's into the Wall Street era, "monetizing" art, which was now frequently more likely to appreciate than stocks and bonds. She helped turn the auction house into a financial institution. Sotheby's had come a long way from its roots in the eighteenth century, when its raison d'être was to provide a place to quickly liquidate estates when people died or fell into debt, a genteel version of a pawnshop. Dede's aristocratic horsey aura and Establishment self-confidence had caught the eye of Taubman. In a classic case of opposites attracting, "Big Al" propelled "Big Dede," who was a towering six feet plus, straight to the top of his new toy.

Dede Brooks was far more "man" than any guy at Sotheby's. I learned this quickly when we met at a corporate retreat that Taubman had arranged at the Mayflower Inn, a Connecticut Relais & Châteaux property owned by Bob Mnuchin, a Goldman Sachs partner who had taken his Wall Street fortune and multiplied it in the art business and was hence able to dabble in baubles like the Mayflower. At Sotheby's retreats we always had to play games designed by some Harvard Business School madman that were supposed to illuminate our corporate strengths and weaknesses. One of these was arm wrestling. We had a kind of lightning round that lasted five minutes. For every takedown, the winner would receive a dollar. The "coach," whoever he was, some MBA surely, sadistically called Dede and me to the fore. I was anything but sporty. In games as a boy, I was always the last to be chosen, the Typhoid Mary of the playing fields. I expected to be humiliated. And by a woman. How ignominious it seemed.

So I tried harder, as hard as I ever had. Dede seemed like Samson, or Goliath. She was so powerful, so intense. I could see how she played to win. I felt like David, the would-be giant slayer. And somehow I hung on. The five minutes, whatever it was, seemed like an eternity. The time went by without either of us pinning the other. We were both beet red. We had fought to a draw. My honor, and that of Europe, had been preserved. Or so I thought. The coach frowned. He excoriated both of us as losers, unable to work together for the greater good of the company. Had we been smarter, had we understood how to cooperate, we could have let each pin the other every second or two and rack up huge piles of dollars for both. By trying to win, we both lost. Get the ego out, get the money in. What a lesson.

I was far more the artist than the businessman. I was happiest on the podium, running the sales, or in the field, planning the sales, courting clients. I didn't want Dede's corporate job. But she wanted mine. She loved being the auctioneer. In fact, she loved doing everything at Sotheby's. She was omnivorous, like the orchestra conductor who also wants to be the piano soloist and play the violin on top of that, and then the trumpet.

Dede's hunger for "having it all" led to numerous departures, such as that of my predecessor, John Marion. John wasn't the only top-level executive for whom life with Dede made Sotheby's too small. Michael Ainslie, who hired me, left in 1993, and Dede took over his position as

CEO. His exit, too, was softened by money. Big Al had taken Sotheby's public at the height of the art market in 1988, and Ainslie, perhaps clairvoyant about the upcoming Japanese 1990 market crash, cashed out to great effect. That did not endear him to Al or to Judy, who was known to remind everyone how rich "they" had made the help, especially Ainslie, who rented a house in Southampton a tad too close to the Taubmans' Long Island barony for Judy's comfort. There were no complaints about Dede, though. Her dynamo style appealed to the quiet Big Al, who may have lived vicariously through Dede's corporate aggressions and bottom-line-enhancing manuevers, while he set about doing what he loved best, which was to "go with the flow." To that end, he spent lots of time in London and completely redesigned the rabbit warren that was Bond Street, ending a century of getting lost as part of the Sotheby's experience.

Dede made her worldwide auction debut commanding the 1996 Jackie Onassis sale, which got Sotheby's the most publicity it ever had. Whatever Jackie had, people wanted it, whether a rocking chair, a tape measure, or a humidor that had been a gift to JFK from the comedian Milton Berle and was inscribed GOOD HEALTH—GOOD SMOKING. Dede gave me a small taste of the action by letting me sell several lots during the four-day April extravaganza, but she, like Armand Hammer, knew the Hollywood way to keep the spotlight on herself. I still had a great time being there. There couldn't have been more of a frenzy if it had been an Elvis auction. Everybody wanted everything, even the junk. I sold a ceramic vase that had held Jackie's deathbed flowers for a small fortune. Then I met Maria Shriver and kissed her hand.

"You must be European," Arnold Schwarzenegger growled at me. "Only Europeans do that sort of thing."

"But you're European, too," I replied. "You must know."

"I do know!" the Terminator crowed. "But I don't kiss them on the hand. I grab them by the hair and kiss them on the mouth."

I was relieved he didn't demonstrate his New World technique.

In London Dede and I became roommates. She was spending as much time in London as I was in New York, prompting one of those MBA bean counters to suggest that sharing one flat was far more economical and efficient than renting two. We found a place right near Bond

Street that we sublet from the Geneva dealer Jan Krugier. We couldn't have been more ill suited, literally night and day. I was out late, often just dozing off from client dinners at Harry's Bar and client dancing at Annabel's, when Dede would arise like thunder at the dawn, usually around 5:30 A.M., to go jogging in Hyde Park.

I suppose I was the nonsense to Dede's no nonsense. I was so impressed at how efficient she could be. It took me far longer to put on my tux for our black-tie dinners at Sotheby's than for her to put on her evening wear. She'd be running numbers at Sotheby's in her simple pearl-necklace-accented day wear, then, realizing we had a fancy-dress meal, she'd dash over to our place and be back in about five minutes, a belle for the ball. Clark Kent didn't change into Superman that quickly.

Somehow I just couldn't be myself around her; I always felt we were competing, for hours, for quiet, for a bathroom, for the kitchen, whatever. After six weeks, I told her the share wasn't working. I had to get my own place. She seemed terribly hurt. It was like a romantic breakup. My new young daughter, by the way, is named Diane Delphine. This "DD," and her older half-sister, Loyse, are the most important women in my life. The other Dede wanted to be the most important woman in my life, and everyone else's. That primacy imperative was the key to her drive, her amazing success, and, in the end, her shocking, Icarus-like fall from grace. Despite the failure of our living arrangement, I could see how many people could find Dede Brooks extremely attractive. She had success, she had power, she had energy, she had presence. She reminded me of Helmut Newton's surprising answer when I asked him who was the sexiest woman he had ever photographed, he of the "big blondes." Margaret Thatcher, Helmut replied, not missing a beat. Dede Brooks was a big blonde, too.

After bailing on the Dede ménage, I went back to staying at the Westbury Hotel a block from the office, which was about as impersonal as a Holiday Inn. Every time I arrived, whether it was my initial visit or my five hundredth, the desk clerk, always a new face, would ask me chirpily, "Is this your first stay with us?" The staff seemed to turn over every single week, and reminded me how important continuity is in any enterprise. That's why I loved patronizing the stylish Mayfair haunts of exclusivity entrepreneur Mark Birley, Annabel's, Harry's Bar, and Mark's, where the servers seemed to have been there since the days of Bertie Wooster and his butler Jeeves. Eventually I found my own place in Mayfair on Dunraven Street, a very cozy bachelor pad that I sublet from Robert Louis-Dreyfuss, the former CEO of Saatchi & Saatchi advertising. Weekends I would fly back to Geneva to spend time with my family, such as it was.

I often worried that Sotheby's could not survive Dede Brooks's brilliant but sometimes oppressive autocracy. Dede was even more worried about beating Christie's. Almost all my time at Sotheby's was spent battling Christie's. On my original tour of duty at Sotheby's, Christie's may have been an annoying afterthought, but it was never the obsession it had now become. After the art market went the precipitous way of the Japanese property market in 1990, Christie's had begun a massive effort to cease being the Avis ("We try harder") of auction houses and displace us as the Hertz. And by 1994, they had succeeded, outgrossing us in sales for the first time since 1954. They would continue to beat us for the remainder of the decade. With the public's mounting obsession with auction records, Sotheby's-Christie's became an iconic ongoing front-page rivalry on the same level as Army-Navy, Harvard-Yale, Oxford-Cambridge, NBC-CBS, Ford–General Motors. Years later, when I tried with Phillips to create a triumvirate out of a duopoly, one journalist said that if Sotheby's was Coke and Christie's was Pepsi, then Phillips was Red Bull.

A lot of the credit for Christie's resurgence was due to its new CEO, Christopher Davidge, who was the antithesis of the Peter Wilson old-boy model and whose ambitions were fueled by what looked like a chip on his shoulder. Davidge was from an old Christie's family, but only in terms of loyal service. His grandfather had been a cashier, his father a porter, his mum a secretary. Davidge had grown up in North London council flats and dropped out of school at sixteen. He made his way up—and up and up—in the gritty printing department that produced Christie's catalogues. Offering efficiency and drive over the class and polish that had always been Christie's trademark, but left it as the perennial Number Two, Davidge was promoted out of the print shop and sent to Hong Kong. There he distinguished himself, rising to head of

Christie's Asia, beating Sotheby's in that increasingly pivotal market and proving that Sotheby's could be vulnerable in the West as well.

Davidge took over as the boss at Christie's King Street, St. James's, headquarters in 1985. The resident swells made fun of his bleached-looking-blond, razor-cut, blow-dried hairstyle, his dandyish Jermyn Street striped shirts and loud ties, his declaration to the *Financial Times* that his greatest extravagance was fancy-grade toilet paper. People at Christie's called him "the butler." Davidge was as different from his counterpart Dede Brooks as he was from the industry standard Peter Wilson. She was an American thoroughbred; he was a Michael Caine character straight out of *Alfie*.

I remember seeing Davidge having a power lunch at Wilton's, the clubby Victorian fish restaurant on Jermyn Street that was a favorite of the auction crowd. He looked so *different* from the rest of the clientele. His hair was *too* groomed, not like that of the proper English gents whose haircuts didn't look like haircuts. He had a beautiful suit, but it was *too* perfect, creaseless, not like the worn look of the proper English gents. You could almost see the muscles bursting forth under those be-spoke threads. Davidge was small but very athletic; he must have spent hours at the gym. In short, and Davidge was short, with a Napoleon complex, the man seemed to be *trying* too hard, a terrible no-no in English society.

Dede Brooks tried hard, too. She strove mightily, but only in business, never socially. She possessed that confident effortlessness that was the hallmark of the well-born American preppie. You couldn't imagine the two of them, Dede and Davidge, making it through lunch together, much less the massive collusion they were charged with that nearly sank their respective ships and wrecked the entire auction business.

Teams of Rivals

I n New York and London, Dede Brooks and Christopher Davidge
were the at-odds couple. In Europe, I had my own sparring partner
in François Curiel, Christie's head of Europe and, as a master of jewelry, the worthy successor to Hans Nadelhoffer in Christie's Geneva
office. The Paris-born, trim, and intense Curiel, whose father was a
jewelry dealer, had started as an apprentice at Christie's in London in
1969 and had ridden the wave of that company's copycat expansion program, opening offices in Madrid in 1972, then New York in 1977, and
then coming back to Geneva in 1989. There he would be my friendly
nemesis in our never-ending quest for important collections to sell.

That was my brief, from Dede Brooks, to "bring home the bacon," as
it was Curiel's, from his new boss Lord Carrington, an Etonian, Peter-
Wilsonian character who as a former secretary general of NATO was
fully versed in the art of war. There was no more delicious bacon, short
of a Francis Bacon, than the first big collection Curiel and I went head-
to-head over. The collector was Albina du Boisrouvray, a mouthful of a
name for a handful of a person. She was the daughter of a French count,
granddaughter of the Bolivian tin king Simón Patiño, and cousin of
Heini's good friend and Gauguin co-venturer Jaime Ortiz-Patiño.

Albina first showed up in my Hotel Beau-Rivage office with a cat in
a basket. A beautiful, elegantly eccentric former model, now in her forties, she had been married first to a Swiss glacier-rescue pilot, then a

French film producer. The reason she had come to see me was that her life had been turned upside down by the recent death of her twenty-four-year-old son, François-Xavier Bagnoud, in a rescue-helicopter crash connected to the Paris–Dakar auto race. She wanted to completely change her own life and had liquidated her Paris production company. Now she wanted to sell her entire inherited art collection—pre-Columbian gold, Impressionists, Old Masters, major jewelry, and more—to create a foundation in memory of her son. This was October 1988. She told me that she was visiting me as well as François Curiel, and that she would render her decision between the two of us the following March.

The most valuable part of Albina's trove was her jewels, supposedly the finest collection in the world after that of the Duchess of Windsor. Despite our recent triumph with the Windsor sale, Curiel and Christie's still had the edge in the gems department. We were in a way the new kid on the diamond (chopping) block. The only advantage I could even try to exploit was that I was from Basel, where Albina owned our great "art hotel," Les Trois Rois. As an art obsessive I knew all the folklore about the hotel, such as the story of Picasso's one night there after being stood up by Paul Klee. I also had some ancient brochures on the hotel that I dug up and gave to her. That gift got her to open up and recount to me that the jewels she was selling meant nothing to her, that they were a "guilt gift" from her father to her unloved mother. This poor little rich girl had many poignant stories to tell, and I had all the time in the world to listen to her. I was hoping the hyperefficient Curiel had less time.

Little things can mean a lot. In March Albina called me and said that she had chosen Sotheby's. She invited me to her home in Zermatt in two weeks to sign the deal. I didn't break out the champagne. Two weeks in art auction competitions can be an eternity. Just as Peter Wilson had stolen the Rosemarie Kanzler house sale from Christie's by out-psychologizing Rosemarie's husband, I knew Curiel was not about to give up and would do all in his power to change Albina's mind. He did. But she didn't.

When I arrived in Zermatt, Albina's chalet had more floral arrangements than a funeral parlor. There were giant bouquets from Lord

Carrington, chairman of Christie's, which Albina, a flower lover, was thrilled to display. My heart sank. I thought she was going to send me away with an "I changed my mind." Instead, she told me that all the flowers in an English spring couldn't make her break her word. I was touched. The auction, which we held in New York, yielded over $100 million and set records for the eighties. More important, the sale resulted in one of the biggest donations ever to Harvard in honor of Albina's lost son.

That was just one round with Christie's. The battle was endless, and always joined, like a never-ending political campaign. It reminded me of the comment in *Variety* about Hollywood mogul Joel Silver, that he would stab *himself* in the back to close a deal. Case in point: One of Sotheby's top business-getters was Prince Dimitri of Yugoslavia, whose specialty was charming jewelry-laden gay divorcées into the Sotheby's fold. In the mid-nineties one of the conquests of the Prince, who was openly gay, was the Lebanese socialite Mouna Ayoub, who had just divorced Saudi billionaire Nasser al-Rashid and wanted to convert some eight to ten million dollars' worth of baubles into cash. The prospective sale was figuratively in the bag, and physically in the safe at Sotheby's, awaiting the auction. To our chagrin, we came to believe that François Curiel was pursuing an affair with Mouna. Why else would she suddenly withdraw the jewels from our safe and put them in Christie's, commissioning them to do the auction?

Curiel conducted a spectacular auction, which yielded over $12 million. Mouna later denied that any hanky-panky had occurred before the sale, saying that she simply was more impressed by Christie's than by Sotheby's and, well, changed her mind. Curiel, she declared, was not her type. He wore trademark rimless glasses, and she never succumbed to men with glasses, no matter how chic. Only *after* she witnessed Curiel's podium magic and saw the $12 million proof of the pudding did she begin to see his romantic virtues, notably at a celebratory postsale dinner in which he happened to take off his glasses. Then, she insisted, she finally saw how handsome he was, and the affair began. No one at Sotheby's believed a word of it. Mouna used the jewelry loot to purchase a "love boat" for her and Curiel, the *Phocea*, one of the world's largest sailing yachts, from French tycoon and Adidas owner Bernard Tapie.

Incapable of making my name as the Don Juan of the auction circuit, I preferred to make my mark as the best auctioneer. I worked hard at it, supercharging my style to match the spectacle that the soaring market of the late eighties had turned into. There was a recovery in the nineties, but it was slow and gradual, unlike the V-shaped recovery that followed the 2008 market crash. For years it seemed like all the buyers were sitting on their hands, and the only bidders were the Nahmad family, who thrived like vampires on market bloodlettings like the nineties depression.

One way I changed the game and tried to pep it up was my decision to stand during auctions. Peter Wilson and the other gavel-bangers were always seated, but I thought that standing would increase the theatricality of the events and thus be a better show for all concerned. I had lobbied Lord Gowrie and Michael Ainslie to allow me to do both Impressionist and modern sales in London, and then I successfully lobbied Dede Brooks to do auctions both in New York and London. This was the first incidence of the bicontinental auctioneer.

My big New York breakthrough came in 1994, with the death of Jean Stralem, the widow of a rich Wall Street banker and the granddaughter of an even richer one, Philip Lehman of Lehman Brothers, who gave the Lehman Collection to the Met. The centerpiece of the Impressionist-modernist hoard was Picasso's 1903 Blue Period portrait of a fellow artist, Angel Fernández de Soto. Dede Brooks had to give away the store in guarantees to beat Christie's for the sale, but that was the price of trying to pull out of the recession we were in. It was like couture being a loss leader to get publicity for prêt-à-porter.

I was dying to do the sale, but Dede was dubious that I could match the stature of Christie's chief auctioneer, Christopher Burge, who was seen as a star in New York. I was not a star. Not yet. But I knew this great collection could make me one. I had to convince Dede to give me a shot. With John Marion gone, who else did she have? And then Dede had to convince the Stralem executors, who had never heard of me. Seeing is believing, she insisted, and flew them over to London on the Concorde to see me in action. They relented. Dede remained relentless. "You better not screw this up!" she warned me.

The beginning of the May 1995 auction went terribly. A few of the works went for their estimate, but many fell short. We still seemed in the grips of this cursed recession that even the Impressionists could not dispel. The Blue Period Picasso was the fourteenth lot. The Stralems had bought it for $22,000 from Knoedler in 1946. Things started slowly. But I had six bidders, some in the hall, some on the phone bank, and I did my best to keep up the tension and keep them bidding.

Eventually it came down to two phone-ins. The whole thing clocked in at six minutes, which seemed like eternity. When the dust settled, I brought the gavel down at $29.1 million. The phone buyer was Andrew Lloyd Webber in London. The price was nearly three times the high estimate of $8–$12 million. It was the highest price paid for a painting since the crash of 1990. Once the Picasso sold, everything else seemed to sell, too, the thundering herd happily at play. I sold Matisse's 1923 odalisque *Hindu Pose* for another record for Matisse, $18.9 million. The total evening's haul for the forty-six paintings (only two did not sell) was $65 million, way above our estimate range of $37–$50 million. The market was back. It was a great night for Sotheby's, and for me.

My job at Sotheby's might seem like a silk-stocking version of "getting and selling" charming countesses into putting their art up for auction, then putting on a show to maximize returns. There was also a thrilling Sherlock Holmes aspect and an altruistic public service component, one case of which colorfully came to fruition in 1995 around the same time as the Stralem sale. Back when I returned to Sotheby's and had made a name for myself as an Iron Curtain expert for the auction I engineered in Moscow, I was contacted by the grandsons of one of the twentieth century's great collectors to see if I could find their family's lost art in Russia and help them get it back. The collector was Otto Gerstenberg, the German insurance magnate who was the J. P. Morgan of German collectors in the pre-Hitler era. The centerpiece of the collection was Degas's masterpiece, his 1875 *Place de la Concorde*.

As war loomed, Gerstenberg, who was not Jewish, asked the National Gallery in Berlin to safeguard his art from possible bombing or other threat. The gallery in turn got nervous and stored the collection in a high-security bunker near the Berlin Zoo. At the close of hostilities, the contents of the bunker, which was located in what was by then Soviet-controlled East Berlin, disappeared. The official word was that the bunker had been burned and the art completely destroyed. Gerstenberg's heirs, Dieter and Walter Scharf, businessmen in Hamburg and Munich, had more than a nagging suspicion that the art still existed and that the Russians had stolen it as spoils of war. In their sixties, the Scharfs first approached me in 1986 to help get to the bottom of the disappearance. They presented me with a long list of titles, Goyas, Renoirs, Picassos, more Degases, a tantalizing list that set me off on a treasure hunt.

Armed with a thick collection of old black-and-white photos of many of the paintings, which were bad but the only evidence I had to work with, I paid visits to my new friends from the Thyssen swap, Boris Piotrovsky at the Hermitage and Madame Antonova at the Pushkin. Both stonewalled me completely. They knew nothing, because there was nothing to know, they declared. They both insisted that the Gerstenberg art had been destroyed. Undeterred, I showed the list to the Ministry of Culture and planted the seed of my persistence. Soon after Boris Piotrovsky died in 1990, I got a call from his son, Mikhail. "Surprise!" he told me, inviting me to come to St. Petersburg and bring the Scharfs with me.

The Scharfs brought not only their families for what might be a momentous event but also Alec Wildenstein, the playboy son of their great dealer Daniel Wildenstein, who had been trying to cut a deal to buy a stake in the missing collection, if it were ever found. Alec was more interested in the live beauties of Russia than in anything on canvas. He partied so late and so hard that after negotiations started, he once fell facedown on the bargaining table in a vodka-caviar coma.

When we arrived in St. Petersberg (Leningrad no more), our first stop was at the office of Mikhail Piotrovsky. Tellingly, the portrait of Lenin that had hung over his father's desk had now been replaced by one of Catherine the Great. Communism was dead! Long live the Empress! Mikhail gave us a grand tour of the Hermitage. We ended up in a large ornate salon, in the center of which was an easel with its back to us. When we reached the front, *voilà!* There was the ghost Degas. On the back was the label with their grandmother's address in Berlin. The brothers, not the crying types, both broke down in tears.

Mikhail took us to another treasure room. There were more paintings there, wonderful, bright Picasso watercolors that seemed as if they had been painted the day before. They were fresh because they had been untouched by daylight for four decades. I felt like a Raider of the Lost Art. Where had they been, I pressed. "I have no idea. We just found them. I'm brand-new here," Mikhail said, hiding behind his father's death as the basis for his plausible denial. In Moscow at the Pushkin, Madame Antonova remained as reticent and reluctant as Mikhail had been gracious. She had been a young commissar stationed in Germany at the time the art was probably moved from there to Moscow and had been rumored to have been in charge as the supposedly destroyed art from the supposedly incinerated bunker was loaded on the secret convoy to Moscow. She would admit nothing. More Gerstenberg paintings had just been discovered in the bowels of the Pushkin as well, Goyas, Daumiers, and more. But again, this was *ars ex machina.*

The new problem was how to get the art back to the Scharfs. The Russians would not budge. It was one thing if the art was in a private collection; a public museum was another matter. The Russians looked at the art as theirs by right, the spoils of war of a victor who had lost a hundred million people to the Nazis. They didn't steal it from Gerstenberg; Hitler and Göring did, and there was no chain of title from Hitler to Stalin. Luckily, the Scharfs were patient men and were thrilled that the art was safe and had not been destroyed.

There were amazingly open talks between Piotrovsky and the Scharfs, who were so grateful that the Russians had taken such good care of their art that they offered a deal to let the Russians keep half of the collection and even offered them a cut of any future sales the Scharfs might make. Given the long Cold War, these cooperative discussions marked a new dawn for cultural diplomacy. Alas, with the ascension of Vladimir Putin in 2000 the Duma regressed to the old hard line and passed a very harsh law declaring the art from Nazi Germany Russia's and Russia's alone. The Scharfs, who loved the art for itself and not merely for *them*selves, were surprisingly understanding of the Russian position.

Like Heini, the Scharfs took pleasure in sharing their art with the world. Hence they found solace in the 1995 blockbuster show Mikhail Piotrovsky mounted at the Hermitage of seventy-five French paintings from the Gerstenberg collection entitled "Hidden Treasures Revealed." "Stolen Booty Exposed!" was the counterheadline of much of the world press, which was up in arms that the Russians were refusing to give the paintings, worth hundred of millions of dollars, back to the rightful owners. I was pleased to have played a role in rediscovering this art and in igniting a debate that remains one of the major topics of our time. Although the rise of Putin has chilled the hopes we all had, because of the reasonableness of men like Piotrovsky, hope still remains for restoration of confiscated art whose original owners were not the Nazis themselves but innocent Jewish victims of the Hitler horror.

In the fall of 1992, with the art market still quicksanded in the post-Japan doldrums, Dede Brooks convened a Bond Street meeting with nine or so of Sotheby's English and European executives to gauge reaction to the notion of raising the buyer's premium. We needed to make money, and this was one way to do it. For the last seventeen years, Sotheby's—and Christie's—had charged a flat 10 percent on all auction purchases. Now, Dede asked what we thought client reaction might be if we raised that premium to 15 percent on the first $50,000, and 10 percent on anything above the $50,000. She was planning to do a similar sounding in New York.

The Continental "we" included myself, Count Christoph Douglas, who headed Sotheby's Germany, and Princess Laure de Beauvau-Craon, who headed Sotheby's France. It was like a grown-up version of the Works of Art course, except now we were getting paid. The English "we" included Henry Wyndham, the chairman of Sotheby's UK, and George Bailey, managing director of Sotheby's Europe. The reason there were so many important-sounding titles was that it was cheaper to hand out titles than hand out money, the latter being in such short supply. Aware of that supply, we all thought it was a great idea to raise the commissions.

In November 1992, Dede Brooks seemed to be following our advice, when the commissions raise was announced. That December, barely a month after Sotheby's made its move, Christie's, par for the historical course, announced that it was matching our raise. "We really had no choice," Christopher Davidge told *The New York Times,* expressing his apology to prospective buyers for hitting them in the pocketbook, "but in the end we felt it was important to be competing with Sotheby's on a level playing field." Twenty years before, the two houses had nearly simultaneously introduced the Continental European concept of the 10 percent buyer's premium. There was a huge outcry from dealers bemoaning how they would all go broke paying these premiums and raising the specter of a conspiracy by the two supposed archrivals to team up and screw "the trade," as the dealers were known. Price-fixing was not illegal in England; the trade soon got over it.

Nobody in the auction world was surprised that Christie's again matched Sotheby's this time. Thus it had always been.

However, *all of us* were beyond surprised, totally shocked, when in 1998 a scandal erupted revealing that Dede and Davidge, supposedly archrivals, were actually the odd couple of the auction universe. American antitrust lawyers were making a huge federal case that "D & D" had conspired to fix the new buyer's premiums, and had made lots of other noncompetitive arrangements as well. Forget Helen Mirren playing Dede Brooks. Dede Brooks could play Helen Mirren. What an amazing act she had pulled off, beseeching us for our opinions on raising those premiums, when in fact the deal—with Davidge—had long been done. Sotheby's and Christie's would both reap millions in the process by holding the (bottom) line in this way. Dede's 1992 summit conference was one massive game of charades.

It had never been a disadvantage to ratchet up rates, and with business being bad, we needed all the revenue we could muster, especially from a price-insensitive elite that would pay anything if they wanted the beauty we were selling. The two firms were such copycats, opening offices in the same cities, chasing the same clients, selling the same art, that charging the same commissions seemed like the natural order of things and did not require conspiracies or cabals. However, America, with its draconian antitrust criminal laws, would not look the other way. Christie's was British owned; hence its top people held to the more permissive British standard. Sotheby's was Big Al's, all-American, and it had to answer to a far tougher source.

When the scandal broke, I had no idea that Dede Brooks and Christopher Davidge conspired to fix anything. As I said, she was such a brilliant actress that she made it all seem spontaneous, the natural order of things. I was grateful that she had not compromised us by involving us in her collusion the way Davidge, it turned out, had compromised his Christie's colleagues by making them aware of what was going on. Nor did I have an inkling whether Big Al and Big Tony (Sir Anthony Tennant, chairman of Christie's) had any awareness of it.

I found it hard to believe that Dede didn't share everything she did and knew with Taubman, who had been her fairy godfather when he rescued her from the ledgers of Citibank and gave her the most glamorous job that any woman, or man, could dream of. In 2000, the FBI would grill me for hours about the matter, and the short answer to some long questions was that I did not know. I was way too busy bringing home the bacon to worry about cooking the books.

The price-fixing scandal, while supposedly having occurred when I was at Sotheby's, did not come to light until I was long gone. After a few more big auctions like the Stralem one, I had reached the conclusion that I had done just about everything one could do at Sotheby's short of being Dede Brooks. Sotheby's at this point was the House of Brooks, if not the House of Mirth. We were still Number Two to Christie's. Our profit margin was barely 1 percent. The company did not seem the wave of the future, but rather the decay of the past. I wanted to be my own man, and not just one of the many striving rulers in Sotheby's army of generals. As much as I loved being our top auctioneer, I had become disenchanted with the Sotheby's bureaucracy and wanted to travel light. Dede Brooks was anything but pleased. Al Taubman was furious. It took Al a decade before he would speak to me again, so incensed was the owner over my decision to leave in 1997. Having given Big Al eleven years of my best efforts, it was time to be on my own.

17

THE WOMEN

To become my own man, I realized, I needed the partnership of a woman. That woman was Daniella Luxembourg, with whom I had worked at Sotheby's when she headed the company's office in Israel. Daniella was the anti-Dede, poor, exotic, completely self-made. What the two women shared was boundless energy and brains. If my image might have been euphemized as the embodiment of Old Europe, Daniella was the quintessence of a brave new world. As a contrast to the countesses and duchesses I had to court to secure their collections, Daniella was a fresh breeze off the Mediterranean.

"Brave" was the operative word in describing Daniella. Born in Poland, Daniella had parents whose families were exterminated by Hitler and who had been imprisoned themselves in concentration camps before emigrating to Israel in 1950, when their daughter was three months old. They lived in Haifa in a prefab asbestos hut. Life was harsh but, compared to Auschwitz, paradise. The brainy daughter of an engineer and a literature professor, Daniella studied French and art history. But she also fought in the Israeli army, which was good preparation for the trench warfare of the art world. After beginning her career in Israel's museums, she was discovered by Peter Wilson's cousin and successor, Lord Westmoreland. In Sotheby's mission to conquer the globe, she was hired to start a branch office in Tel Aviv.

Daniella rose to the occasion and mobilized Israel's emerging wealthy class to buy art. However, after she was promoted and transferred to my Geneva office, she had a falling-out with Dede Brooks. The contretemps occurred when Dede vetoed an auction Daniella was setting up in Austria of recently uncovered stolen Jewish art, whose owners were now dead, to benefit the living Jews of Austria. Dede felt the auction had "blood on its hands" and ceded it to Christie's, which sold the works for a then-record $10 million. Her frustration with Sotheby's threw Daniella in league with me. In 1997 we pooled our estimable Rolodexes and started our own company in Geneva, de Pury & Luxembourg.

It was our very first day in business. Daniella and I were sitting in our barren, temporary headquarters in Geneva. We were a shoestring operation, wondering who, if anyone, would drop in. Imagine our surprise when the first call of the day was from Ronald Lauder, probably the most influential collector in the world, in New York. A longtime friend of Daniella's, Ronald got straight to the point. Tell Krugier, he told her, that I want to buy that Picasso study.

Krugier was Jan Krugier, one of the preeminent Geneva dealers, whose Mayfair flat was the locus of my ill-fated share with Dede Brooks. The Picasso in question was a four-foot metal scale model of a fifty-foot-tall steel work for a public square in Chicago, a city the artist loved the idea of, without ever having visited it. Ronald was willing to pay $2.5 million for the piece. Daniella hung up. We called Krugier and made the deal. In an instant. We couldn't believe how easy it was. We had hit a grand slam our first time at bat. Being a dealer was wonderful! In one day we had accomplished what would have taken forever at Sotheby's. Alas, our elation was brief. Three days later the elation became deflation. In our discussions with Lauder, we figured out that the Picasso he wanted was not Krugier's but a different one. We had a case of mistaken identity.

It was almost biblical: The Lord giveth, the Lord taketh away. Jan Krugier's wrath was infernal, something out of the Old Testament. I had thought he was a friend. I had known him for years. That friendship was ended by what he saw as a breached contract. Even if we hadn't had time to memorialize it on paper, a deal was a deal. Jan's rage was choleric. He threatened to send in the lawyers. We saw our reputation going up in smoke. Jan's trademarks were his fedora and his cane. We feared that he would beat us with the latter item.

Ronald Lauder was more than sympathetic about the mess he had inadvertently landed us in. He offered to make a large donation to create a school for Jewish children in Poland, where Jan had been interned in Auschwitz, in Jan's name. After the war, Jan had gone to Paris to become an artist. His best friends, Giacometti and Matisse, convinced him to become a dealer instead. With his deep connections, this was not a man to cross. And cross him we had.

Ronald's offer fell on deaf ears. We went in person to see Jan with the olive branch. He threw us out. For years Jan turned away whenever he saw us. Jan died in 2008. The ultimate irony would have been if Ronald Lauder had, in the end, purchased the "wrong" Picasso from Jan's estate. Even at a dozen times the original price, I still doubt that Jan, wherever he is, would ever have forgiven us. P.S. In the actual auction at Sotheby's London, the Picasso ended up selling at a far lower price than the $2.5 million we mistakenly thought was ours.

Despite this false start, the new dealership managed not only to survive but to thrive. Notwithstanding our problems with Jan, we prided ourselves on our skills in courting and cosseting private clients. Those skills paid off; between 1998 and 2000, de Pury & Luxembourg soon became one of the hot shops on the Continent, selling some of the most important paintings to come on the market during that time, triple-A works by Van Gogh, Renoir, Klimt, Picasso, Brancusi, and more. We were so hot that we attracted the attention of LVMH's Bernard Arnault. The French luxury titan could not stand to be bettered by his archrival, Francois Pinault, who had bought Christie's in 1998 for $1.2 billion. Their competition was iconic, like Sotheby's and Christie's. If Pinault had an auction house, so must Arnault. The logical one was Sotheby's, but Taubman wouldn't sell. So Arnault decided to create his own Sotheby's from the building block of Phillips, a fusty London gallery that had a long history but no pizzazz. Founded in 1798 by Harry Phillips, the chief clerk of the founder of Christie's, James Christie, Phillips prided itself on having done auctions for Napoleon Bonaparte, Beau Brummel, and the post-guillotine estate of Marie "Let them eat cake"

Antoinette. That was a long time ago. And that's where Daniella and I came in, to provide the sizzle and turn the auction wars from a two-house battle into a three-house free-for-all.

I had first met Bernard Arnault when I was on the board of directors of Gucci, and he and Pinault had engaged in a vicious takeover battle. Pinault technically "won" by acquiring Gucci, but Arnault made over $700 million in the battle and was anything but a sore loser in a deal that closed two days before 9/11's body blow to the luxury market. I had gotten a taste of Arnault's passion, which was very different from Pinault's, though equally intense. Arnaunt was elegant, cerebral, aloof, and unfailingly polite. Pinault was hands-on, exuding warmth and passion but equally as steely and determined as Arnault.

I was impressed at the way LVMH had courted the art world and integrated art into its campaigns. Louis Vuitton's use of Richard Prince, Murakami, Kusama, and others had made it chic and cool for luxe brands to associate themselves with art. Arnault, who had bought Phillips sight unseen for the bargain-basement price (compared to Pinault's layout for Christie's) of $121 million, was a man on a mission, a mission of art. That was my kind of man.

Arnault's refined and impeccable taste was on display when I met with him in his penthouse office atop the Dior building on Avenue Montaigne. The food and wine were worthy of any nearby three-star temple of gastronomy. Arnault lived, spoke, and talked culture. His French Canadian wife was a concert pianist. He played well himself. He played me like a baby grand when he urged me to join him as his partner in Phillips. "You need a *stage*," he told me, "which you lack now." He knew how much I loved auctioning, and how I now missed it. He pressed all the right buttons. When I told him that I had a partner, he said, "She's *my* partner now." The new company would be called Phillips, de Pury & Luxembourg. Daniella and I would have 25 percent, LVMH 75 percent. This was the dream backer of all time. We knew we could compete with the giants. We were in the game, big-time.

The original idea for Arnault's Phillips was that it would be much more profitable than the duopoly, which was burdened by overhead and bureaucracy. The two items that most ate into the auction house bottom line were catalogues and staff. Catalogues could cost over $70 each, and, depending on the importance of the sale, the house could send out as many as fifteen thousand of them. With a lot of sales throughout the year, that could add up fast. The other bottom-line destroyer was staff, and nobody had more staff than the duopoly—many old retainers, old boys, old girls, family ties, a Noah's Ark of dead weight. We knew an elegant perfectionist like Arnault would never skimp on catalogues, but where the dead weight was concerned, particularly the British dead weight, he expected Daniella and me to be as ruthless as Hercules in cleaning out the Augean Stables.

The best-laid plans often go astray. With the deep pockets and even deeper ambitions of Monsieur Arnault, our desire for simplicity was instantly upended into complexity. Aside from our London headquarters, LVMH had taken on a lavish New York space at the corner of Fifth Avenue and 57th. I moved into the St. Regis, Daniella into an East Side town house that had belonged to Pierre Matisse, the art-dealer son of the great Henri, and we planned our first auction for spring 2001. To put us on the New York map, it had to be huge, and this one couldn't have been bigger. It was the collection of Heinz Berggruen, the renowned art dealer whom I had met as an apprentice to Ebi Kornfeld in Bern and got to know even better through his friend Heini Thyssen.

Like Heini in his move to Madrid, Heinz had moved a spectacular collection across borders. One of the greatest of all postwar dealers in Paris, Heinz was courted and convinced to transfer his collection to Berlin, a city he, as a Jew faced with the Holocaust, had been forced to flee. Berlin's creation of a museum for Heinz, and his acceptance of their offer, was a gesture of forgiveness and reconciliation that made him an international art star. "I am not French or German," Heinz liked to say. "I am European." He also liked the situation in Berlin, whose politicians set up a grand apartment for him above the museum. He could see his paintings every day. "I can say good morning, and I can say good night, and I can sleep well knowing that they are with me."

Heinz had initially decided to retire in Geneva and give his collection to Switzerland. In 1987 I had arranged for Heinz's art to be shown at a museum in Geneva. Unfortunately, some overzealous eagle-eyed Swiss customs officials noted that there were no proper import papers on a few of the lesser works and confiscated the art until all t's were crossed. A deeply insulted Heinz forthwith sold his new Geneva apartment, moved out of Switzerland, and began flirting with England for a time until Germany made him the great offer. The Swiss bureaucracy thus cost their country one of the treasure troves of the world.

To get the collection he wanted to sell now, I knew that another great offer was essential. Heinz loved money. Luckily, Monsieur Arnault had money and was willing to spend it on a guarantee that would top anything either Sotheby's or Christie's might offer. In Hollywood, it's called "buying a gross." Disney did it, when it got into the non-animated feature-film business under Michael Eisner, spending a fortune on advertising to get people into the theaters. All their early films were hits, but they still lost money, until the world took Disney seriously. So it would be with Phillips, de Pury & Luxembourg. I used all my history and a lot of LVMH's money to lure Heinz to us, confident it would be worth it. Bernard Arnault and I flew to Berlin and closed the deal with Heinz in Berlin's Paris Bar, which is something out of *Cabaret,* the old prewar Berlin of Dietrich and decadence.

Donning my good-luck Caraceni suit and my Swiss-bankerly white shirt and dark tie, I ate the single apple that had become my sole pre-auction sustenance and superstition and stepped up on the new, made-especially-for-Phillips podium to auction my heart out. I sold Cézanne's stunning *Montaigne Sainte-Victoire,* the view from his studio in Aix-en-Provence, for $38 million, as well as forty other masterpieces for Heinz. I sold other non-Bergguen art as well, like two Renoirs from leveraged-buyout king Henry Kravis. The final tally was $124 million. It may have been below the guarantee to Heinz, but it wasn't hay. The world was watching. That was the point. Phillips had demonstrated that it could sell paintings in the "heavyweight" category of Impressionist and modern art, in which it previously had zero track record.

That same year, on September 11, I can remember precisely where I was when I first became aware of the unfolding tragedy. I was in Paris walking through the serene Jardins des Tuileries, heading toward the LVMH offices on the Avenue Montaigne, when I got a cell phone call telling me that one of the Twin Towers had fallen. At Monsieur Arnault's office atop Dior, he, Daniella, and I sat there mesmerized watching on television the second tower go down in flames, and, as we would soon learn, our dreams for Phillips go up in smoke. That night the Dubuffet show's opening dinner at the Centre Pompidou that Arnault had planned was canceled. Two days later the LVMH lawyers called with the grim tidings. The world had changed. They wanted out.

The fall of the towers was something of a metaphor for the fall of my marriage. However, while I pride myself on being highly decisive on the job, I was as indecisive about leaving my home as I had been about leaving the Sotheby's of Peter Wilson for Baron Thyssen, and later leaving Thyssen for the Sotheby's of Al Taubman. I had been unusually decisive about leaving the Sotheby's of Dede Brooks. It was much easier to leave my job than to separate from my wife, because I had become paralyzed by the fear of losing the love of my children, which meant more to me than anything else.

I was so depressed that in my search for clarity I signed up for ten sessions with a female psychiatrist in Geneva. The therapy only made things worse. Then an Indian princess in Montreux introduced me to her fortune-teller. Desperate times, desperate measures, desperate man, you must think. Actually this wasn't my first encounter with the occult. In my Heini days, his dear pal Henry Ford took a third wife, Kathleen, a lively and unpretentious Michigan girl and former model whose first husband had been a Chrysler assembly line worker. Kathy was devoted to astrology, and she got Henry hooked on the stars.

Henry Ford didn't make a move without consulting their fortune-teller, who was anything but a Gypsy. In fact, this lady seemed more like a Ford CEO. Once when I came to give an art lecture at the Detroit Museum, Kathy gave me the gift of a session, and this woman was amazing. The fortune-teller knew about the lecture, and everything else that was going on in my life, about Isabel, about Daniella, about Phillips. I wanted to go back to her for help, but she had died of cancer.

Thus I eagerly accepted my Indian gift, a clairvoyant whose name was Carmen Bietenharder. She wore a white robe and had her white hair in a mannish crew cut and was always accompanied by the little shih tzu that had been a gift from her client Elizabeth Taylor when Carmen had lived in Hollywood for twelve years. She told me that her dog and I shared the same birthday, which had major significance, though I'm not sure what. Carmen arrived at our new de Pury & Luxembourg offices in 1998. She put a séance cloth on a table and spread out her cards.

Our assistant entered in the middle of the card reading, catching Daniella and me together in an in-flagrante of mysticism, and thought we had gone mad. But Carmen was right on the money. She understood all of Daniella's and my private turmoils. She helped me where the psychiatrist had failed; she took the guilt away. She made me decisive. I found the courage to leave my house and get a separate apartment in Geneva, though not yet the divorce I so feared. I was, in my late forties, something of a new man. And then I met Louise MacBain.

I first encountered Louise in the summer of 2000, when things couldn't have been going better for me, personally and professionally. Carmen had given me courage and clarity, Daniella and I were doing great business in Switzerland, and Bernard Arnault was on the horizon with the offer that would change me from being a mere employee of Sotheby's to one of its chief rivals. I was in Long Island to conduct the charity auction of the Texas-born avant-garde playwright Robert Wilson's Watermill Center. That weekend my friend the Vendome Press art publisher Alexis Gregory took me to a lunch at a mansion on Gin Lane, the most prestigious address in all the Hamptons (this was South).

The home, where Woody Allen filmed *Interiors,* belonged to Louise MacBain, who had to be one of the most beautiful super-rich women I had ever met. Barely forty, strawberry blond, sleek, and regal, Louise was a Canadian, but the only time I could detect her accent (in French or English) was when she spoke to Canadian guests or help. All Alexis had told me was that she ran a global empire that published down-market magazines selling classified ads and that she was interested in "getting into art." I heard that all the time about rich people, so I didn't get too excited, but I did get excited by Louise's looks and charm and the fact that she changed her luncheon seating to put me next to her. In terms of her slender, delicately sculpted, perfect fair looks, Louise reminded me a bit of Denise Shorto, Heini's third wife. But while Denise was a party girl, Louise was dead serious, as well she might be for having made the fortune she had.

I got the impression Louise was single and ran this empire all by herself. After lunch Alexis disabused me of that notion. The company, called Trader, Inc. (sounded like Murder, Inc.), had been founded by her still-very-much-married husband, John MacBain. They had three children. However, Louise was an active, equal partner and interested in new technology. Accordingly, she wanted to put her ad mags on the Internet, and she also wanted to bring the Internet to the antediluvian art world, where we were still sending each other big packets of Ektachromes. Would I meet her at her Geneva mansion and advise her?

There was no art to speak of in that expensive *Interiors* house, so I had no idea what her taste ran to, if it ran at all. All I noticed was that it seemed to be running to me, at which I was highly flattered. Nor did I quite follow what she was talking about for technologizing art. Her dialogue was a cross between Carlos Castaneda and *The Wall Street Journal*, spiritual New Age meets the Fortune 500. Whatever, her beauty and success forced me to lean in and try to figure it out. She wanted to be cutting-edge, and she thought I might help her. Southampton, Geneva, art, tech . . . why not?

I was especially excited because Louise's Geneva mansion had been bought from Heini's dear friend and art co-venturer Jaime Ortiz-Patiño. Jaime, the golf king, had built a private nine-hole course around the house, which he had filled with great art that he eventually gave me carte blanche to sell for him. I had had great luck with anything Patino: Jaime's sale, Jaime and Heini's Gauguin sale, Albina du Boisrouvray's jewelry sale. Being superstitious, and now more so than usual given my success with the clairvoyant Carmen, I saw those past successes as a sign from above.

Back in Geneva at my villa of good luck, there were butlers with gloves and fancy servants Louise told me had previously worked for French president Jacques Chirac at the Élysée Palace. I was disappointed to see how conventional Louise's taste in art was, and how different and cold the house looked with Jaime gone. There was a medium-quality Chagall, a minor Signac. In time I would tell Louise how different her taste was from mine. Her response was to *change* her taste to mirror mine. When I also candidly mentioned to her I wasn't a huge fan of the work of her Southampton decorator, Alberto Pinto, she had the house redone by François Catroux, whose work I did like. She could be a chameleon. Such flattery of imitation would get her everywhere, at least at the beginning of things.

All my sugarplum visions were derailed when, at the house, I first met Louise's impressive dynamo husband, a Canadian Rhodes Scholar and Harvard MBA. I also learned a little of Louise's background. Louise Blouin was from a very normal Quebecois French Catholic family that ran an insurance agency. Her older sister had married big-time to the son of Paul Desmarais, a north-of-the-border Warren Buffet billionaire who controlled the Power Corporation of Canada, an energy conglomerate. John MacBain worked for Power and met Louise through her sister. In 1987 John had left Power and, with Louise, started Hebdo Mag (no relation to the Paris *Charlie Hebdo*), which quickly grew to encompass over three hundred classified-ad publications. The couple seemed to have a Midas touch in business, something both alien and awesome to the artist in me, and had homes everywhere. Louise was fascinated by culture and society. John preferred running marathons.

John indulged Louise in her expansion interests into the art realm. They flew me around Europe in their private plane exploring possibilities, including a trip to Monte Carlo, where I introduced Louise to my friend Helmut Newton so she could talk to him about doing a photographic campaign for her ad business. From the first time I saw Helmut's shots in *Vogue,* I knew this was someone I had to meet. To do so, I invited him to be part of my Sotheby's lecture series in Geneva, where I immediately bonded with him and his wife, June, a serious photographer herself under the name Alice Springs, taken from her native Australia.

All our business talk must have had a yin-yang aphrodisiac effect. One day we were alone in my office at sunset, with its sexy Andrée Putman décor and its romantic sunset view over Lake Geneva. Suddenly a spontaneous kiss ignited what would become a major flame. I called it "a kiss with consequences." We had a teen expression, *Elle achètera les rideaux maintenant.* She'll be buying curtains now. And she did, curtains by François Catroux.

Because John and Louise worked so closely, our burgeoning affair took on French-farce characteristics. John, whom I really liked, which complicated the matter even further, was too intelligent not to be suspicious. On a trip to London, we all stayed at Claridge's. I noticed John strolling the halls outside my suite with a frequency that belied the notion of looking for an ice machine. I presumed his perambulations were to see if Louise might show up. Instead, an English woman I had been occasionally seeing happened to arrive. That may have assuaged John's suspicions momentarily, although it inflamed Louise's competitiveness, as John informed Louise about this "girlfriend." Louise, always proprietary, was furious that I was "cheating" on her.

The farce got really intense one night when three couples had a dinner together in Geneva: Louise and John; Daniella Luxembourg and her husband, Boubi; and Isabel and I, who had not gotten divorced yet. Despite Carmen's clarifying clairvoyance, I was still in Hamlet mode. I knew what I wanted to do, but I was still afraid to do it. Naturally everybody hated each other. Louise put on "If I Had a Hammer" after dinner. It was the theme song of a recent humorous video a friend had produced of me conducting an auction. While it wasn't exactly "our song" where Isabel and I were concerned, it certainly wasn't "our song" for me and Louise, but that seemed to be the way Isabel was viewing Louise's proprietary disc jockeying.

Boubi Luxembourg, an architect, was a direct descendant of the Marxist theorist and martyr Rosa Luxemburg. The liveried servants and Louise's queenly style brought out the radical revolutionary in him. I was surprised he didn't set the villa on fire. I remember introducing Daniella Luxembourg to the Duc de Luxembourg at an auction in the Duchy, and seeing them joke about coming from "different branches."

After dinner John MacBain took me for a spin in the new Ferrari Louise had given him for his fortieth birthday. Spin is not the right word. It was more like a kamikaze death dive. Again, I had flashbacks of the Christopher Walken scene from *Annie Hall* that I had played out once before with a jealous Sandor Berkes in Lugano. This time, though, a jealous John MacBain was driving much more dangerously. I staggered out of the car, amazed to be alive.

When I flew in the jet with Louise and John, under the guise of their getting into the art business, there was lots of tension in the air. They might argue about anything and everything, including Louise's playing *Elton John's Greatest Hits* as cabin music at a deafening volume. Still, Louise was a fabulous organizer, arranging a fantastic trip on the yacht of a Greek tycoon that sailed from Helsinki to St. Petersburg, so we could enjoy the white nights. It was John, Louise, and their kids, and me by myself. When John and the children went home, Louise stayed on with me on terra firma to pursue our art research.

In St. Petersburg we ran into a "biker club" that included Jeremy Irons and Guggenheim director Thomas Krens and rode motorcycles around the enormous square of the Hermitage at 3:00 A.M. I knew in my heart that our affair was too hot to handle. I knew in my heart that it would end badly. But somehow, as with any bad addiction, I could not stop. On another ostensible "family" trip to Russia in Louise's plane with Eve Scharf, whose Gerstenberg grandfather-in-law's art I had helped relocate at the Hermitage, another of our companions was Elise Goulandris, the widow of Greek tycoon Basil Goulandris. These two wise women summoned me to the bar of our hotel in Moscow. Together, the two Sybils warned me that they saw what was going on. They told me as a friend that what they saw was "a bad idea."

Louise was nothing but impulsive. Early on, she told me she wanted to separate from John and be with me. Displaying an outsider's vulnerability to both flash and pedigree, Louise had had other intense romances, her first with Laurent Junot, the playboy brother of Philippe Junot, himself a playboy who had married Caroline de Monaco. Louise had had a previous husband, the heir to a Canadian tobacco fortune. That was intense, too, and very brief.

Louise was not afraid to cut and run. She was ready to do it again, with me. I was forty-nine, she was forty-two. She was not burdened with the same sort of decisional paralysis that had often plagued me in my personal life. She would change her life on a dime. That decisiveness was very sexy and belied Louise's cool, controlled Grace Kelly façade. Our new romance played out in the most romantic spots, as we jetted between continents, grand luxe hotels, and the resorts of the richest and most famous, my ego fortified by being pursued both by Louise and by Bernard Arnault. She rented us a "love nest" town house in Chester Square in London. I later found her an even bigger mansion in Holland Park that she bought from one of the two "official" wives of the Sultan of Brunei. She then sold the Holland Park house to Goga Ashkenazi, a world-class adventuress connected to the ruler of Kazakhstan. In a short time both Louise and Goga would both become the close friends of Prince Andrew. It was the stuff of novels, albeit by Danielle Steel.

The only thing bringing me back to earth was the tragic and sudden illness of my brother David from pancreatic cancer at fifty-seven. I was always in his shadow as "David's younger brother." The smartest, most charismatic, most charming man I have ever known, blood or no blood, he had become one of the top diplomats in Europe, Switzerland's top trade negotiator, and sat on the boards of several giant concerns, including Nestlé and Credit Suisse. We had just celebrated his birthday in Basel with his Peruvian wife, who was leaving for Lima to visit her family the next day. No sooner had she flown off, David's doctor called him in to tell him that he had pancreatic cancer, with six months at most left to live. His only chance, and it was a slim one, was a major operation. David, as was his wont, took the chance. His wife, who had turned around from Peru, arrived at the hospital to be told the operation was a great success. It may have been, but the problem was that David never woke up from the anesthesia and was put on life support. A few days later the plug was pulled.

While David was dying, my theology professor brother, Albert, was celebrating his sixtieth birthday, at which I was asked to give a speech. Because David's wife didn't want anyone to know David was sick, we had to create the illusion that we were one carefree happy family. So, as at an auction where no one was bidding, I did what the French call *faire bonne mine àmauvais jeu,* put on a good face at a bad game. It was bad indeed. I gave the birthday all-is-fine speech on December 22, 2000. David died on December 26. My father had also died, of a sudden heart attack, in 1997, and my mother was a flame that was gradually fading. That I was the next generation was painfully clear, and I wanted to do my best to uphold my family's impossibly high standards.

Right after David died, Louise flew me by Concorde to meet her in St. Barts, where she had rented the yacht of the Swiss watch tycoon Jorg Bucherer. The previous renter was Puff Daddy. The bling was everywhere, though my recent loss had kept me out of a blingy mood. I did my best to focus on my new brief at Phillips and on mounting our challenge to the duopoly. Louise told me she wanted to support our effort, maybe even join it in some way. I did my best to sell Louise to

Daniella, who herself was on the verge of a divorce and in the midst of a forbidden romance of her own. I had no idea how much we would soon need Louise business-wise.

I spent a great part of 2000 and 2001 flying back and forth to Los Angeles to line up our next blockbuster sale at Phillips. This was the Smooke collection. The lately departed Smookes were one of the great property dynasties of Los Angeles, Eli Broad before Eli Broad. Like Broad, and unlike most fat-cat, sports-mad, beachy Angelinos, they married money and culture. Nathan and Marion Smooke were among the founders of the Los Angeles County Museum of Art. They had a fabulous collection of early twentieth-century German and French paintings. We paid a huge guarantee to their heirs to get the right to sell them, just as we had with Heinz Berggruen. I knew the press would criticize us for "buying a gross." But they had criticized Michael Eisner for doing the same thing, and now Disney was ahead of Fox and the rest. We hoped we could end up similarly situated in the art market.

We knew Phillips could never be all things to all buyers like Sotheby's and Christie's, so our business strategy was to compete elite, to focus on the highest-end Impressionist and modern art, the works that got the big headlines and the big bucks. Let Sotheby's sell comic books, baseball cards, movie posters, dolls. Let Sotheby's sell Jackie Onassis knickknacks. Let Sotheby's choke on its bureaucracy. We intended to run a lean, mean operating machine, no more than 150 employees, compared to the thousands at Sotheby's and Christie's. Nobody was better at luxury than Bernard Arnault. We would be true to his exclusive spirit. As Daniella put it to one reporter, "If you want a couture dress, you don't go to Macy's."

Daniella and I had to aim very high to compensate for Monsieur Arnault's false start with Phillips. His first sale, in May 2000, before he signed us, was a disaster. The paintings were weak. Moreover, he had hired as the sale's mistress of ceremonies Sharon Stone, whose star had dimmed somewhat since the flash of 1992's *Basic Instinct*. Sharon roamed the aisles like a game-show hostess, and actually sat in the laps of some bidders, trying to elicit some life from a dead audience. One of the laps she sat on was that of David Nahmad, who was so used to being around beautiful women that even Sharon in his lap could not elicit a bid if the art wasn't right for him. Sharon is irresistible as a charity auctioneer, but her vivacious technique was simply not suited to a serious commercial sale like this. The auction was a bomb. Monsieur Arnault then and there realized he had to "go pro." It was good for Daniella and me, but we knew we couldn't make one false move. The pressure was enormous. Then again, I tended to thrive on pressure, so I welcomed the challenge.

Obviously, no one could have anticipated 9/11, an event that shocked even the world's highest rollers. While François Pinault owned Christie's through his private holding company Artemis and not through the publicly traded PPR, Bernard Arnault owned Phillips through the very publicly traded LVMH. Even before 9/11, 2001 was a difficult year for the global luxury industry. Although the financial press wasn't focusing on what Pinault was doing with Christie's, there was a fair amount of print questioning whether it made sense for LVMH to invest so heavily in an area that was clearly not part of its core business.

The guaranteed contract with the Smooke family was in place in late August. It could no longer be changed. On September 12 neither Bernard Arnault, Daniella Luxembourg, myself, nor anyone else would have recommended any longer that we sign it. Bernard decided that, in this suddenly upside-down world, the whole enterprise didn't make economic sense. He wanted out, with a capital O. Daniella and I were informed that LVMH wanted to immediately start negotiating their exit. That famous Italian movie title *Seduced and Abandoned* said it all. Our new Phillips, dePury & Luxembourg was like a horse galloping at full speed that was suddenly brought to a screeching halt. I was trying hard to remain in the saddle.

I was a global nomad now, living downtown in the Mercer Hotel. Daniella was still in the 64th Street Matisse town house. We had a crash course trying to prepare for the Smooke sale and for the Arnault exit. At the same time LVMH was unloading us, it was also ditching its other new auction-house acquisitions, Bonhams in London and Tajan in Paris. Based on Arnault's actions, it seemed that the art market was about to go the way of the Twin Towers on Wall Street. Confidence was not inspired.

We spent a great deal of that awful fall in the white-shoe law offices of Debevoise & Plimpton with Louis Begley, who had somehow managed to balance two seemingly incompatible careers, one as a hard-charging corporate lawyer and the other as a sensitive novelist (*About Schmidt*). Despite his WASPy firm and blue-chip aura, Begley was actually a Polish-born Jew, like Daniella. Begley had grown up in Brooklyn and made it through Harvard, the hard way. He had headed the Debevoise office in Paris, so he seemed to speak our language and understood both art and Europe.

Despite the horrors of terrorism in our midst, the Smooke sale gave New York a needed dose of the glamour and luxury that Manhattan does better than anywhere. I was on the podium at our new headquarters auctioning at my most vivacious to a packed house of five hundred swells who ran the gamut from Las Vegas's Steve Wynn to New York's Ronald Lauder, who was about to inaugurate his own Neue Galerie on 86th Street in these parlous times.

The final sale totaled $86 million, not far below its estimate. Only five works did not sell, but each of these orphans broke my heart; they were *my* orphans now, not Sotheby's orphans. It was personal. But the real bottom line, and the one the press seized on, was the rumor that we had paid in guarantees way over what we had netted. This hurt, and ensured that Bernard Arnault, that savviest of investors, would not have second thoughts about getting out of the auction business.

Not that Bernard Arnault "took a haircut." Just by waiting a few years, he was able to sell the inventory of top artworks he had assembled, including some wonderful Klimts and the like, for substantial profits over his costs. The main reason he got out wasn't the money; it was the scrutiny of Phillips being a public company, owned by LVMH, that was excoriated by the financial press because an art house was not considered compatible with LVMH's *core* business, which was fashion. The year 2001 turned out to be one of the worst ever in the annals of luxury. Even billionaires are sensitive to what the newspapers of the world are saying about the way they make their billions.

Despite the efforts of Louis Begley, we were being bullied to a pulp by Arnault's phalanx of LVMH attorneys. The fact that LVMH had pulled out was a stigma, a scarlet letter that no company could expect to recover from, the ultimate vote of no confidence. Daniella and I had gone from having our own very successful business, with low overhead and high profits, to becoming the sudden owners of a conglomerate's business with high overhead and no profits. That is, if we wanted to go on, which we did. Trying to raise money for something as nonessential as an auction house would never be easy. After 9/11 it was madness. If Bernard Arnault could not save Phillips, who could?

What about Louise? She had kept pushing to be involved; I kept pushing back to avoid mixing business and pleasure. We seemed madly in love at this point. She had proven herself to be a business genius. And what did I need? A business genius. And one with deep pockets. She could be the white knight no one else wanted to be. Louise had met me because she wanted to get into the art business. She had wanted to be part of my life, and my life was Phillips. Now she could have her chance. What could have been more perfect?

Louise had not been installed in our offices for a day when the cracks began to show. On day one Daniella had agreed with me, "Yes, we've found the formula." On day two, Daniella retracted all her praise. "This is a disaster," she exclaimed. Daniella and I had grown so close we were like the same person. We completed each other's sentences. So how could I love Louise and Daniella hate her? Easy. Here was a case study in the perils of mixing business and pleasure, particularly when there was little business to mix. In return for our making her CEO of Phillips, de Pury & Luxembourg, Louise, who expected to be an equity partner, had promised a substantial and essential cash infusion. She had so far not put in a penny, and Daniella believed she never would.

Furthermore, Louise, who was a neophyte when it came to art, was not content to stay on the business side. She wanted what she perceived as the glamour of the "artistic" side. But that was Daniella's side, and Daniella was rightfully proprietary about it. Within a month we had to retain another lawyer, a partner at Coudert Frères in Paris, to come in and act as a sort of marriage counselor between Daniella and Louise. The first day he was on the job, he spent seven hours conferring with Louise. "He totally agrees with me," Louise exulted to me afterward. Then he spent hours with Daniella. "He totally agrees with me," Daniella also exulted.

The next morning the Coudert lawyer reported back his inescapable conclusion: Louise must go. I did my best to try to play King Solomon between my partner and my girlfriend. It was a thankless task. Neither woman had what one would call a small ego. Combined, the two were way too big for me. And Daniella was correct. Louise, notwithstanding all her assurances, would never invest in the company. She wouldn't put her money where she claimed her heart—and her art—was.

As for the heart part, our supposed marriage-track affair was derailed by Isabel's refusal to give me the divorce that my clairvoyant had given me the courage to seek. I had even hired one of the top lawyers in Europe, Marc Bonnant, who represented the divorcing wives of Russian oligarchs, and billionaires like Lily Safra in Monaco, in the case of the mysterious death of her husband Edmond. But even Bonnant couldn't make my case. Under Swiss law, both spouses have to appear before the judge and declare they want the divorce. Isabel refused. "I'm doing this to *protect* you," she insisted outside the courthouse. To this day I am grateful to her for that refusal. With partnership, both in life and at work, out of the question, the romance with Louise came to an end.

Within seven months of joining Phillips in 2002, Louise was out; Daniella was also looking toward the exit. Ronald Lauder, one of the most brilliant of businessmen, had analyzed Phillips and found it unsalvageable. He advised her to leave. That was seemingly the kiss of death. When Daniella quit, she was followed by the head of our photography department. I was then summoned to the lobby of the Mercer by five of my other department heads. Were they leaving, too? Before I could begin to despair, they told me quite the opposite. *If you are willing to fight on, we will fight with you.* Their loyalty gave me courage and strength.

I must give credit where credit is due. My "Fab Five" were Brook Hazelton, my CEO; Michael McGinnis, worldwide head of contemporary art; Michaela Neumeister, head of business development and also in charge of German-speaking countries; Aileen Agopian, director of contemporary art; and Sean Cleary, chief operating officer. Not one of them was over thirty-five. I knew I couldn't rebuild the business without them. Accordingly, to reflect their essentiality, I decided to give the group 30 percent of the equity in the company, in effect making them my partners. From 2003 until 2008, no one left, as together we would make one of the most unexpected comebacks in the annals of the art business.

My evolving relationship with Louise is a prime example of how art can make strange bedfellows out of the deepest of lovers. Before Louise joined Phillips, de Pury & Luxembourg, we used to have the most romantic times in Paris. She was renting a superb apartment on the Rue Saint-Honoré directly across from the British Embassy. Huge windows opened onto one of the most splendid gardens in the heart of the city. We'd go for endless night walks and always end up at the Café de Flore, where we'd sit inside with the truly chic Parisian habitués (never on the terrace with the tourists) and order boiled frankfurters followed by chocolate eclairs and laugh at how unhealthily and un-Michelinly we were eating and loving it. Then we'd go around the corner to La Palette and have more drinks while being insulted by the famously rude *patron*. It was fun to see Louise, who was very controlling and dowager-like for such a young woman, relax for once and live like a peasant rather than Marie Antoinette.

By then it might have been two in the morning, and we would begin our peregrination back to the Right Bank, going window-shopping at the irresistibly seductive vitrines of the Rue de Seine. One night, after Louise had joined the firm and we were still trying to make peace (and money), we were stopped short by what we saw in the window of Vallois, a store that was the temple of Art Deco. For me it was love at first sight— two giant ceramic vases by Jean Besnard, whose heyday was in the 1950s. They were the best vases I had ever seen, and I waxed rhapsodic to Louise about how much I loved them. I don't *think* she was jealous over these inanimate objects, though I was so carried away, she might have been.

The next day I called Madame Vallois, who told me she regretted that the vases were *reserved*. They were not for sale. As I was not a privileged customer, I accepted defeat, but not totally. Every few weeks I'd call and ask about the vases. Always reserved. When I was next in Paris, now on my own, as the business affair had begun to poison my love affair, I'd go in person to Vallois hoping to change my luck. Still reserved, I was told. Eventually I got angry. I offered to pay for them, full price, on the spot. I was rejected. The next day, after my solitary nightcap-cum-insult at La Palette, I strolled by to see my unrequited loves. They had vanished from the vitrine. The morning after, I came into the store and was told that the vases had been sold. I never felt so rejected.

A while later, still in 2002, Louise was gone from me and from Phillips, and I was totally on my own. I received in the mail a magnificent catalogue from Christie's for the upcoming auction of the Karl Lagerfeld collection. It made me wax nostalgic over a Lagerfeld auction I had done in Monte Carlo of his Memphis furniture. Nostalgia quickly gave way to mystery when I turned a glossy page and saw my two true loves, the Besnard vases I had coveted. I understood why Vallois would favor Lagerfeld over me. He was without question one of the most brilliant individuals in any category I have ever met. However, the Christie's sale was so soon that there had been no real time for the vases to have gone to Lagerfeld. They had to have gone from Vallois straight to Christie's. Without trying to fathom motives, I was thrilled that finally here was my chance to acquire the vases.

I was on the phone that auction night as a bidder. Nothing was going to stop me now. These vases, I vowed, would never escape me. My vows were put to the test by another obsessive bidder. Whatever I bid, the other person topped me. The prices became astronomical. I was driven, and I understood Paul Mellon's dictum at that first great Peter Wilson sale: What was price where beauty was concerned? Eventually, I shot the moon, and the vases were knocked down to me. A record was set for Jean Besnard. I felt conflicted. I had gotten what I wanted, but I was furious with myself for overpaying, and then some. Soon I saw a press cutting from a German newspaper saying how thrilled Lagerfeld was with the sale, particularly of the Besnard vases. He had more Besnards to sell; he could only win.

Not long after, I ran into someone I knew from Christie's who whispered, in deep confidence, the most unimaginable treachery in my burning ear. The opposing bidder was Louise MacBain. Hell hath no fury like a collector scorned. I still have those wonderful vases, but they're in storage. The silver lining here is that the prices for Besnard have continued to soar beyond the highway robbery and lover's ransom that I had paid. The moral is that if you buy the best and if you can stay the course, in the long run, you will not overpay.

Louise MacBain continued to dog me. Her bids for the Besnard vases were chump change compared to her next expenditure designed to stick hard and deep in my craw. In March 2003, Louise purchased the bible of the art trade, *Art & Auction* magazine, which at the time was to art what *Women's Wear Daily* was to fashion. Just as that latter journal's imperious owner, John Fairchild, would have his pets and his pariahs, whom he would either pan or not mention at all, I feared that there was no way I could get objective coverage if *A&A* was controlled by Louise, who still seemed to have a score to settle. I guess I was being sensitive, because by the time Louise bought *A&A*, I was at a low ebb in my career.

My ultimate defeat in trying with Phillips, de Pury & Luxembourg to challenge the duopoly occurred on 57th Street in 2002. *Faire bonne mine à mauvais jeu.* I did it for my dead brother. Now I would be doing it for my dead auction house. That old French expression, a darker take on grace under pressure, would become my mantra on November 4, 2002. That date, which will live in infamy in my calendar, was my own Pearl Harbor, the worst auction of my life. I was always superstitious about auctions, and the monsoonal thunderstorms that evening augured ill. They drenched the stylish crowd of several hundred people who had jammed into the Phillips auction room on West 57th Street. I had thought the huge turnout was a good thing, but in retrospect I realize that I had drawn a crowd who were there not to buy art but to see the spectacle of my being fed to the lions. Thumbs down.

I had high hopes that night for our Impressionist sale. Louise and Daniella were in their Mexican standoff, and the rent was killing, but the art was great, assembled by Michel Strauss, Sotheby's distinguished head of Impressionist art, whom we had recently hired away. The art would save Phillips, and me. We were expecting a sale of at least $50 million that evening. It started with a Monet, *Japanese Bridge at Giverny*. It was offered at $6.5 million. Nobody wanted it. I refused to give it away. "Passed," I was forced to declare. That was the cruelest word in the auction lexicon, and it was law, rather than any tradition, that forced me to intone this declaration of humble pie. In the eighties, David Bathurst, the first head of Christie's New York, had told the press certain pieces at auction had been sold, for millions of dollars. The seller sued, claiming the pieces had not been sold at all. The seller prevailed; Bathurst resigned in disgrace, and later died at fifty-four, while shooting in the moors in Scotland. My first "pass" was the beginning of a humble-pie-eating contest. I said the P-word over and over that endless evening, as the cruel buyers just sat on their hands. We had seventeen paintings valued at over a million dollars. Only one sold.

The entire auction yielded $6.9 million, barely enough to keep the lights on in this vast and costly house that LVMH had built and abandoned. A bad game indeed. In retrospect the paintings that Strauss had put together for the sale had mostly been on the market before and not sold. There was a lack of freshness. But that was hindsight, and hindsight was no better than blindness. Walking down Madison Avenue, I could feel the gloating and thrill of schadenfreude, the sorrow and the pity. Many people crossed the street just to avoid me. But I had to keep smiling and make the promise of a better day to the press, to our clients, wherever they were, to our enemies. The crazy thing for me was that this was no act. I should have felt like Napoleon at Waterloo. Instead, I felt like MacArthur on Corregidor. *I shall return.* Phillips had been around since 1798. It was not going to die on my watch. Was I delusional? Maybe, but if you love art, and you believe in art, you always know that art will come back, and take you along with it.

18

MY OLIGARCHS

———————

The year 2002 was not my favorite. I lost Louise. I lost Daniella. My auction house looked dead. And the man who made the career that seemed to be dying with Phillips did the unthinkable. That ultimate force of life Heini Thyssen gave up the ghost in April. He was eighty-one, and I thought he would go on forever. He had had a series of strokes, and while some might say his oenophilia had led to his demise, I would have to give my diagnosis as terminal litigation. He had spent much of the time since I had left him in a donnybrook of a lawsuit in that off-shore haven of Bermuda. As usual, the only winners were the attorneys. But oh, how they won. Having been suffering from a similar illness in my legal dealings with LVMH, I was a totally sympathetic mourner, as well as being a brokenhearted honorary member of the family.

I attended the small funeral at the Schloss Landsberg, outside of Dusseldorf, the ancestral castle where Heini was buried with his father and his grandfather. My most vivid memory, aside from the sparcity of attendees given Heini's multiplicity of supposed friends, was the schloss's amazing Art Nouveau master bathroom. The *salle de bain* had been imported, tile by tile, from the 1900 Paris World's Fair, which introduced this new style to a breathless world. Standing among the graves, I thought back on the origins of the family's collecting. All Heini's grandfather, the chicken-wire maker turned steel baron, had in the way of art was reproductions of seventeenth-century Dutch painters.

The only notable art he had was his sculptures by Rodin, who had been a great friend of his grandfather. Heini had arrayed these white marble statues around his indoor pool when he redecorated Daylesford for Denise to resemble a decadent Roman bath.

I was more than sad. I recalled, once Tita joined the scene and the cash flow started to dry up, how Heini's accountant, Signor Guscetti, begged me to make Heini stop buying so much art. I did try. In vain. Each year Heini would make a New Year's Day resolution to curtail his buying. That resolution would be broken, shattered, by January 5. Art collecting has been called the "beautiful illness." There in the imperial gloom of Landsberg Castle, I was certain that this beautiful illness was not what killed my friend. It was what kept him alive.

I looked around at the children, the ex-wives, the current Baroness Tita, Miss Spain, who would be bringing more than a title home to Madrid. She would be bringing a collection, maybe the best in the world. There was an American game show called *Family Feud*. This was the aristo-version, kinky as could be. The child most like Heini was Francesca, who had gone from being the party girl of Steve Strange to being the Archduchess von Habsburg, courtesy of her husband, Karl, the direct descendant of the Holy Roman Emperor. Karl's title was as unassailable as Heini's contested Hungarian one was vulnerable. Titles aside, Heini had inadvertently stolen the show at his daughter's wedding by coming dressed as a Cossack. Never a dull moment.

Now the legal battle was over, the spoils shared by half the solicitors in London. On his imperial deathbed, he'd called the whole thing off. The kids would get the money; Tita and Spain would get the art, in what would be the biggest transfer of culture since Napoleon brought half the treasures of Europe to the Louvre. Everyone had wanted Heini's collection, from Margaret Thatcher and Prince Charles to Helmut Kohl to the Getty to the National Gallery to Disney (!). But Spain got it; such was the power of Tita, of beauty over art.

The Landsberg funeral was months before my own personal death by auction that November. At this point, I could still hold my head up. After all, I owned a major auction house, didn't I? After November, I couldn't make that claim. I faced abject defeat. Accordingly, I retreated and retrenched. In 2003 I closed the 57th Street gilded albatross and moved the house—now, with Daniella having left, called Phillips de Pury—down to a low-rent concrete warehouse in Chelsea on West 15th Street, far west, wild west. The Meatpacking District, pre–High Line hipness, was a wasteland of mean leather bars and abandoned abbatoirs. I had to let go of the Old Masters and Impressionists and even modern art, for which I lacked the resources necessary to compete with Sotheby's and Christie's. I decided to focus on the art of the last twenty-five years; call it ultra-contemporary. While most people defined contemporary as starting in the seventies, I used the eighties as my cutoff, if only to further tighten what was of necessity a very tight focus. I thought this was where I had the greatest upside potential, and, in this case, I turned out to be dead right.

I had seen the emergence of the new wave led by Koons and Hirst and had a gut feeling that their enormous prices, which the old-time art critics derided as a flash in the Wall Street pan, were just the beginning of a landslide. I would also keep Phillips involved in photography and design. I would live, and sell, in the now. I would make my pared-down, tiny staff, whoever was brave enough to be loyal to me, stakeholders in the new Phillips de Pury. It would be a sort of cooperative. Phillips de Pury would become a guerrilla auction house.

I somehow succeeded despite the art world's most dire predictions. My embrace of the new turned New York's Chelsea into a new version of the London Chelsea of the Beatles and Stones, a King's Road by the Hudson. Obsessed with pop music, I pumped my playlists through the galleries. Some clients did complain, but they got over it. At the 2015 spring sale at Christie's, the one that totaled just under a billion dollars and broke all records, what was playing? Pop music. The change had come.

My auctions at Phillips, which were surrounded by wild parties, rock concerts, and assorted other "happenings," turned stars into superstars. My alchemy was to put the exploding, untrammeled wealth of Wall Street and hedge-fund collectors into the ever-bulging pockets of not only Koons and Hirst but a growing profusion of new big names like Richter, Murakami, Prince, Fischer. And it wasn't just painters who partook in this gold rush. Designers like Ron Arad and Marc Newson became stars as well, and photographers like Andreas Gursky and Helmut

Newton entered a stratosphere of price and respect that they never ever expected. It was a new age where the starving artist morphed into Croesus, and almost all of the new superstars were introduced at Phillips.

One sale that epitomized the new Phillips was the 2005 auction of the art of my old friend Princess Gloria von Thurn und Taxis, aka "the punk princess," also aka "Gloria TNT, the dynamite socialite." Gloria was only in her early twenties when she married Bavaria's Prince Johannes von TNT, who was thirty-three years her senior, openly bisexual, and a master of irreverent practical jokes that cemented his friendship with Heini Thyssen. Once at an all-white ball at his Versailles-sized castle in Regensburg, the Prince poured red wine onto the chair of Princess Margaret, visiting from London, so as to create an embarrassing stain on the royal derriere.

Gloria was one of the world's great party givers. Few fetes could compare to her 1986 birthday bash for the Prince, where the birthday cake was festooned with sixty phalluses made of marzipan, and the people who ate them included Mick Jagger and Jerry Hall, Al and Judy Taubman, Malcolm Forbes, Adnan Khashoggi, Ann Getty, and of course Heini and Tita. Keith Haring had designed all the plates on which the guests dined, and these plates became collector's items. On another occasion, Gloria had Michael Jackson there as her guest. How many castles can boast a guest list that included both Prince and Michael Jackson? Gloria loved New York and loved its contemporary art scene, hanging the works of eighties wunderkinder like Jeff Koons, Keith Haring, and Cindy Sherman in her suite at the castle, which she had redecorated by a hip Irish interior designer.

When the Prince died in 1990, following a failed heart transplant, he left Gloria with over $500 million in debt, turning her overnight into a poor little rich girl. Now Gloria had to sell a lot of that art to pay the late Prince's debts and tax bills. I was there for Sotheby's to auction it off, at two huge sales, one in Geneva in 1992, and another at a marathon five-day "house sale" in the castle itself in 1993. I did the kickoff session and then the third day and was planning to leave, when Gloria, seized with separation anxiety, called Al Taubman himself and ordered him to hold me hostage at the Regensburg podium until the last bibelot had been auctioned off. Big Al, who rarely called anyone and had Dede

Brooks do his dialing, rang me directly and firmly instructed me to stay put.

A similarly flattering request, or rather demand, had been put to me at the three-day Palazzo Corsini house sale in Florence, where the Princess Corsini insisted that I do the honors at every sale on every day. When the Sotheby's lawyer tried inserting a "health permitting" escape clause in the auction contract, the Princess counter-argued for her right to inspect the doctor's medical certificate if I somehow tried to malinger my way out.

When I was resurrecting Phillips, I created a hip, young advisory board with Gloria as a charter member, alongside her royal hipster counterpart Francesca Thyssen; Lapo Elkann, who was Gianni Agnelli's grandson and heir to Fiat; the art-collecting designer Marc Jacobs; LA art maven and *The Young and the Restless* soap-opera magnate Maria Arena Bell; super-photographers Mario Testino and Jurgen Teller; architecture trophy hunter Aby Rosen; and former Sex Pistols manager Malcolm McLaren.

Phillips de Pury was the anti-Sotheby's, the *Animal House* of the art world, and thrilled to be driving the uptight people crazy. In 2005 we had sales of slightly over $100 million compared to Sotheby's $2.7 billion and Christie's $3.2 billion. Size didn't matter; I wasn't fighting the duopoly any more. I was fighting for survival, and in 2005 my Phillips turned a profit for the first time in the five years since I had begun my crazy trip there. Nobody in New York or London believed I could pull it off.

By the time my life had turned upside down, Gloria had turned her own inside out. She became a born-again Catholic, the closest female friend of Regensburg's homeboy Cardinal Joseph Ratzinger, who became Pope Benedict XVI. With that privileged access to the Vatican, plus an eyebrow-raising love affair with her Italian counterpart Princess Alessandra Borghese, whose mother was heiress to the San Pellegrino water and Citterio prosciutto fortunes, Gloria had moved to Rome to be with her new passions.

I divined that Gloria was ready to sell some more art, and that I was the ideal person to sell it for her. We had a great track record; we had history and friendship. Nonetheless, I couldn't help but worry she would still pick Sotheby's, because she and Johannes were such close friends of Al and Judy Taubman. Realizing that I was my own best emissary, I went to Rome to talk to her about it, bringing Michaela Neumeister, one of my "Fab Five" loyalists, of whom Gloria was most fond. I was, too, but I didn't realize how fond, until Michaela and I fell in love and got married, several years later, in 2009.

At the Hotel de Russie near the Piazza del Popolo we ran into Nicolas Berggruen, bon-vivant son of Heinz and a dear friend. Nicolas is a chocoholic, as is Gloria, so we indulged in an all-afternoon sugarfest at the hotel's dining room, after which Gloria would have let me sell anything I wanted. For the auction, to be held in 2006, I got Jurgen Teller to go to the castle in Regensburg and create the most provocative catalogue in the history of auctions. On the back cover he had, in a parody of Bavarian gemütlichkeit, a shot of Princess Gloria dressed as a barmaid holding a turkey leg in one hand and a beer stein in the other. Gloria was game for anything.

Sometimes Jurgen's games could get him, and me, into trouble. For a jewelry catalogue I commissioned him to do for Phillips, he festooned all the members of his family with our precious stones, including his baby boy. In the drop of a lawsuit we got a threatening letter from a children's protective organization accusing us of child molestation and exploitation. For the same auction, he delivered a jewelry catalogue in a cardboard pizza box. Jurgen loves combining the riduclous with the sublime, and his unorthodoxies helped create the identity I wanted for Phillips.

So did our sale of Gloria's glorious eighties art. The sale was preceded by a delicious and festive dinner in our Chelsea offices toplined by Tom Ford and Marc Jacob, followed by a dance party with Gloria's favorite eighties band, Kid Creole and the Coconuts. The celebration endeared us to the fashion-driven New York press, as did Gloria, who was a mainstay of Condé Nast. Highlights of the sale were Jeff Koons's kitschy wood sculpture *Yorkshire Terriers*, Paul McCarthy's subversive *Santa Long Neck*, and Keith Haring's *Self-Portrait*. Because every single item in the auction sold, the Gloria event was what they call in the trade a "white glove sale." In the duopoly, in the rare case when everything sells, the auctioneer is given a commemorative pair of white gloves. As I was the chairman of my own house, I thought it would be unseemly to make the gift to myself. Nonetheless, I was as proud as a new father. Phillips had indeed been reborn. Long live Phillips de Pury. At least as long as I could keep it afloat.

With the aid of my young CEO, ex–Goldman Sachs banker and Harvard MBA Brook Hazelton, who was proof that the combination of Harvard and hip was not oxymoronic, I enjoyed such an unexpected renaissance in New York that I also did a similar makeover of Phillips London. Brook is now president of Christie's America, proof of my eye for talent. At the London Phillips flagship, I turned a dowager into a go-go girl. I celebrated this 2006 unveiling in a former Post Office building in Victoria, which Phillips shared with ex-Gucci-ites Tom Ford and über-designer Marc Newson, with a decadent feast from star chef Jamie Oliver and a concert from the Human League. Even without the Concorde, I lived a Concorde lifestyle, splitting my time between Claridge's in London and the Mercer Hotel in New York, always mixing it up, high and low. Eventually the success of our new glamour caught the eye of the contemporary-art-obsessed new superclass of Russian oligarchs.

No one had better Russian bona fides than I. I had begun moving in this new fantasy world that my own efforts to "open up" the old Soviet Union had helped usher in. This was the world of "Dasha and Masha," the two young and gorgeous twin tsarinas of the Russian art elite. Dasha was, and is, Dasha Zhukova, the consort of the London-based billionaire Roman Abramovich, arguably the world's most eligible bachelor, who created the ultra-hip Garage Museum in Moscow. Masha, Dasha's rival for the modern Catherine the Great—or Peggy Guggenheim—position, was, and is, Masha Baibakova, daughter of property billionaire Oleg Baibakov. Masha is a cultural impresario whom I met when she was introducing young Russian artists to the world at Moscow's Chocolate Factory. While Dasha grew up a middle-class émigré in LA, went to UCSB, then met her prince, Masha was born a princess in Moscow. She lived everywhere, graduating from Barnard, Harvard Business School, the Courtauld, the Sotheby's training course. While Dasha's mission was to bring Koons and Hirst to the Russian masses, Masha's was to refine the mass taste by exposing it to emerging artists both from her home and abroad, like LA's Sterling Ruby.

I quickly got to know all the oligarchs who had an interest in art. They would become even bigger buyers of contemporary art than the American hedge-funders. Because their wealth was so new and so sudden, they were not in thrall to the Sotheby's-Christie's Establishment and were open to outliers like myself, particularly if I had what they wanted. They were a colorful lot, these "Wild Easterners." Take Victor Pinchuk. A brainy Russian-born metallurgical engineer who got rich from his patents, which created his giant company Interpipe, Pinchuk mixed wealth and politics, a surefire combo, by marrying the daughter of the president of the Ukraine.

Pinchuk and I shared an obsession with Japanese culture, which was my entry point. Pinchuk had created a magnificent Kyoto temple of a home outside Kiev, an odd juxtaposition that made it all the more dramatic. I tried to sell Pinchuk a Kabakov for his great collection, but he said no. While Kabakov was born in the Ukraine, he pretended to be Russian. His lack of national pride was a deal breaker if you are married to the Ukrainian president's daughter. Not that Pinchuk is stuck in Kiev. He helped mount the Jeff Koons show at Versailles, and he made headlines for his fiftieth birthday party in the French Alps, where he was fed by Alain Ducasse and entertained by Cirque du Soleil.

Then there is Vladislav Doronin. If Vladimir Putin had to change places with any of the billionaires he has helped spawn, he would surely choose Doronin. The self-styled James Bond of the Russian oligarchy, Doronin is Putin's own Platonic ideal of himself. Both are Leningradians, both fitness fanatics, both audacious; Doronin even looks like a Hollywood version of the man who made him a king. The most worldly and Westernized of all the eastern tycoons, Doronin lives perhaps the biggest life on the planet. He just broke up with Naomi Campbell in favor of Luo Zilin, Miss Universe China. Miss China has reportedly been dethroned now, at least in Doronin's heart, in favor of a Russian beauty. He owns prime real estate across the globe, his holdings epitomized by his recent acquisition of the super-luxe Amanresorts chain.

Doronin is a relative youngster. He was born in 1962. His best American friend is Leonardo DiCaprio. They both are extremely interested in art. We met at Art Basel, through the late billionaire oil trader Marc Rich, for whom Doronin had worked early in his career. Rich was notoriously pardoned by Bill Clinton over trading violations with Iran, though the controversy was so great that he never came back to America to enjoy that pardon. Doronin loves Pop Art. Like other oligarchs, he built his estimable collection in record time. Like Pinchuk, Doronin gives amazing parties. He invited me to his birthday fete at the Jodhpur Fort in India, thrown by Naomi Campbell and studded with her fellow supermodels Karolina Kurkova, Eva Herzigova, Kate Moss. The entertainment was provided by Chaka Khan and Diana Ross, who, while singing "I Will Survive," fell off the stage and disappeared for a suspenseful few minutes. However, she reappeared and finished the song. A few days later I saw a picture of her in a large cast in the *Daily Mail*. What a trouper. In India, we all rode elephants and dressed as rajahs. Doronin didn't have to pretend.

And then there were *my* oligarchs, the Mercury Boys. Given that the Russians and I spoke the same language, it was a perfect fit when the Mercury Group bought into Phillips in the dog days of the America financial crisis in 2008. Famed for its Luxury Village, the world's ultimate shopping mall in the Beverly Hills of Moscow, Mercury was founded by the "two Leonids," Friedland and Strunin, very poor Jews who got very rich when the Iron Curtain fell. What a success story. The two Leonids, one rounder, one thinner, went to kindergarten together. In the nineties they were street peddlers, selling lacquer boxes and babushkas to tourists. They worked their way up to opening a booth at the Radisson SAS Hotel. There they started selling watches, and the rest is history, as they rode the tidal wave of Russian wealth and status-symbol acquisitiveness.

My deal with these new capitalists of the old Communism, whom I met through the Paris dealer Albert Benhamou and began flirting with in 2007, was closed on a yacht in the harbor of Saint-Tropez, replete with more starlets than the Cannes Film Festival. The two Leonids, both in their early forties, dressed less like tycoons than like low-budget tourists in polyester tracksuits. Still, their champagne tabs were as high as Heini Thyssen's wine bills, and their entourage of models, starlets, whatever, you never knew, was larger than *Playboy*'s Hugh Hefner's in his prime. At La Voile Rouge beach club in Saint-Tropez, where a lot of the closing festivities went on, the two Leonids got their kicks by shaking up bottles of the finest vintages and then spraying the costly bubbly on all the patrons, most of whom were topless anyhow and didn't mind.

The two Leonids were initially not interested in art; they were interested in money. They saw Phillips de Pury as a natural extension of their retail empire, one more luxury brand. Again, administration being my weak suit, I was delighted to have such hard-nosed moguls at the helm, minding the store. I was less than thrilled, however, when, to oversee the business side of their new acquisition, they brought in the least likely CEO in the history of the auction world. This was Bernd Runge, who had started *Vanity Fair* in Germany for Condé Nast and had been selected as Germany's Media Man of the Year in 2003. Runge knew nothing whatsoever about art. That was one of the problems of being in the business of art, but in Hollywood, most of the executives don't know anything about movies, either, and the show goes on. Runge looked like a more malevolent version of Dennis Hopper in *Blue Velvet*.

Those looks were not deceiving. In 2004 Runge was unmasked as a spy for the East German Secret Police, or Stasi, from 1981 to 1989, beginning when he was a student at Moscow University. Operating under the code name "Olden," Runge was said to have even spied on his own sister, who was trying to escape from East Germany. The Newhouses, who owned Condé Nast, kept Runge on, dismissing his "distant past" as irrelevant to his business success. Likewise, the two Leonids, having grown up being spied upon, were not troubled by Runge's Stasi background. I was, and I told the Leonids my reservations. "He gets results" was their reply. One of these results was that between 2008 and 2012, thirty-six employees left Phillips.

Working side by side with a Stasi spy had its challenges, but nowhere nearly as many as starring on a reality television show. The show was Bravo's *Work of Art: The Next Great Artist*, which was the cable network's attempt to clone its enormously successful *Project Runway* for the art world and discover the next Warhol, with ratings to match. The main producer was *Sex and the City*'s Sarah Jessica Parker and her company, Pretty Matches, which teamed up with an LA production company called Magical Elves. What names in showbiz! I was "discovered" by one of Sarah Jessica's producers who had seen me doing an auction at Phillips and thought I had "star quality." When William Morris Endeavor descended upon me, I felt like Lana Turner being spotted by a casting agent at Schwab's Drugstore in Hollywood.

Naturally all my Establishment friends said absolutely no way. You can't turn art, sacred art, into a spectacle. And naturally, because I saw what a spectacle art, particularly contemporary art, had become, I said yes. My role was the show's mentor, to encourage the contestants to be the best artists they could be. That was far less cruel than being a judge. That discerning task went to a highly qualified threesome. There was Jeanne Greenberg-Rohatyn, a second-generation gallerist from St. Louis who had married the son of super-banker and ex-amabssador to France Felix Rohatyn. There was William Powers, another gallerist who was the masculine half of a New York "power couple" with the fashion designer Cynthia Rowley. And there was the *New York Magazine* art critic Jerry Saltz, half of another power couple with Roberta Smith, art crtic of *The New York Times*.

Casting the show was a marathon, as eleven hundred artists descended upon us, camping out outside our studios to present their five-minute videos and do a brutal two-minute interview to make their mark. It was the equivalent of speed dating and just as unfair. I noticed that the ones who made the cut to the initial eighty, which would in turn be winnowed to fourteen, were the first six we saw after our lunch break, when our hypoglycemia had been assuaged. So much for objectivity.

I enjoyed getting to know Sarah Jessica Parker. For a big star, she seemed terribly nervous. Every time she was scheduled to appear on camera, she was a wreck and often turned to me for moral support. She was in the same state I was in every time before an auction. However, since this was not an auction but the make-believe that was reality TV, I was out of my element and thus as cool as a cucumber, which deeply impressed Sarah Jessica. I guess it was because my life didn't depend on Bravo, because it was just for fun. However, once the cameras rolled, the nervous Miss Parker was as smooth as silk, a true star, while the cool Mr. de Pury often came across as the fumbling, bumbling amateur that he was.

The show ran for two seasons. Although it was ultimately not renewed for a third, each episode was seen by over a million viewers. Very few artists in history have had an exhibition seen by so many. The show, if considered a failure relative to *Project Runway,* was in my mind a qualified success. *Work of Art* was a testament to the power of television and the new media, and it was proof that Louise MacBain was indeed ahead of the curve in her ambition, inchoate as it may have seemed, to marry art and the Internet. Like Heini Thyssen, I wanted to get art seen by as many people as possible. While our contestants weren't Rembrandts, neither was Jeff Koons when he was starting out.

By 2012, although my oligarchs and I had surfed the tidal wave of the last financial cataclysm, I came to the conclusion that I had enough of Harvard-Business-School-think, or even Stasi-think. The oligarchs wanted new headquarters in London. They wanted to get bigger. They wanted, as Bernard Arnault had wanted, to challenge the duopoly. That was always an auction person's holy grail. I, on the other hand, was ready for change and for the halcyon days of high flying and low overhead, where all I needed was a cell phone and the trust of my clients. The work of the dealer can be in *charming* people to buy, while that of the auction house can be in *scaring* people to sell. There's a lot of charm, and seduction, in the scaring, but dealing, and building collections, is the stuff of dreams, rather than the stuff of estates.

My life seemed to be lived in ten-year cycles, and the Phillips cycle, begun in 2001, was reaching its limit. Single for a long time after having in 2004 secured my divorce from Isabel, who felt she didn't have to protect me anymore, I married someone of whom Isabel, and our four grown children, wholeheartedly approved. This was my Phillips cohort, Michaela Neumeister, a brilliant Stanford doctoral student whose family owns the preeminent Munich auction house Neumeister. She loves art as much as I do. We quickly had a daughter, the non-Brooks DD. In late 2012 I sold my remaining interest in Phillips to my comrades at Mercury, and I embarked on a new adventure that is certain to be as eventful as all my previous ones.

19

COURTING MEDICIS

I was worried that having Jeff Koons and Damien Hirst in the same desert tent would be too much fame in too small a space. After all, even more than a tent, it would take a country far bigger than Qatar—Greenland, maybe—to hold the egos of the two most successful living artists on earth. Whatever might happen, I was thrilled to be able to see the spectacle, and thrilled to be going to Qatar. I had been invited to the opening of the Damien Hirst retrospective show that had been presented at the Tate Modern and now, in expanded form, was coming to Doha. That was one invitation no one in the art world would ever refuse, including Jeff Koons, who was there in homage to his rival in "bigness." Not to make too grandiose an analogy, it would be equivalent to Michelangelo declining an invitation to go to Florence. Qatar is the Florence of Arabia, and its Sheikha Al Mayassa, at thirty-one, the sister of the Emir and a worldly Duke graduate, is a desert Catherine de Medici. When it comes to art, no other woman is close to her influence, and no other country is more ambitious.

The public highlight of the art fest was the dramatic unveiling of fourteen monumental sixteen-foot-tall bronze Hirst sculptures depicting the cycle from conception to birth. The art stood in front of the Cesar Pelli–designed Sidra Medical and Research Center. (Doha, the ultramodern Persian Gulf–side capital of this oil barony, is full of the temples of starchitects—Pei, Hadid, Nouvel, Herzog, and de Meuron, among many.) The private highlight was a desert odyssey worthy of T. E. Lawrence. We rode through a barren landscape of endless towering sand dunes in a caravan of twenty-five Land Rovers for nearly two hours to a romantic full-moon-lit tent-city oasis, greeted by dark men in white robes and a herd of ships of the desert so numerous that we dubbed the oasis Camel-lot.

The main tent had been transformed, in honor of Hirst, into a pharmacy, a nod to his late iconoclastic Notting Hill art-restaurant. As we were in a holy land, no alcohol was served. We didn't miss it. Instead, waiters brought around platters of hypodermic syringes filled with a dazzling array of fresh-squeezed and exotic fruit juices. A newly salubrious dimension was thus added to "shooting up." The tahini bacchanal of local lamb and rice dishes was something out of *The Arabian Nights*; the black-tie jazz band and the fox-trots they played were out of *The Great Gatsby*. In short, the evening was a fusion of Mecca and West Egg. We danced, we ate, we rode camels, we flew falcons perched on our arms by the birdmen of the desert, and we discreetly looked for art opportunities, buyers and sellers.

There were 150 guests, half local, half international. The Qatar women, all in black, hooded, and veiled, were a study in how much you could learn about someone through her eyes and the cut of robes that at first blush seemed identical but on close inspection bore infinite nuances. If you're in the art business, you learn to pay close attention. God is in the details. Among the Westerners were a panoply of tip-top collectors and dealers. Given the distances involved, the balance was predictably more heavily European than American. But the real focus was on the art stars, Hirst and Koons. It was like putting Michelangelo and da Vinci in the same room, or Picasso and Matisse. What would it be like? Would there be fireworks?

The reality was far less combustible than anyone would have thought. I had known both artists from their early days, when Hirst was a bad-boy art student in thrall to adman/art patron Charles Saatchi and Koons was a commodities trader manqué in thrall to the Italo-Hungarian porn star Cicciolina. Both had risen to the top by mixing outrageously original art with marketing wizardry. Hirst seemed like something out of *A Clockwork Orange*, shaking up the proper English art world the way fellow bad boy Gordon Ramsay was shaking up the heretofore nonexistent English food world.

So was Koons, at fifty-five a decade older than Hirst. Koons understood that the buyer was king (or emir), and managed to make everyone there feel like the most important person on earth. When I first met Koons, he was dressed like Elvis. I had invited him to be part of my lecture series at Sotheby's in Geneva, where he shocked the audience by showing nude sex art featuring a veritable Kama Sutra of himself and Cicciolina. Like a Hollywood star before he had quite become one, Jeff had made a special dietary request, a "virility menu" designed for him by none other than Arnold Schwarzenegger, red meat, oysters, and such, which we served to all the attendees. After Jeff's sex-loaded presentation, everyone asked for a second helping.

In Doha, two decades later, Jeff was dressed for fiscal success and as happily married as any suburbanite, minus the cheating. Even Hirst had put aside his menacing skull-decorated T-shirts and was wearing a proper suit. Courting Medicis, of any era, demanded perfect behavior, and both artists fell in line, praising each other to the heavens. Competition? Never! In the current art market, everybody wins, and wins big, and the customer is always right.

Courting Medicis is now what I do, and every week seems to bring a trip to Qatar, Shanghai, or some other Neverland where fantastic people indulge their fantasies by collecting art. I'm there to help. As a key component of this continuing courtship, I continue my passion for auctioneering by conducting charity auctions all over the world. In terms of *counting* Medicis, no big night at Sotheby's or Christie's could have overshadowed the sheer volume of titanically rich and powerful art lovers who assembled at Saint-Tropez in July 2015 for the auction I conducted for the Leonardo DiCaprio Foundation. LDCF has become a juggernaut in supporting environmental concerns and preserving both wildlife and wildlands with a heady, Hollywoody combination of highlife and nightlife. In terms of separating the men from the boys, as it were, while admission to a Sotheby's or Christie's auction is free, a ticket to Leonardo's Show of Shows cost £12,000, or nearly $19,000 dollars. That 650 people paid the price this night to get into Leonardo's party is testimony to how big—and how generous—the oft-derided "1 percent" actually is.

Just as Los Angeles has become, in my view, the most important city in the world where art is made, Hollywood is no longer sneered at as a cultural Mojave Desert. Gone are the days when art collectors in the film colony were as sparse as Ivy League, or even college, graduates. In the fifties, Edward G. Robinson and Billy Wilder were virtually the only serious collectors in Tinseltown. Stars like Elizabeth Taylor may have had great art on the walls of their Bel Air mansions, but they were most likely to have been fabricated by the studio prop department. Today the stars and the moguls have discovered the joys of collecting, and right at the head of the new Hollywood Art Pack is Leonardo DiCaprio. The Wolf of Wall Street is also the Sage of Bond Street, the Midas of Madison Avenue, the star as connoisseur.

I had first met Leonardo the year before at the amfAR (American Foundation for AIDS Research) gala that had been taking place for twenty years as the major non-film event at the Cannes Film Festival. There I had had the pleasure of "selling Leonardo," auctioning off the privilege of walking the red carpet at the Oscars with this dashing five-time Oscar nominee. The extra frisson here was that on the highest-bidder's walk of fame, Leonardo might actually win the Acadamy Award for the first time.

An even bigger frisson, if such is possible, at the 2014 amfAR gala, was my auctioning Damien Hirst's glass-caged mammoth skeleton, *Gone but Not Forgotten,* for $15 million, a major record for any charity auction. It was the single largest donation ever made by any artist to a charity. No guest at any charity dinner, no matter how many Michelin stars were at play, had ever bid over $3 million for art. But on this night I got Len Blavatnik, the London-based, Ukrainian-born oligarch who owns the Warner Music colossus, to step up and set a record in buying Hirst's mammoth mammoth. I suppose Leonardo liked what he saw, for he soon invited me to helm his foundation's first auction that July. I couldn't say no, and the start-up was, like everything Leonardo touches, a vast success, raising $26 million for the benefit of the planet.

So here I was in Saint-Tropez, in the midst of a record heat wave that made the Riviera seem more like the Sahara. Michaela and I were totally jet lagged, having flown in from the Hamptons, where we had just been honored by the Rush Philanthropic Arts Foundation, headed by America's reigning hip-hop mogul, Russell Simmons, and his two equally talented brothers Joseph "Rev. Run" Simmons, of Run-DMC, and the visual artist Danny Simmons. Their mission had been to expose inner-city kids to the arts, and my wife and I, easy converts to the cause, had done all we could to aid the foundation, building a bridge from the galleries of Chelsea to the streets of Harlem. For most others in the art establishment, it was a bridge too far, and the Simmons brothers never forgot how we two European foreigners were there to get them the attention they deserved when many Americans were not. Rush's other three honorees were the comedian Dave Chappelle; the director of *Selma,* Ava DuVernay; and Wangechi Mutu, a fine African-born artist now living in America. Although we may have looked like the odd couple out in a largely African American crowd dressed fabulously for the Roaring Twenties Gatsby-themed event, we loved being the exotica for a change. Naturally, I did "sing for my supper," doing my auction-ioneering before dancing the night away, after which we dragged our tired bodies to JFK for a commericial flight to Nice.

Courting Medicis doesn't always mean traveling like one, though once we arrived, we were lodged in great style on the yacht of the Sebastian Kulczyks, the son and daughter-in-law of the richest man in Poland, Jan Kulczyk, the cornerstone of whose fortune was owning the first Volkswagen dealership in the country. Jan Kulczyk, who had helped transform his country from Communism to capitalism and was a major benefactor of Warsaw's Museum of the History of Polish Jews, very sadly died unexpectedly a week after we were his son's pampered guests.

But there was little time for being pampered. I had an auction to do, and I was as nervous as I always am, whatever the venue. Every auction seems like my first, and I am always plagued by high anxiety, which is good and keeps me on my toes. Never one to rest on his laurels, Leonardo wanted the 2015 auction to raise even more money than the one the previous year. He wanted more lots, and whatever Leonardo wants, Leonardo gets. I worked closely with the two masterminds of the event, like myself both enlisted by Leonardo because of the amazing job he had seen them do at amfAR. One was the producer Andy Boose, an ex-rocker who had once performed under the name Rene Risque before starting an events company that became the brains behind all the amfAR benfits now taking place across the globe.

Getting to be Andy's and amfAR's auctioneer had been as much of a chain-letter/domino effect as being discovered by Leonardo. Six years before at amfAR, I did a brief auctioneer cameo when Thomas Flohr, a friend of mine who owned the sky-high plane-rental service VistaJet, asked me as a favor to guest-auction at amfAR two paintings he had donated to the event by the Austrailian graffiti artist Richard Hambleton. I got up, made my sale, and sat down, auspiciously at a table that included Kanye West and Kim Kardashian. Within minutes, Harvey Weinstein, the moving force behind the money raised for amfAR, was right there at the table demanding that I resume the podium and sell his lots. I've been doing the honors at amfAR ever since, and the honor is all mine.

The other amfAR man on Leonardo's A-Team is Milutin Gatsby, a massive and compelling Eastern European who is the fund-raising chairman of AmFAR. The name itself is unique, a combination of Serbian muscle and Fitzgerald fantasy, and it cannot go without notice that Leonardo did play Gatsby, a name that is as "full of money" as Daisy Buchanan's voice. Milutin is "full of money." He is a master of obtaining donations. As amfAR's and now Leonardo's "money wrangler," his duty is to round up oligarchs and make sure they not only buy those £12,000 tickets but also bid oligarchically on the lots that I put up for sale.

What a job Milutin did. He had assembled tycoons from every corner of the globe. You could call the group the "titanic thousand," Asian electronics billionaires, African oil chieftans, Amercan hedge-funders, the usual Russian suspects, all leavened with the supermodels of the world. At one point I wasn't sure whether I was at a charity auction or a Victoria's Secret convention. Naomi Campbell, Heidi Klum, Petra Nemcova, Irina Shayk, Jessica Stam, and Chrissy Teigen were just the most famous of the eye candy that filled the huge tent at the Domaine Bertaud Belieu, a Gatsbyesque vineyard next to the polo club of the magical Côte d'Azur village where Brigitte Bardot became the beach goddess of her generation in *And God Created Woman*.

The Hollywood celebrities, that certain guarantor of worldwide publicity (no one is more media-savvy than superstar Leonardo) included Sylvester Stallone, Goldie Hawn and daughter Kate Hudson, Adrien Brody, Orlando Bloom, Marion Cotillard, and the star-maker himself, Harvey Weinstein. The art world was represented by Larry Gagosian, the Nahmad family, my old friend Anh Duong with African art collector and Fiat scion Jean Pigozzi, and Budi Tek, the Indonesian agricultural billionaire who has built amazing museums in Jakarta and Shanghai and is considered the Asian Eli Broad.

Among the corporate power elite were Steve Schwarzman of the Blackstone Group, who has a nearby villa, Los Angeles supermarket magnate Ron Burkle, music's charitably ubiquitous Len Blavatnik, shipping's Idan Ofer (the Israeli Onassis), fashion's Tommy Hilfiger, and blingdom's Laurence Graff. The night was as hot socially as it was climatically. The stars, however, were the exception. Otherwise the rule was the anonymity of power—high leverage, low visibility. Our table was typical: the Polish Kulczyks, the Sasan Ghandeharis (he a Kazakh oligarch), and Thomas Leclerc (he a shopping-mall developer, the French answer to Big Al Taubman). If you've never heard of them, that's precisely what they want.

This was an auction in a sauna. I had never been so hot. When I took the rostrum at 9:00 P.M. I had forsaken my normal uniform of navy Caraceni suit for jeans and an untucked white linen shirt. During the course of the marathon auction, which went on until 2:30 A.M., I repaired backstage to change that white shirt four times. I was constantly drenched and so revved up that I even forgot to eat my good-luck apple before the bidding began. I broke my normal rule of Evian-only to gun down a glass of the local rosé to de-tense myself. I think what I ate on the Kulczyk yacht was a steak, for the protein, but it may have been pasta, for the carbs. Whatever, like a competitive athlete on the eve of the Olympics, I needed all the energy I could summon up.

Some of the backstage tension was broken by Leonardo's favorite magician, an Israeli named Lior Suchard who could psychically bend spoons and forks like Uri Geller and read minds like nobody's business. He asked Sylvester Stallone, whom he had never met, to think of his first girlfriend so he could guess her name. The first clue he asked for was how old Stallone was when love hit him. "Eight," the star growled. Suchard scribbled something down, then asked Stallone the name of his inaugural amour. When Stallone gave the name, Suchard whipped out the paper with the young love's name written on it. The crowd was awed. Suchard went on to outdo himself by similarly guessing the name of Stallone's wife's first boyfriend.

Finally, I took the stage, introduced by Leonardo, and began my show. The auction had three components. First, there were the "money can't buy" experiences, like getting to attend all the major Hollywood awards with Harvey Weinstein. Twenty hands went up, compared to maybe five or at most ten for a Picasso at Sotheby's. A very rich and pretty young woman from China won Harvey with a bid of a million euros. Roger Federer donated a tennis match, and Prince Albert of Monaco came to join me onstage to offer a place on one of his Arctic expeditions. The American realty hegemon Tom Barrack of Colony Capital paid €12 million for some more real estate—a lot on the super-eco-resort Leonardo is building on Blackadore Caye, his private island off Belize. Milutin Gatsby had done his job well. For every lot, there were lots of bidders, and they spent wildly.

The second component of the sale was traditional works of art, some pieces, like a Warhol and a Banksy, donated by Leonardo himself. The Nahmads donated a Monet. A huge replica of Rodin's *The Thinker* sold for €1.5 million. The Marianne Boesky (daughter of insider-trader Ivan) Gallery in New York donated a Frank Stella statue, which did well, and Michael Chow, who has recently added canvases to his woks as a sphere of passion, was overjoyed when a painting he donated sold for €450,000. Finally, there was the pièce de résistance, a private concert by Elton John, of which Sir Elton gave the Saint-Tropez crowd a taste. John Legend added to the thrill by singing two songs at the same piano. The taste must have been good, because not one but two Elton concerts were sold to Asian billionaires for €3 million each.

By 2:30 A.M. the auction was over. We had raised a record $40 million. That entitled me to celebrate by dancing—with my wife—until dawn. The blue-chip DJ, a one-name show in a bowler hat named Cassidy, had DJ'ed at President Obama's inauguration as well as Jay Z and Beyoncé's wedding. He was a star, too, just like everyone else here. The adrenaline kept me up until we returned to the Kulczyk yacht at dawn. The next night we were still stoked enough to attend another huge party given by the Reuben brothers, London's answer to Donald Trump in the property business. There was no point in trying to rest up, because, like those all-night diners, I think I have a sign on my back, WE NEVER CLOSE. The next day I was up at dawn to catch the Delta flight back to JFK and then a car back to the Hamptons for still another charity, this time the Robert Wilson arts extravaganza at his Watermill Center, where I had been conducting the auctions for the last twenty-one years. I ask not for whom the gavel tolls. I know it tolls for me.

Given all my decades of auctioneering and all those banging gavels, one would think that I was beyond stage fright and sale anxiety. Not so. For all my triumphs, like these three back-to-back summer auctions, there have been some disasters, most notably that "Black November" sale at Phillips in 2002. But there were plenty of others. For instance, I once did an auction at a Swiss castle for a charity called La Main Tendu, or the Outstretched Hand. The Clenched Fist would have been a better appellation. The room was full of Geneva bankers, many of whom I knew, all of whom were tight as a drum. Almost none of these rich but frugal Calvinists would bid a franc. So I took the matter into my own outstretched hands and did the bidding for them. Thank you, Didier, how generous of you, Jacques, the world will be better for your charity, Henri. My own annoyance forced me into a desperate measure, and good ended up being done.

Far worse was another Swiss auction in my family's hometown of Neuchâtel. The wife of one of my childhood friends asked me as a favor to do an event to raise money for Parkinson's disease. Naturally, I was delighted to help. However, when I arrived, I quickly realized that most of the attendees were victims of Parkinson's and, on top of that, were people of very limited means. In auction parlance, there was "no money in the room." In plain Eglish, it was heartbreaking. There was no way I could use my skills to part these people from assets they did not have. I tried to make the evening as light as possible, but I couldn't have gone home more depressed.

Fortunately, where charity auctions are concerned, the highs greatly outweigh the lows. Some good charity auctioneers are dreadful at regular auctions, and vice versa. I would like to think that I happen to be good at both. I really cut my charity teeth in the AIDS crisis in the eighties, which hit the art world especially fast and hard. I helped organize evenings in Geneva nightclubs, auctioning Lakers jerseys and basketballs autographed by the first sports legend to come out with HIV, Magic Johnson. But it was the untimely death of Thomas Ammann, who was well on his way to becoming the Duveen of his time, that galvanized the art world to take major action.

The seminal moment came at Art Basel in 1990, two years before Elizabeth Taylor founded amfAR, when she and Audrey Hepburn took to the stage together to ask the collectors to step up and help. It was only a silent auction that night. I was asked up to that stage as well, to explain to bidders the rules of the game. To be in the presence of these two legends, whose beauty was exceeded only by their goodness, was my Francis of Assisi moment that converted me, once and forever, to the charitable cause. Doing good simply feels even better than doing well, and, besides, there are no buyer's commissions to worry about.

20

THE CUTTING EDGE

W hen I get the inevitable queries, "What are you doing next?" or "Where is art going?" I finally have an easy answer. I am going, and art is going, where everything else in the world is going. To the Internet. At first glance, art and technology may seem like strange bedfellows, particularly if you subscribe to Heini Thyssen's Old Master–centric view that the only great, or collectible, artist is a dead artist. However, the current explosion of contemporary art as the place where the big money is is proof that even the hidebound, ultra-traditional, change-resistant art world, the world that spawned me, is ripe for a revoltion. In October 2015, wanting to surf that new wave, I kicked off a new venture called de Pury (keeping it simple) to do super-quality single-owner sales of great collections on the Internet.

I was inspired to this endeavor by my very first "house sale" of the Rosemarie Kanzler collection, which I did in Geneva with Sir Peter Wilson in 1977. People loved coming to the great house on Lake Geneva, seeing the collection, of art, furniture, and sculpture as a whole, a whole that was even greater than the sum of its great parts. Collectors loved house sales. They got inspiration from them. They got ideas of how to display the art they might own. I wanted to tap into that inspiration. My brainstorm was to take the house sale to the Net, to create a virtual house sale, and then combine it with a physical house, a brick-and-mortar entity where prospective bidders could come and see the collection in the flesh, as it were. It seemed like a tall order, a huge challenge. But I love tall orders and huge challenges. Here's how I did it.

To begin with, I began thinking about the state of the art market in tech terms. On one hand, you had eBay as the largest flea market in the world. On the other hand, there were the ancient auction houses, Sotheby's, Christie's, my Phillips, still nipping at their heels. In the middle there was almost nothing, like the *New Yorker* Saul Steinberg cover of an America with only New York and California and a void in between. My calculations also took account of the art-market pyramid, at whose pinnacle there were maybe fifty people who could spend over $100 million on a work of art, but at a million dollars, there were probably several thousand, like the people at the Leonardofete in Saint-Tropez. Buying a painting for a million dollars used to be on the front page of *The New York Times*. Of course, the base of the pyramid is eBay, and is vast. There was a lot of room in between to make a mark.

My bête noir at Sotheby's, and the one beast I tried to exterminate at Phillips, was overhead—the huge staffs, those expensive catalogues that had to be hand-messengered to the collectors' multiple homes, the staggering 25 percent buyer's premium. The Net was the Promised Land of No Overhead. Yet no one had seemed to figure out how to sell "bourgeois art," that is, art that is priced in that vast chasm between $10,000 and $1 million, on the Internet effectively. The pioneering effort here was made by Artnet, founded by the German Hans Neuendorf, which is remarkably valuable as a price guide. Its auction efforts have not taken off.

Nor have those of Artsy, the brainchild of a twenty-something Princeton grad named Carter Cleveland who created something compellingly called the Art Genome, so compellingly that he attracted formidable investors like Larry Gagosian, Dasha Zhukova, and Wendi Murdoch (Rupert's ex). The idea here is the same as the music services like Pandora: If you like *this* piece of art, then you will also like *these*. It's a great idea. However, in execution, there is a mediocre selection that is something of an insult to your stellar taste.

Another of these sites waiting—and waiting—to take off is Artspace, which was recently sold to financial titan Leon Black, whom I rank with Ronald Lauder as one of America's greatest collectors, and whose deep,

deep pockets are an entrepreneur's dream. Artspace sells art on the Net, but it doesn't do auctions.

Then there is Paddle8, named after the lodestar of exclusive Manhattan nightlife Bungalow 8 and founded by my dashing young Phillips discovery and protégé Alexander Gilkes. Paddle8's goal is to sell art in the $1,000 to $100,000 range, which is quite different from my higher-end focus. If you judge a site by the company it keeps, Paddle8 will be a smash. Gilkes's investors include Damien Hirst, Jay Jopling of White Cube, Matthew Mellon of *those* Mellons and Jimmy Choo, and the Wertheimer family that owns Chanel. Gilkes's success so far is in the online hosting of charity auctions, but the nature of the charity beast is non-profit, so to make a profit Paddle8 will have to sell art—lots of art, given its target range—to the public, a challenge that remains to be met.

I looked at the fashion houses, which, like the art houses, were initially skeptical of the Net. Who would buy couture *online*, they had all haughtily sniffed. Then Net-a-Porter came along and showed how wrong everyone was. Next the site 1stdibs did the same thing with high-end contemporary furniture. People loved ordering expensive clothes and expensive furniture online. Why not expensive art? Of course, this "why not" moment might have never happened were it not for a confluence of fortuities. To begin with, I had the pleasure to meet in London Klaus Hommels, a Swiss-based German who is considered one of Europe's leading tech "angels." Klaus was a ground-floor investor in such success stories as Skype, Spotify, and Facebook. We had a lot in common, and began looking for things to do together.

The second fortuity was that my dear friend Baroness Marion Lambert called me at roughly the same time looking for advice about selling her formidable art collection. Her husband had just died, and her son wasn't interested in the art, so Marion asked me to help her get proposals from the Big Three auction houses for a prospective auction. As a family, the Belgian Lamberts had taste as good as anyone else in Europe. A branch of the Rothschilds, they founded the Banque de Bruxelles in 1840 and financed King Leopold in colonizing the Congo (now Zaire). Marion, a regal Dutch woman, was married to Baron Philippe, who died in 2011 and had amazing homes in Geneva, Gstaad, and Greece. Philippe's brother Baron Leon Lambert lived in a grand apartment above the bank's Brussels headquarters that contained one of Europe's finest art collections. He had a very untimely death from AIDS in 1987, a high-profile demise that, like that of his friend and dealer Thomas Ammann, served to transform the disease into perhaps the preeminent charitable cause of the latter twentieth century.

Marion has been one of the world's leading collectors of photography. She had housed her massive collection at the family bank, then called Banque Bruxelles Lambert. When an overly fastidious bank director publicly objected to turning his finance house into a museum, Marion came to me at Phillips to sell the collection in 2005. The result was one of the major photography sales in history. We called it Veronica's Revenge, a reference to St. Veronica, whose iconic veil famously contained the afterimage of Christ, an image that some consider the first photograph, the absence of a camera notwithstanding.

Such is faith, and such is the faith Marion Lambert placed in me after deciding that none of the three bids to sell her collection met with her approval. The collection was as eclectic as Marion and just as unorthodox, with the common denominator being her impeccable taste. There was eighteenth-century furniture, twentieth-century decorative design, and contemporary art including Christopher Wool's finest abstract work, the most expensive of all the pieces, estimated at over $9 million. There was couture, and there was even a car, an Italian fifties Topolino, an even mini-er Fiat that you could almost pick up like a bicycle. There were over four hundred pieces in all, a lifetime of innovative elegance. Christie's had come in with a very bespoke, state-of-the-art proposal. Sotheby's was also elaborate, but felt like it came from a template and was less personal. Phillips, which I thought would have tried harder, was the least impressive. I recommended that Marion choose Christie's.

Instead she chose *me*. "You do the auction," she told me. I laughed, thinking she was joking. She wasn't. Where, I asked her. I didn't have an auction house to sell from anymore. "On the Internet," the Baroness, who is no more computer literate than most other royals of her generation, said confidently. But no collection of that magnitude had ever been sold on the Net, I said, trying to reason with her. "You be the first," she insisted.

It all made me think back to the advice that had been imparted to me in my early Peter Wilson days at Sotheby's: "You have to eat your cookies while they're being passed." The sweets tray was on the table. The tray became even sweeter with the last fortuity. My wife, Michaela, had been trying to have us meet Arnaud Massenet, the cofounder of Net-a-Porter, for the last year and a half. One of her closest friends was also close to Massenet and had been promising to make the match. Promises, promises. With the Baroness's cookies at hand, Michaela called her friend on the carpet, and the match was finally made. We had dinner with Arnaud in London at Alfred's (as in Dunhill), a private club on Davies Street in Mayfair, close to Sotheby's and across from Larry Gagosian (Larry is everywhere).

Arnaud, who grew up in Paris but got his MBA from the University of North Carolina and worked for Morgan Stanley, turned out to be not only an international business wizard but a passionate art collector as well. Because of his success in rebutting all the negativity of the fashion world toward Net-a-Porter, he understood instantly what we were trying to accomplish and felt we could do it. It was Kismet. We needed an expert to move ahead, and now we had one. We decided on the spot to join forces—Arnaud, Klaus Hommels, Michaela, and me—and plan for a fall 2015 launch with the Baroness's collection. We enjoyed a big tray of cookies for dessert.

In planning the sale, which we titled "A Visual Odyssey—Selections from the LAC (Lambert Art Collection)," we decided that we would fuse ether with bricks and mortar by creating a "house" for the "house sale" that prospective buyers could visit, in the flesh. And what a house we found. This was Ely House, at 37 Dover Street in Mayfair, completed in the Revolutionary year of 1776 as the London residence of the Bishop of Ely. Considered one of the finest town houses in the metropolis, the bishop's urban palace had recently become the headquarters of Mallett, one of the most venerable of all antiques dealers.

We decided to rent Mallett for two weeks prior to the sale and were fortunate that one of Marion's best friends was the mega-decorator Jacques Grange (the Mark Hotel in Manhattan; the homes of Saint Laurent, Lagerfeld, Valentino, and Pinault). We enlisted him to turn Ely House into Maison Lambert for two magic weeks, during which we would have experts, professors, curators, and critics come in to give colloquia on various themes arising from the diversity of treasures the Lamberts had assembled. The auction itself would be held live at Mallett and streamed over tablets and smartphones.

What we intended to create was a one-time Brigadoon-like arts festival in the middle of Mayfair that would become our template for future de Pury online sales. Instead of physical catalogues, we will have physical exhibitions, hopefully in New York, Los Angeles, Shanghai, Dubai, wherever great collections and great collectors may be. And to sweeten the pot, our buyer's commission rate on items up to $2 million will be 15 percent, compared to the 25 percent of the Big Boys. There will be no minimum price guarantees to the Baroness, or to future sellers. The goal is to be light on our feet and light on buyers' wallets.

Down the block at 40 Dover Street, in another imposing town house, was the Arts Club, founded in 1863 by Dickens and Trollope and visited over the years by the likes of Degas, Monet, and Whistler, and now by the likes of Gagosian, Hirst, and Koons. Dover was Art Street, the heart of Dixie of the international art world. By creating our own "Lambert House" at Mallett, we were sure to get a lot of fancy traffic and a lot of glittering word of mouth.

As the auction neared, we realized that, notwithstanding our great expertise in modern and contemporary art, there were other aspects of the Baroness's uniquely diverse collection where there were experts greater than we. When it comes to eighteenth-century French antique furniture, which was a highlight of the collection, there was no greater expert than Charles Cator of Christie's, whose strength in the Lambert Collection's Asian art and Japanese screens also exceeded our own. With our highest duty to our client, the Baroness, to get the best result possible, we all agreed that it would behoove us all to make our auction a joint venture with Christie's. We were delighted that Christie's agreed to join the team.

The groundbreaking Internet-intensive aspect of the auction remained. What made it unique was that I had the pleasure of conducting my first auction on the premises of Christie's, on King Street in London. I shared the podium there with Christie's formidable auctioneer Jussi Pylkkanen. Jussi took the first third of the auction, the "old stuff" from before 1970. I did the rest, which lasted a marathon four and a half hours, because there were over 300 lots. It gave me the proud distinction of having presided at auctions at all three of the major houses, Sotheby's, Christie's, and Phillips. The end result made me even prouder. There was enthusiastic bidding, both by phone and on the Internet, and in the end, the sale totaled an impressive $22.9 million. All's well that ends well, and we intend to be out on the virtual cutting-edge again in the very near future.

As thrilling as *selling* art has been and will always be, an even greater thrill is *making* art. I started out wanting to be an artist, and there's nothing more gratifying to me than to discover emerging artists before anyone else does. When I ran Phillips, I not only reveled in discovering new artists but also pioneered the selling of items like design and photography that had never been auctioned before. Ron Arad, Marc Newsom, and the late Helmut Newton have all thanked me—and have done so profusely—for putting them on the auction map. If I am not the Christopher Columbus of the art world, I do love the excitement of exploration, of being the first.

For instance, I may not have been the first person to discover Gerhard Richter, now probably the most important—and expensive—living painter in the world, but I certainly felt like it. I'll never forget being overwhelmed, decades ago, when I first was exposed to Richter's works at an exhibition in Sils-Maria, in the Swiss Alps, at the home of Friedrich Nietzsche, curated by the boy-wonder curator Hans-Ulrich Obrist. Richter at this point was a long way from becoming the Superman of Art, but the Nietzschean location confirmed my immediate instinct that something big was before me.

I conveyed my enthusiasm to that oracular dealer Thomas Ammann, but he wasn't sure. "You may have a point" was all he allowed me. I was thrilled to have been right. Richter's works sell in the tens of millions, and his abstract works, the ones that mesmerized me, sell for more than his representational pieces. Because Richter worked in such a wide diversity of styles, including photography and sculpture as well as painting, no one could pigeonhole him. His diversity was initially a liability. If only I had purchased a truckload!

Another bandwagon I am proud to be one of the first to get on is that of my fellow Swiss Urs Fischer. Barely into his forties, Fischer, I believe, is the main artist to emerge from the current decade. He can be to the 2010s (whatever they are called) what Koons was to the 1980s, Hirst to the 1990s, Cattelan to the 2000s. At Phillips I was always looking for the next Richter or Fischer, showcasing emerging artists in the press-unheralded day sales and doing my best to slip them into the evening sales where somehow, I hoped, the fickle art press might discover them and aid their emergence. One of these artists I was particularly proud to midwife was Mark Bradford, whose collage art was as compelling as his résumé. Mark had grown up on the edge of the Los Angeles ghetto, where his mother owned a beauty salon. Even though the family escaped to Santa Monica, the salon remained, and Mark became a hairdresser there after high school. Only at thirty did he go to art school, at the super-prestigious incubator of talent, Cal Arts, which is to art what Cal Tech is to science.

Mark bloomed late but mightily, aided by his discovery by the influential New York–based Italian collector Principessa Kika Borghese, whose deepest interest was in African American art. Mark's first auction sale, at Phillips, was for a huge-for-a-beginner $180,000, and his price has soared from there. One of his pieces is in the Lambert Collection, and he has been commissioned to do a $2.5 million piece on the Constitution for the new American Embassy in London. Never forgetting his roots, Mark took over his retired mother's hairdressing salon and turned it into his studio. I remember being crippled with lumbago at the Bel-Air Hotel on one of our annual visits to LA to visit emerging artists. Michaela told me it was too bad I was so sick, because she was going to visit Mark at the studio. Like a cripple going to Lourdes, I dragged my aching self out of my sickbed and joined her. I'd like to say that the art healed me; maybe it did.

Mark has a great personality, which goes with his work. That's not always the case. I usually prefer to see the art first so that the current cult of personality doesn't influence me. Nonetheless, one of the beauties of collecting contemporary art is that you can visit the studios and get to know the artists, *pace* Heini Thyssen. In the past few years Michaela and I have been spending every August in Los Angeles, which we view as the most vibrant art center in the world today. What Paris was to the Impressionists, or the Surrealists, for that matter, LA is to contemporary artists. The light is perfect, the space is relatively cheap, the collectors are legion and influential, the culture is open-minded and open-armed, and downtown, which is where the art is, is no longer armed and dangerous but more cutting-edge than even Berlin.

A case study is one of the artists we found during one of our LA "endless summers," Alex Israel. We were introduced to Alex by China Chow, daughter of Michael, who was one of my colleagues on the *Work of Art* Bravo series, on which she was the host. Her description intrigued me. Alex, whose work focused on the cult and culture of celebrity, was the only artist in the world whose studio was at a studio—a film studio, that is, Warner Bros. to be exact. How perfectly, quintessentially LA that seemed. Accordingly, Michaela and I set out to meet him. We drove the freeways, the 405 to the 101 to the 134, in the much-mocked LA parlance, got our pass from the studio gatekeeper, who seemed to have been there since the *Sunset Blvd.* days of Gloria Swanson, then were chauffeured around the lot, past a diversity of cinematic ecosystems, from the Wild West to the Roaring Twenties to suburbia to outer space, until we reached a vast hangar that Alex Israel called his artistic home.

We were greeted by a slight, quietly eloquent cool cat whose thick, dark sunglasses are as much a trademark as those clear frames of Michael Chow, and perhaps even more so, since Alex has created his own luxury sunglass company, Freeway Eyewear. As a brand, Alex is simply following in the Warhol tradition. Alex knows his traditions, he knows his art, and he knows his business. The product of West Los Angeles comfort and luxury, Alex Israel went east to Yale, then boomeranged back west for an MFA at USC. Then he went east again, to get to know the art market from the inside, with jobs under Tobias Meyer at Sotheby's, at the gallery Hauser & Wirth, and as an assistant to the late artist Jason Rhoades.

Only after this decadelong apprenticeship was Alex prepared to step out as an artist himself. Aided by the army of technicians, prop masters, and workmen on the Warner lot, he led off with a series of pastel panel paintings that some critics described as resembling the sets of the porn films that made the San Fernando Valley the Hollywood of the porn world. Europeans, who tend to have a weakness for all things cinema, high or low, ate these up.

The early Alex then did a performance art series called *As It Lays*. The title was an homage to Joan Didion; the series was an homage to Warhol. On the pastel set, Alex, in his dark glasses and Teddy Boyish suit, serves as an affectless, deadpan interviewer, with the emphasis on dead. He does ten-minute sessions with often over-the-hill but once highly famous local celebrities, including Phyllis Diller, Cheryl Tiegs, Jon Peters, Marilyn Manson, Oliver Stone, Bobby Shriver, and others. The list is less a barometer of the interest in art of these erstwhile legends than a testament to Alex's vast local network.

It isn't just local. Everywhere Michaela and I travel, we seem to run into Alex. We saw him at the Liebieghaus Museum in Frankfurt for the opening of the exhibit there of Alex's admitted role model Jeff Koons. There, with Koons's gilded staute of Michael Jackson and his chimp Bubbles displayed amidst the classical museum's Egyptian funerary, Alex appeared *deus ex machina,* with his powerful Paris dealer, the stunning half-French, half-Thai Almine Rech, whose husband is Bernard Picasso, grandson of Pablo. This is art royalty.

We also ran into Alex, and his parents, in Rome for his joint show with Kathryn Andrews at Larry Gagosian's new Eternal City headquarters, housed, appropriately enough, in a former bank near the Spanish Steps. If Alex has a middle name, I bet it's Network. When Alex appeared on the cover of the art magazine *Purple,* he got Jeff Koons to Instagram a picture of himself holding up a copy of *Purple* with Alex on it. Such is validation in the art world.

The self-profiling has more than paid off. In 2014 one of Alex's pastel sky paintings sold at Christie's for $1 million. Two nights later, another sold at Phillips for $750,000. Where can he go from there? Somehow, I'm not worried. We last saw him at a party given by Rosette Delug, the Turkish-born blond-bombshell doyenne of the Los Angeles contemporary art scene, trustee of the Hammer Museum and former trustee of MOCA, resigning only when Eli Broad seemed to be buying the place.

Delug lives in a fifties mansion in Trousdale filled with the hundreds of pieces of great art she has acquired in her short life as a collector: Ruschas, Baldessaris, LA's greatest hits. Even the obligatory LA pool is a work of art, with Lawrence Weiner's text work *Stretched as Tightly as Possible: Satin & Petroleum Jelly* emblazoned on the pool floor. She began collecting only in 2001 and loved it so much that she once disguised herself as an installer with overalls and a fake badge to get the jump on the crowd at Art Basel. Delug's parties are A-ticket and are considered performance pieces in themselves, featuring spray-painted Playboy bunnies and the like. That night, of course, there was Alex Israel, with China Chow, who was importuning him to marry her so she could change her name to China Israel.

Michaela and I love to discover new artists like Alex Israel. We also love to collect them. In the course of our travels, we meet high achievers in just about every field, but we always seem to like the artists the best. I suppose it takes one to know one. Again, it's much more interesting befriending an artist before a consensus develops. Being a taste-maker is its own reward. It makes you feel good, just as having Russian oligarchs fighting over your work and bidding into the eight figures makes the artists feel good. Money brings recognition, and what artist doesn't want to be recognized? That is the calculus of taste. So be it.

From the beginning of my career in the business of art, I always saw myself as an artist in a dealer's suit. As my first mentor, Ernst Beyeler, told me, I had a physical, rather than an intellectual, approach to art. What really turned me on was never the history, and never the money, but rather the absolute pleasure of seeing and being around great art. If my pleasures had been otherwise, I would be a lot richer than I am, and I would have a huge home to display the art I do collect.

Not that I am anti-money. No collector I have ever met is proud that the art he has bought has gone down in value. There is no reverse chic in falling prices. I have, on the other hand, met critics who, certainly in the case of emerging artists, are suspicious of rising prices. To them I have one word only: *Bollocks!* By that logic collectors should be dumping their Picassos and Matisses en masse. I buy with love, and I hope and pray everything I buy will go up. An art addict, I buy, when I can, two or three new pieces a month and store them in a Swiss freeport, waiting in vain to build my own Villa Favorita, which I know will exist only in my dreams. Meanwhile, I have my art to comfort me. It's my guiding obsession, and really the only thing I know about. I have put all my eggs in one basket, the basket of art. Too bad they're not Fabergé . . .

LIST OF ILLUSTRATIONS

FAMILY JEWELS. Motörhead Ed, London 2005

NIGHT CAPS. Reprinted with permission of the author

EVERY LITTLE BREEZE SEEMS TO WHISPER LOUISE. Bertrand Rindoff Petroff / Getty Images; Artwork: © 2015 The Andy Warhol Foundation for the Visual Arts, Inc. / Artists Rights Society (ARS), New York

LITTLE EINSTEIN. Reprinted with permission of Albert Oehlen

LOW PROFILE. Reprinted with permission of Claude Mercier

BARONIAL. Reprinted with permission of the author

THE TWO HEINIS. Reprinted with permission of the author

HECTOR EN FAMILLE. Reprinted with permission of the author

HEAVY HITTERS. © Royal Academy of Arts, London; artwork: © 2015 Estate of Pablo Picasso / Artists Rights Society (ARS), New York

CAPTAIN MARBLE. Reprinted with permission of Jeff Koons

THE ENABLER. Reprinted with permission of the author

TEAM PLAYERS. © M. Schlemmer; reprinted with permission of the author

LIVES OF THE PARTY. Reprinted with permission of the author

JUDY AND BIG AL. Reprinted with permission of the author

HUNGARIAN RHAPSODY. Reprinted with permission of the author